Certification Study Companion Series

The Apress Certification Study Companion Series offers guidance and hands-on practice to support technical and business professionals who are studying for an exam in the pursuit of an industry certification. Professionals worldwide seek to achieve certifications in order to advance in a career role, reinforce knowledge in a specific discipline, or to apply for or change jobs. This series focuses on the most widely taken certification exams in a given field. It is designed to be user friendly, tracking to topics as they appear in a given exam. Authors for this series are experts and instructors who not only possess a deep understanding of the content, but also have experience teaching the key concepts that support readers in the practical application of the skills learned in their day-to-day roles.

More information about this series at https://link.springer.com/bookseries/17100

Certified OpenStack Administrator Study Guide

Get Everything You Need for the COA Exam

Second Edition

Andrey Markelov

Apress®

Certified OpenStack Administrator Study Guide: Get Everything You Need for the COA Exam

Andrey Markelov
Stockholm, Sweden

ISBN-13 (pbk): 978-1-4842-8803-0   ISBN-13 (electronic): 978-1-4842-8804-7
https://doi.org/10.1007/978-1-4842-8804-7

Copyright © 2022 by Andrey Markelov

Managing Director, Apress Media LLC: Welmoed Spahr
Acquisitions Editor: Divya Modi
Development Editor: James Markham

Cover Image: Courtesy of Freepik.com

Distributed to the book trade worldwide by Springer Science+Business Media New York, 233 Spring Street, 6th Floor, New York, NY 10013. Phone 1-800-SPRINGER, fax (201) 348-4505, e-mail orders-ny@springersbm.com, or visit www.springer.com. Apress Media, LLC is a California LLC and the sole member (owner) is Springer Science + Business Media Finance Inc (SSBM Finance Inc). SSBM Finance Inc is a **Delaware** corporation.

For information on translations, please e-mail booktranslations@springernature.com; for reprint, paperback, or audio rights, please e-mail bookpermissions@springernature.com.

Apress and friends of ED books may be purchased in bulk for academic, corporate, or promotional use. eBook versions and licenses are also available for most titles. For more information, reference our Special Bulk Sales–eBook Licensing web page at www.apress.com/bulk-sales.

Any source code or other supplementary materials referenced by the author in this text are available to readers at www.apress.com. For detailed information about how to locate your book's source code, go to www.apress.com/source-code/. Readers can also access source code at SpringerLink in the Supplementary Material section for each chapter.

Printed on acid-free paper

To my wife, Elena, for her love and support

Table of Contents

About the Author

Andrey Markelov is an experienced Linux and cloud architect who has worked for large international companies (Red Hat and Ericsson, currently). He has written and published more than 50 articles about Linux and Unix systems services, virtual systems, and open source (Linux Format RE, Computerra, PCWeek/RE, and others). Andrey is the author of several OpenStack and Kubernetes books. He has taught Microsoft and Red Hat–authorized courses for over 15 years. Andrey has been a Red Hat Certified Architect since 2009 and is also a Microsoft Certified System Engineer, Cisco Certified Network Associate, Novell Certified Linux Professional, and VMware Certified Professional. Although Andrey has been working with cloud computing for a decade, he avoids clouds in real life by enjoying private piloting as a hobby.

About the Technical Reviewer

Ilya Alekseyev has 20 years of experience in IT, including cloud computing, DevOps, big data, HPC, system and software architecture, software development, and development team management. He has experience in open source software development and community development for OpenStack projects. For several years he has held a volunteering position as OpenStack Ambassador. He worked in companies such as Nutanix, Nvidia, Mirantis, Grid Dynamics, and others. He has participated in OpenStack-related projects for PayPal, NTT East, Lattelecom, and other companies. He has also organized a series of OpenStack meetups and conferences.

CHAPTER 1

Getting Started

What Is the Certified OpenStack Administrator Exam?

The Certified OpenStack Administrator (COA) is the first professional certification offered by the OpenInfra Foundation. OpenStack's website states that it's designed to help companies identify top talent in the industry and help job seekers demonstrate their skills.

The COA certification is available to anyone who passes the exam. No mandatory learning is required. However, the Certified OpenStack Administrator is a professional, typically with at least six months' OpenStack experience. It is very important to gain practical skills in working with OpenStack before taking the exam. If you read this or any other books or if you watch any video courses with no practice, you will likely fail your exam. Practice, practice, practice is the only way to successfully reach the exam goals.

The following are some quick facts about the exam.

- The duration is three hours.

- The price (at the time of writing) to take the exam is $400.

- The exam is performance-based. You may use a graphical interface or the command line.

- The exam is available anywhere in the world through the Internet.

© Andrey Markelov 2022
A. Markelov, *Certified OpenStack Administrator Study Guide*,
https://doi.org/10.1007/978-1-4842-8804-7_1

- A proctor monitors candidates virtually during the exam session via streaming audio, video, and screen sharing.

- The certification is valid for 36 months after the passing date.

This book is organized to cover all COA exam requirements, which are publicly available at www.openstack.org/coa/requirements. They are also shown in Figure 1-1 in short form.

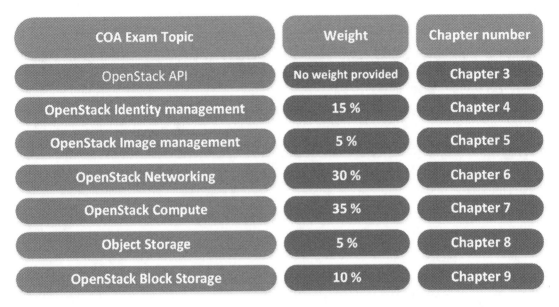

COA Exam Topic	Weight	Chapter number
OpenStack API	No weight provided	Chapter 3
OpenStack Identity management	15 %	Chapter 4
OpenStack Image management	5 %	Chapter 5
OpenStack Networking	30 %	Chapter 6
OpenStack Compute	35 %	Chapter 7
Object Storage	5 %	Chapter 8
OpenStack Block Storage	10 %	Chapter 9

Figure 1-1. *OpenStack COA exam requirements*

Exam objectives are subject to change. Please visit the COA exam website for the most current listing of exam objectives. Even if you don't plan to take the COA exam, this book can be a useful tutorial for OpenStack operators.

Tips for COA Exam Preparation

After successfully going through this book's contents, you should read the *OpenStack Foundation Certification Candidate Handbook for OpenStack Foundation Certified OpenStack Administrator (COA)*. This guide is available from the COA website at www. openstack.org/coa/. It contains all the instructions and conditions you need to know before taking the exam.

The day before the exam, it is better to rest and not to study until late evening. Try to schedule the exam for the first part of the day when your brain is fresh.

The handbook tells you to launch `http://docs.openstack.org` to access the technical documentation. Take some time to investigate the information. You do not need to memorize everything, but it is good to know what the documentation website contains.

It is probably better not to type long names of projects, volumes, directories, and so forth but instead copy them from the exam task list to the command line during the exam. You can avoid mistypes and errors if you do so.

Candidates should ensure that their webcam can be moved in case the proctor requests that the candidate scan their surroundings to check for potential violations of exam policy.

Using one of the terminal multiplexers is highly recommended because the exam terminal has a single console. You can use the `screen` command or the more advanced `tmux`. Take your time to practice with one of them. Using `tmux,` you can start a new session with the following command.

```
# tmux new
```

If the connection is lost, you can rejoin a session using the following command.

```
# tmux attach
```

Figure 1-2 shows the `tmux` display. Table 1-1 lists the most common shortcuts for `tmux` commands.

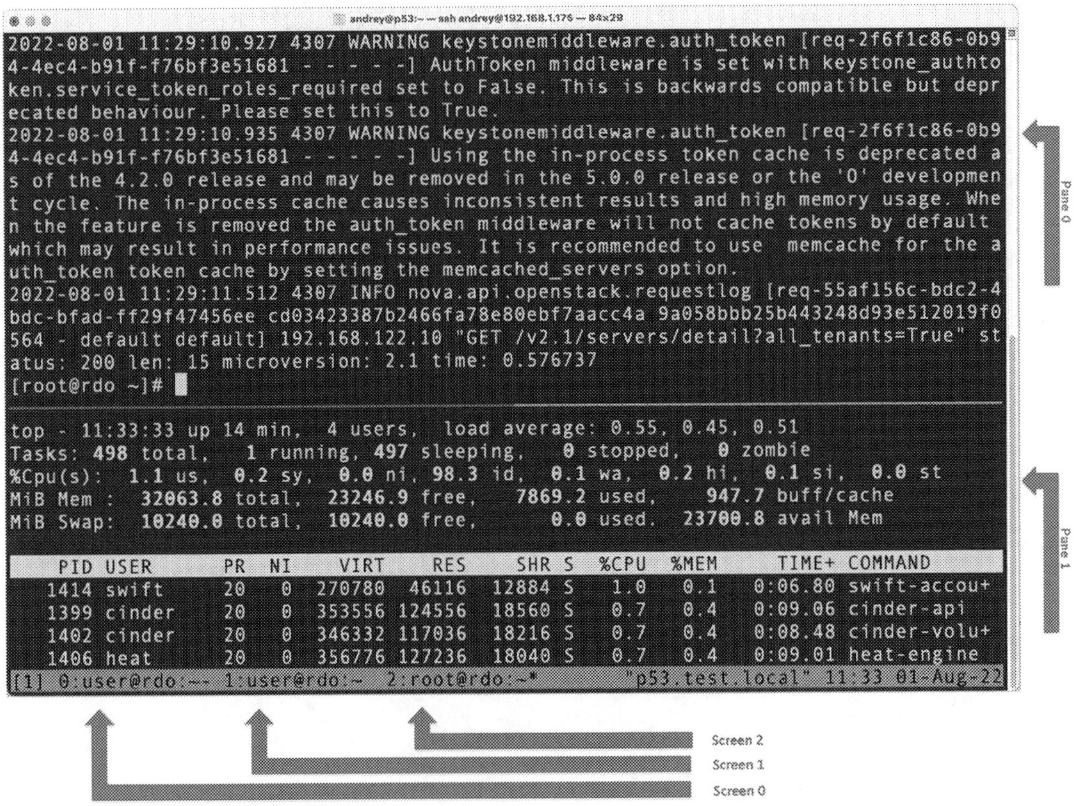

Figure 1-2. *The* `tmux` *screen multiplexer*

Table 1-1. *Some* tmux *Command Key Bindings*

Command Key Bindings	Action
Ctrl-B ?	Show screen with help.
Ctrl-B d	Detach from the session.
Ctrl-B s	List sessions.
Ctrl-B c	Create a new window.
Ctrl-B n	Change to the next window.
Ctrl-B p	Change to the previous window.
Ctrl-B 0…9	Select windows 0 through 9.
Ctrl-B %	Create a horizontal pane.
Ctrl-B "	Create a vertical pane.
Ctrl-B ↑↓→←	Move to pane.

Other OpenStack Certifications (Red Hat)

This book may help you prepare for other OpenStack certifications, but it does not contain any specific information beyond the COA exam. Exam objectives can be different. The comparison in Table 1-2 is purely for information purposes only. It is accurate at the time of writing but is always subject to change.

Table 1-2. *Comparison of OpenStack Certifications*

Vendor	COA	Red Hat
Certification name	Certified OpenStack Administrator	Red Hat Certified Specialist in Red Hat OpenStack
Exam availability	Worldwide (through Internet connection)	Worldwide (through Internet connection)
Performance-based	Yes	Yes
Vendor-neutral	Yes	No
Certification validity	3 years	3 years
Passing score	70%	210 out of 300 points
US exam price	$400	$400
Source of information	www.openstack.org/coa/	www.redhat.com/en/services/training/ex210-red-hat-certified-system-administrator-red-hat-openstack-exam

Mirantis Certified Administrator for OpenStack certification was mentioned in the first edition of this book, but it no longer exists. In October 2019, Mirantis became the new administrator of the upgraded Certified OpenStack Administrator (COA) exam.

Before delving into a discussion of OpenStack, let's determine what is meant by *cloud computing*. The National Institute of Standards and Technology's (NIST) definition is considered the established definition in the industry.

> *Cloud computing is a model of providing widely accessible and convenient access via the network to the common set of adjustable computational resources on demand (such as networks, servers, data storage, applications, and services). These resources can be promptly allocated and released with minimum customer efforts spent on management and interactions with the service provider.*

The service models shown in Figure 1-3 are defined by five essential characteristics, three service models, and four deployment models. It includes self-service, general access to the network, a common set of resources, flexibility, and calculation of use. Service models differ by the level of customer control of the provided infrastructure and include the following.

- In **infrastructure as a service (IaaS)**, the user has control over all levels of the software stack above the cloud platform—virtual machines, networks, and space volume at the data storage system— given to the user. The user is an administrator of the operating system and all the work above it to the applications. OpenStack is an example of IaaS.

- In **platform as a service (PaaS)**, the cloud can exist "inside" the cloud of the IaaS model. In this case, the user controls the level of the platform applications built, for example, applications servers, libraries, programming environment, and databases. The user does not control and does not administer virtual machines and the operating systems deployed on them, data storage systems, and networks. Pivotal Cloud Foundry and Red Hat OpenShift are examples of PaaS.

- In **software as a service (SaaS)**, the user level of control is only for the application itself. The user is unaware of the virtual machine and the operating system and only works with the application. Examples of such products are Google Docs and Microsoft Office 365.

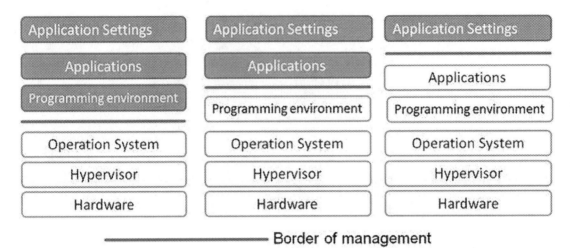

Figure 1-3. *Cloud service models*

The following are four deployment models of cloud platform implementations.

- In a **private cloud**, all the infrastructure is deployed in the data center and defined as a division of one company or a group of companies.

- In a **public cloud**, any company or even a person can be a customer of cloud services. This is the integration model the cloud service providers use.

- A **community cloud** is used when a community of companies with common tasks is the customer (common tasks can be missions, safety requirements, policies, or compliance with different requirements).

- A **hybrid cloud** is a combination of two or three types of clouds, where various loads can be in a private, public, or community cloud.

OpenStack can be a foundation for the cloud in all four deployment models.

Understanding the Components That Make up the Cloud

The OpenStack project, also called a *cloud operational system*, consists of several projects developing separate subsystems (see Figure 1-4). Any OpenStack installation can include only a part of them. Some subsystems can be used separately or as part of any other open source project. Their number is increasing from version to version of OpenStack project, both through the appearance of new ones and the functionality split of the existing ones. For example, the nova-volume service was extracted as a separate Cinder project.

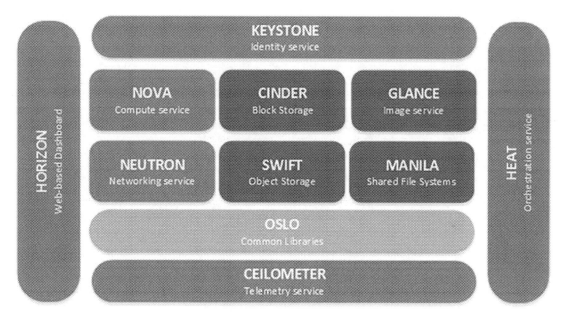

Figure 1-4. *OpenStack architecture and components*

Each project has its own documented set of *representational state transfer application program interfaces* (REST APIs), command raw utilities, and "native" Python interfaces, providing functions similar to the command raw utilities.

One of the basic services is Nova, OpenStack's compute service, which is installed on all cluster computer nodes. It manages the level of abstraction of virtual equipment (processors, memory, block devices, network adapters). Nova provides the management of instances of virtual machines addressing the hypervisor and giving such commands as it is launching and stopping.

It's important to note that OpenStack technologies are independent of the hypervisor. Support is implemented through the appropriate drivers in a Nova project. OpenStack development and testing are primarily for Kernel-based virtual machines (KVMs). Most execution is also implemented on top of the KVM hypervisor.

KVM has been a part of the Linux kernel since 2007, requiring virtualization hardware support on servers with standard architecture (AMD-V or Intel VT-x). Currently, KVM is adapted for usage with several different platforms, for example, PowerPC. QEMU (short for *quick emulator*) is used for input/output devices for emulation in GNU/Linux.

You can check whether the support is turned on and the processor supports one of the technologies by executing the following command.

```
$ grep -E ' svm | vmx' /proc/cpuinfo
```

You should see svm or vmx among the flags supported by the processor. Also, if you execute the command, you should see two kernel modules loaded into the memory.

```
$ lsmod | grep kvm
kvm_intel              143187  3
kvm                    455843  1 kvm_intel
or
$ lsmod | grep kvm
kvm_amd                 60314  3
kvm                    461126  1 kvm_amd
```

The kvm is the module independent of the vendor, and the kvm_intel or kvm_amd executes VT-x or AMD-V functionality, respectively. Pay attention to the fact that virtualization hardware support could be disabled in the basic input/output system (BIOS) by default. As examples of corresponding settings for AMD and Intel processors, you can see Figures 1-5 and 1-6.

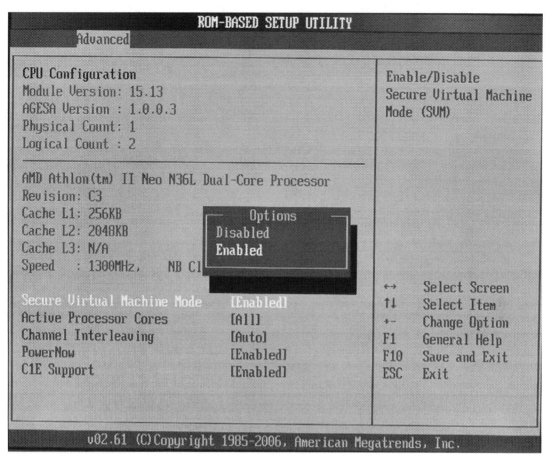

Figure 1-5. *Example of enabling virtualization hardware support in BIOS (AMD CPU)*

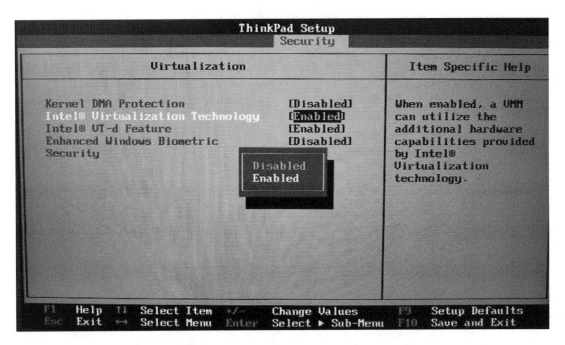

Figure 1-6. *Example of enabling virtualization hardware support in BIOS (Intel CPU)*

Neutron, OpenStack's networking service, is responsible for network connectivity. Users can create virtual networks and routers and set up Internet provider (IP) addresses. One of the mechanisms provided by Neutron is called a *floating IP*. Thanks to this mechanism, virtual machines can get externally fixed IP addresses. Such functionality has a network capability balancer as a service, a firewall as a service, and a virtual private network (VPN) as a service that can be obtained through connecting modules.

Keystone, OpenStack's identification service, is a centralized catalog of users and services they can access. Keystone performs as a united authentication system of the cloud operating system. Keystone checks the validity of users' accounts and the accordance of users to the OpenStack projects and roles. And if it's compliant, it gives the token for access to other services. Keystone runs a services catalog/directory as well.

Glance, OpenStack's image service, runs the catalog of virtual machines' images, which users can use as templates to run instances of virtual machines in the cloud. This service also delivers backup functionality and snapshot creation. Glance supports various formats, including vhd, vmdk, vdi, iso, qcow2, and ami.

Cinder, OpenStack's block storage service, can be used by running instances of virtual machines. This is permanent data storage for virtual machines. Snapshots can be used for data saving and restoring or cloning. In most cases, data storage based on GNU/Linux servers is used together with Cinder. However, there are connecting modules for hardware storage.

Swift, OpenStack's object storage service, is one of the original OpenStack projects. Originally it was called Rackspace Cloud Files. This service allows users to store files. Swift has distributed architecture, allowing horizontal scaling, redundancy, and replication for failover purposes. Swift is oriented mostly to static data, such as virtual machines' copies, backup copies, and archives.

Ceilometer, OpenStack's telemetry service, is a centralized information source based on cloud metrics for monitoring data. This component delivers the billing ability for OpenStack.

Heat, OpenStack's orchestration service, has the main task of application life cycle provision in cloud infrastructure. Using the template in AWS CloudFormation format, this service manages all other OpenStack services, allowing the creation of most types of resources (virtual machines, volumes, floating IPs, users, security groups, etc.). Heat can also automate application scaling using data from the Ceilometer service. Templates describe the relationship between the resources, allowing the Heat service to make API OpenStack calls in the right order, for example, to create the server and connect volume to it.

Horizon, OpenStack's dashboard service, allows management of cloud resources through the web console.

The History of the OpenStack Project

OpenStack, a cloud operating system, was established in June 2010 as a project that connected NASA's Nova virtual server development system and Rackspace's Swift data storage system. The first version, under the code name Austin, was released in October 2010.

The Glance image storage service and Nova and Swift appeared in the Bexar version. The Essex version added the Horizon management web console and the Keystone identification service. The Folsom version added the network service, originally named Quantum, and the Cinder cloud block storage service. The Heat orchestration service and Ceilometer service were added in the Havana version.

It's important to understand that OpenStack is a development project. The website, `www.openstack.org`, doesn't provide any reference for distribution; otherwise, different vendors could create their own distributions based on this project code.

At present, OpenStack is developed under the control of the OpenInfra Foundation (named OpenStack Foundation before 2021), which includes 110,000 members in 187 countries.

To easily evaluate each vendor's contribution to the OpenStack project, visit `www.stackalytics.com`. The Mirantis company created this service to get the statistics and measure the company's engineers' contributions to the project and its separate parts. Then all the rest of the OpenStack developers began to use it. The top five contributors are Red Hat, IBM, HP, Rackspace, Mirantis, and Huawei.

Before going further, it may be interesting to look through the portal (`www.openstack.org/enterprise/`), where you can find examples of OpenStack usage in production operations at some of these enterprises.

As stated earlier, OpenStack is a cloud infrastructure development project but not a product. However, many companies participating in OpenStack development create their products and distributions based on its code, often using their proprietary components. This situation is similar to GNU/Linux distributions' creation. Some examples of OpenStack distributions with links for downloading are shown in Table 1-3.

Table 1-3. *Download Links for OpenStack Distributions*

OpenStack Distribution	URL
Red Hat OpenStack Platform (60-day trial)	`www.redhat.com/en/technologies/linux-platforms/openstack-platform`
RDO by Red Hat	`www.rdoproject.org`
Mirantis OpenStack for Kubernetes	`www.mirantis.com/software/mirantis-openstack-for-kubernetes/`
Ubuntu OpenStack	`https://ubuntu.com/openstack`

You can find an up-to-date complete list of major distributions on OpenStack's Marketplace tab at `www.openstack.org/marketplace/distros/`.

For the lab environment, I recommend RDO. RDO (RPM Distribution of OpenStack) is a project on open OpenStack distribution creation sponsored by Red Hat. Unlike Red Hat commercial distribution, the RDO support cannot be bought with Red Hat

OpenStack Platform (RH OSP). The interrelation between RH OSP and RDO is very similar to the interrelation between Red Hat Enterprise Linux (RHEL) and Fedora. RDO is called up to create a community for Red Hat developments. In the latest versions of RDO, Manager, based on OpenStack Ironic and OpenStack TripleO projects, is offered to be used for installation. RDO can be deployed on top of RHEL and its derivatives (CentOS, Oracle Linux, etc.).

Summary

This chapter discussed the COA exam and tips for preparation and provided a high-level overview of OpenStack and its history.

In the next chapter, you'll learn how to create your own virtual test environment.

CHAPTER 2

How to Build Your Own Virtual Test Environment

This chapter describes how to install a virtual lab in preparation for the Certified OpenStack Administrator exam. You will use the DevStack, PackStack, or MicroStack tools for this installation. This chapter does cover exam questions.

Installing Vanilla OpenStack with the DevStack Tool

You have a lot of options for how to create your test environment. I introduce several of them in this chapter. First, let's look at the most generic method of OpenStack installation. In this case, you install all services from scratch on one PC or virtual machine. You can use one of the common GNU/Linux distributions, such as Ubuntu, Fedora, or CentOS. Since this method is very generic, you probably need some adaptations for your particular environment. More specific examples are given later in this chapter.

I recommend using a virtual desktop environment, such as VirtualBox, VMware Workstation, or KVM with Virtual Machine Manager, also called virt-manager (see Figure 2-1). Virtual Machine Manager is probably the best if you use GNU/Linux as a host. I recommend at least 16 GB of memory for VM, where you install all the OpenStack services.

© Andrey Markelov 2022
A. Markelov, *Certified OpenStack Administrator Study Guide*,
https://doi.org/10.1007/978-1-4842-8804-7_2

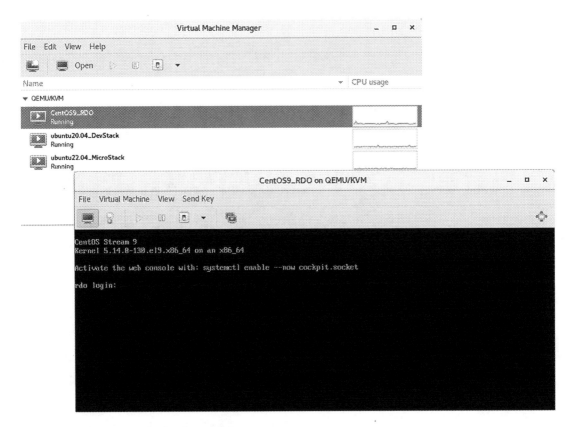

Figure 2-1. *Virtual Machine Manager*

First, you need the OS installed with access to standard repos. Then you need to get the DevStack tool from GitHub. The main purpose of this tool is to prepare the environment for OpenStack developers, but you can use it to create this learning environment. The following instructions are for the most recent Ubuntu LTS releases.

The following creates a stack user to run DevStack by changing the ownership of /opt/devstack to the stack user, installing the Git tool, and downloading DevStack.

```
user@devstack:~$ sudo useradd -s /bin/bash -d /opt/stack -m stack
user@devstack:~$ sudo chmod +x /opt/stack
user@devstack:~$ echo "stack ALL=(ALL) NOPASSWD: ALL" | sudo tee /etc/
sudoers.d/stack
stack ALL=(ALL) NOPASSWD: ALL
user@devstack:~$ sudo -u stack -i
stack@devstack:~$ git clone https://opendev.org/openstack/devstack
Cloning into 'devstack'...
```

```
remote: Enumerating objects: 25233, done.
remote: Counting objects: 100% (25233/25233), done.
remote: Compressing objects: 100% (3470/3470), done.
remote: Total 49012 (delta 24602), reused 21763 (delta 21763),
pack-reused 2377
Receiving objects: 100% (49012/49012), 9.60 MiB | 8.30 MiB/s, done.
Resolving deltas: 100% (34874/34874), done.stack@devstack:~$ cd devstack
```

DevStack uses a special file located in the root directory with instructions that describe how to configure OpenStack services. You can find several examples on the DevStack website (http://docs.openstack.org/developer/devstack/), or you can use the following minimal example of the local.conf file.

```
[[local|localrc]]
ADMIN_PASSWORD="apress"
SERVICE_PASSWORD="apress"
RABBIT_PASSWORD="apress"
DATABASE_PASSWORD="apress"
SWIFT_HASH=sOM3hash1sh3r3
SWIFT_REPLICAS=1
LOGFILE=/opt/stack/logs/stack.sh.log
SCREEN_LOGDIR=/opt/stack/logs
```

Now you need to run the stack.sh script from the devstack directory and wait for it to load.

Here is an example.

```
stack@devstack:/opt/devstack$ ./stack.sh
...
=========================
DevStack Component Timing
 (times are in seconds)
=========================
wait_for_service       12
pip_install           172
apt-get               254
run_process            25
dbsync                  6
```

```
git_timed              989
apt-get-update           1
test_with_retry          4
async_wait              82
osc                    213
--------------------------
Unaccounted time       183
==========================
Total runtime         1941

==================
 Async summary
==================
 Time spent in the background minus waits: 361 sec
 Elapsed time: 1941 sec
 Time if we did everything serially: 2302 sec
 Speedup:  1.18599

This is your host IP address: 192.168.122.7
This is your host IPv6 address: ::1
Horizon is now available at http://192.168.122.7/dashboard
Keystone is serving at http://192.168.122.7/identity/
The default users are: admin and demo
The password: apress

Services are running under systemd unit files.
For more information see:
https://docs.openstack.org/devstack/latest/systemd.html

DevStack Version: zed
Change: bd6e5205b115fb0cafed7f50a676699a4b9fc0fe Increase timeout waiting
for OVN startup 2022-07-03 22:30:41 +0200
OS Version: Ubuntu 20.04 focal.
```

Installation can take some time. In the end, you can source OpenRC in your shell and then use the OpenStack command-line tool to manage your environment. The process can be different in different environments or with different versions of OS. You may probably have to debug some errors. For a more predictable way of installing, see the next section.

Installing RDO OpenStack Distribution with PackStack

PackStack (https://wiki.openstack.org/wiki/Packstack) is another tool that can be used to install OpenStack. The main purpose of PackStack is to prepare OpenStack's test environments with rpm-based distributions. Under the hood, PackStack uses Puppet modules to deploy one or several OpenStack nodes. The easiest and most predictable way to use PackStack is with CentOS Stream 9. The other option to use with PackStack is Red Hat Enterprise Linux.

Let's start with OS preparation. First, you must install CentOS Stream 9 with the `Minimal` or `Server with GUI` option. I recommend that the `Server with GUI` option have a local browser in case you want to access services not exposed externally by default. For example, you can mention the RabbitMQ console.

Next, add additional repositories that contain the last version of OpenStack and some supplementary packages.

```
# dnf config-manager --enable crb
# dnf install -y centos-release-openstack-yoga
```

After adding the repos, you should update the packages and reboot your test server.

```
# dnf -y update
# reboot
```

With older versions of CentOS or RHEL, you must disable Network Manager and enable the Network service. But since CentOS Stream 9 is used, it is okay to skip this step. Now everything is ready, and you can install the PackStack tool.

```
# dnf install -y openstack-packstack
```

There were known issues with SELinux policies when this chapter was written. For a workaround, please disable SELinux enforcing mode.

```
# setenforce 0
```

To keep SELinux in permissive mode after reboot, you must edit the /etc/sysconfig/selinux file. It should contain the following line.

```
SELINUX=permissive
```

Now you can just run the packstack --allinone command, but I recommend another change to generate the answers file for PackStack.

```
# packstack --gen-answer-file answer-file.txt
```

Now you are ready to edit the answer-file.txt. This file contains a lot of different options. Some of them are documented in Table 2-1.

Table 2-1. *PackStack Options*

Option with Example	Definition
CONFIG_<name of component>_ INSTALL=y	Specify y to install the OpenStack component. <name of component> can be CINDER, GLANCE, NOVA, NEUTRON, and so forth; for example, CONFIG_SWIFT_ INSTALL=y.
CONFIG_DEFAULT_ PASSWORD=password	This is the default password used everywhere (overridden by passwords set for individual services or users).
CONFIG_NTP_SERVERS= 192.168.1.1,192.168.1.2	This is a comma-separated list of NTP servers.
CONFIG_CONTROLLER_HOST= 192.168.122.10	This is a comma-separated list of servers on which to install OpenStack services specific to the controller role.
CONFIG_COMPUTE_HOSTS= 192.168.122.10	This is a list of servers on which to install the compute service.
CONFIG_NETWORK_HOSTS= 192.168.122.10	This is a list of servers on which to install the network service.
CONFIG_AMQP_BACKEND=rabbitmq	This is the service used as the AMQP broker; usually rabbitmq.
CONFIG_AMQP_HOST= 192.168.122.10	This is the IP address of the server on which to install the AMQP service.
CONFIG_AMQP_ENABLE_SSL=n	Specify y to enable SSL for the AMQP service.
CONFIG_USE_EPEL=y	Specify y to enable the EPEL repository (Extra Packages for Enterprise Linux). You need to do that if you are using CentOS or Oracle Linux.

(continued)

Table 2-1. (*continued*)

Option with Example	Definition
CONFIG_KEYSTONE_ADMIN_ PW=password	This is the password for the identity service admin user.
CONFIG_KEYSTONE_DEMO_ PW=password	This is the password for the identity service demo user.
CONFIG_GLANCE_BACKEND=file	This is the storage back end for the image service (controls how it stores disk images). Valid options are file or swift.
CONFIG_CINDER_BACKEND=lvm	This is the storage back end for the block storage service. Valid options are lvm, gluster, nfs, vmdk, or netapp.
CONFIG_CINDER_VOLUMES_CREATE=y	Specify y to create the block storage volumes group. PackStack creates a raw disk image in /var/lib/cinder and mounts it using a loopback device.
CONFIG_CINDER_VOLUMES_SIZE=20G	This is the size of the block storage volumes group.
CONFIG_NEUTRON_FWAAS=y	Specify y to configure OpenStack Networking's firewall-as-a-service (FWaaS).
CONFIG_NEUTRON_VPNAAS=y	Specify y to configure OpenStack Networking's VPN-as-a-service (VPNaaS).
CONFIG_SAHARA_INSTALL=y	Specify y to install the OpenStack data processing service (Sahara).
CONFIG_HEAT_INSTALL=y	Specify y to install OpenStack orchestration service (Heat).
CONFIG_TROVE_INSTALL=n	Specify y to install the OpenStack database service (Trove).
CONFIG_SWIFT_STORAGE_SIZE=2G	This is the size of the object storage loopback file storage device.
CONFIG_PROVISION_DEMO=y	Specify y to provision for demo usage and testing.

It is best to at least change the following options.

```
CONFIG_DEFAULT_PASSWORD=password
CONFIG_KEYSTONE_ADMIN_PW=password
CONFIG_KEYSTONE_DEMO_PW=password
CONFIG_PROVISION_DEMO=y
```

You should certainly use your own password instead of `password`. If you want to play with Heat, OpenStack's orchestration service, I advise you to enable it. Heat is not required for recent versions of the COA exam, but you can still find corresponding labs in this book's appendix.

```
CONFIG_HEAT_INSTALL=y
```

It can also be wise to point your host to an external NTP server, especially if you add additional nodes in the future. The time must be synced among all the nodes.

```
CONFIG_NTP_SERVERS=<IP address of NTP server>
```

Now you are ready to run PackStack.

```
# packstack --answer-file answer-file.txt
```

You must wait until PackStack completes all of its tasks. It can take 10 to 20 minutes. While working, the tool reports all that is happening at each stage. The following is an example.

```
Welcome to the Packstack setup utility
The installation log file is available at: /var/tmp/packstack/20220711-
154722-Oggeuec9/openstack-setup.log
Installing:
Clean Up                                        [ DONE ]
Discovering ip protocol version                 [ DONE ]
Setting up ssh keys                             [ DONE ]
...
Applying Puppet manifests                       [ DONE ]
Finalizing                                      [ DONE ]
 **** Installation completed successfully ******
```

Additional information:
 * Parameter CONFIG_NEUTRON_L2_AGENT: You have chosen OVN Neutron backend.
   Note that this backend does not support the VPNaaS plugin. Geneve will
   be used as the encapsulation method for tenant networks
 * Time synchronization installation was skipped. Please note that
   unsynchronized time on server instances might be problem for some
   OpenStack components.
 * Warning: NetworkManager is active on 192.168.122.10. OpenStack
   networking currently does not work on systems that have the Network
   Manager service enabled.
 * File /root/keystonerc_admin has been created on OpenStack client host
   192.168.122.10. To use the command line tools you need to source
   the file.
 * To access the OpenStack Dashboard browse to http://192.168.122.10/
   dashboard .
Please, find your login credentials stored in the keystonerc_admin in your
home directory.
 * The installation log file is available at: /var/tmp/packstack/20220711-
   154722-0ggeuec9/openstack-setup.log
 * The generated manifests are available at: /var/tmp/packstack/20220711-
   154722-0ggeuec9/manifests

Tip   You can re-run PackStack with option -d if you need to update the configuration.

The PackStack log output contains the IP address and URL of the OpenStack dashboard, where you can connect using the admin or demo username and your password.

Using the command line, you can source one of the RC files, /root/keystonerc_ admin or /root/keystonerc_demo, and execute some test commands. For example, let's get a list of the hypervisors.

```
# source keystonerc_admin
# openstack hypervisor list
+----+--------------------+-----------------+----------------+-------+
| ID | Hypervisor Hostname | Hypervisor Type | Host IP        | State |
+----+--------------------+-----------------+----------------+-------+
|  1 | rdo.test.local     | QEMU            | 192.168.122.10 | up    |
+----+--------------------+-----------------+----------------+-------+
```

If you have enough resources for additional compute virtual machines, you can add a server at the PackStack configuration and re-run the installation. For the second new server, you can repeat some of the steps you did for the first server.

```
# dnf config-manager --enable crb
# dnf install -y centos-release-openstack-yoga
# dnf -y update
# reboot
# setenforce 0
```

And again, to keep SELinux in permissive mode after reboot, you must edit the /etc/sysconfig/selinux file.

```
SELINUX=permissive
```

At the first server where you initially deployed PackStack, you need to add the IP of the second server to the CONFIG_COMPUTE_HOSTS configuration parameter.

```
CONFIG_COMPUTE_HOSTS=<First_server_IP>,<Second_server_IP>
```

Ensure that the key CONFIG_NETWORK_HOSTS exists and is set to the IP address of your first host.

Run PackStack at the first server again, specifying your modified answer file. This time, you are also asked for the root password at the second server.

```
# packstack --answer-file answer-file.txt
Welcome to the Packstack setup utility

The installation log file is available at: /var/tmp/
packstack/20220728-142909-5oau1d25/openstack-setup.log
```

```
Installing:
Clean Up                                        [ DONE ]
Discovering ip protocol version                 [ DONE ]
root@192.168.122.84's password: <enter the password>
```

After the second run, ensure that you have two compute nodes.

```
# source keystonerc_admin
# openstack hypervisor list
+----+---------------------+-----------------+----------------+-------+
| ID | Hypervisor Hostname | Hypervisor Type | Host IP        | State |
+----+---------------------+-----------------+----------------+-------+
|  1 | rdo.test.local      | QEMU            | 192.168.122.10 | up    |
|  2 | rdo2.test.local     | QEMU            | 192.168.122.84 | up    |
+----+---------------------+-----------------+----------------+-------+
```

Installing Ubuntu OpenStack with MicroStack

MicroStack (https://microstack.run/) allows you to create an OpenStack test lab. It is a Canonical project based on the snap tool (https://snapcraft.io/). MicroStack quickly installs OpenStack on a single machine. The supported services include Glance, Horizon, Keystone, Neutron (with OVN), and Nova.

Note   You cannot run all the labs in this book using MicroStack! You must use other options for the Cinder, Swift, and Heat examples in this book.

The installation step consists solely of installing a MicroStack snap.

```
user@microstack:~$ sudo snap install microstack --beta
[sudo] password for user:
microstack (beta) ussuri from Canonical✔ installed
```

The next step is initialization. It automatically deploys, configures, and starts OpenStack services.

```
# sudo microstack init --auto --control
...
2022-07-17 16:09:48,508 - microstack_init - INFO - Adding cirros image ...
2022-07-17 16:09:51,217 - microstack_init - INFO - Creating security group
rules ...
2022-07-17 16:09:59,982 - microstack_init - INFO - Configuring the Cinder
services...
2022-07-17 16:10:50,669 - microstack_init - INFO - Running Cinder DB
migrations...
2022-07-17 16:11:04,620 - microstack_init - INFO - restarting libvirt and
virtlogd ...
2022-07-17 16:11:30,231 - microstack_init - INFO - Complete. Marked
microstack as initialized!
```

For better usability, add an alias to the microstack.openstack command.

```
user@microstack:~$ sudo snap alias microstack.openstack openstack
[sudo] password for user:
Added:
  - microstack.openstack as openstack
```

Now you can run some OpenStack commands.

```
user@microstack:~$ openstack hypervisor list
+----+---------------------+-----------------+-----------------+-------+
| ID | Hypervisor Hostname | Hypervisor Type | Host IP         | State |
+----+---------------------+-----------------+-----------------+-------+
|  1 | microstack          | QEMU            | 192.168.122.100 | up    |
+----+---------------------+-----------------+-----------------+-------+
```

Summary

This chapter discussed installing a virtual lab in preparation for the Certified OpenStack Administrator exam. You can choose between the DevStack, PackStack, or MicroStack tools for this installation.

The next chapter delves into OpenStack APIs.

CHAPTER 3

OpenStack APIs

This chapter describes how to use the OpenStack CLI and dashboard. The chapter does not cover exam questions.

Using the OpenStack CLI

OpenStack comes with many client utilities. Most services have their own command-line interface (CLI) utility, which has the same name as the service itself. Some of these utilities will become obsolete because of the universal OpenStack CLI, which this book mainly uses.

You can use the packet manager to identify installed clients.

```
# rpm -qa | grep python.*client
python3-keystoneclient-4.4.0-1.el9s.noarch
python3-cinderclient-8.3.0-1.el9s.noarch
python3-novaclient-17.7.0-1.el9s.noarch
python-openstackclient-lang-5.8.0-1.el9s.noarch
python3-neutronclient-7.8.0-1.el9s.noarch
python3-openstackclient-5.8.0-1.el9s.noarch
python3-glanceclient-3.6.0-1.el9s.noarch
python3-barbicanclient-5.3.0-1.el9s.noarch
python3-swiftclient-3.13.1-1.el9s.noarch
python3-designateclient-4.5.0-1.el9s.noarch
python3-heatclient-2.5.1-1.el9s.noarch
python3-mistralclient-4.4.0-1.el9s.noarch
python3-troveclient-7.2.0-1.el9s.noarch
python3-ironicclient-4.11.0-1.el9s.noarch
python3-zaqarclient-2.3.0-1.el9s.noarch
```

© Andrey Markelov 2022
A. Markelov, *Certified OpenStack Administrator Study Guide*,
https://doi.org/10.1007/978-1-4842-8804-7_3

```
python3-saharaclient-3.5.0-1.el9s.noarch
python3-octaviaclient-2.5.0-1.el9s.noarch
python3-manilaclient-3.3.0-1.el9s.noarch
python3-magnumclient-3.6.0-1.el9s.noarch
python3-aodhclient-2.4.1-1.el9s.noarch
python3-gnocchiclient-7.0.4-2.el9s.noarch
```

Some of the packages do not belong to OpenStack. For example, Prometheus-client or google-api-client do not. But most of the RPMs include the name of the OpenStack service in the package name. For a full list, refer to `https://wiki.openstack.org/wiki/OpenStackClients`. At the time of writing, only the Keystone client was marked as deprecated. Most clients have an internal help section that can be printed with the `help` option followed by a subcommand. The following is an example.

```
$ glance help image-create
usage: glance image-create [--architecture <ARCHITECTURE>]
                           [--protected [True|False]] [--name <NAME>]
...
```

Universal `python3-openstackclient` has an interactive mode. This mode is indicated by the `(openstack)` prompt.

```
$ openstack
(openstack) help
Shell commands (type help <topic>):
===================================
cmdenvironment  edit    hi       l    list  pause  r    save  shell      show
ed              help    history  li   load  py     run  set   shortcuts
Undocumented commands:
======================
EOF  eof  exit  q  quit
Application commands (type help <topic>):
=========================================
aggregate add host          object list                 volume unset
aggregate create            object save
aggregate delete            object show
...
```

Use the following code to get help with the keypair create subcommand.

```
(openstack) help keypair create
usage: keypair create [-h] [-f {html,json,json,shell,table,value,ya
ml,yaml}]
                      [-c COLUMN] [--max-width <integer>] [--noindent]
                      [--prefix PREFIX] [--public-key <file>]
                      <name>
Create new public key
positional arguments:
  <name>                New public key name
...
```

Horizon's Architecture

I assume that you have used Horizon, OpenStack's dashboard, since Chapter 1. For first-time OpenStack users, it is probably easier than using CLI. However, you need to know that Horizon gives access to only about 70% to 80% of its overall functions. In certain situations, you are forced to use CLI. Figure 3-1 shows the login page for the OpenStack dashboard.

But what is it?

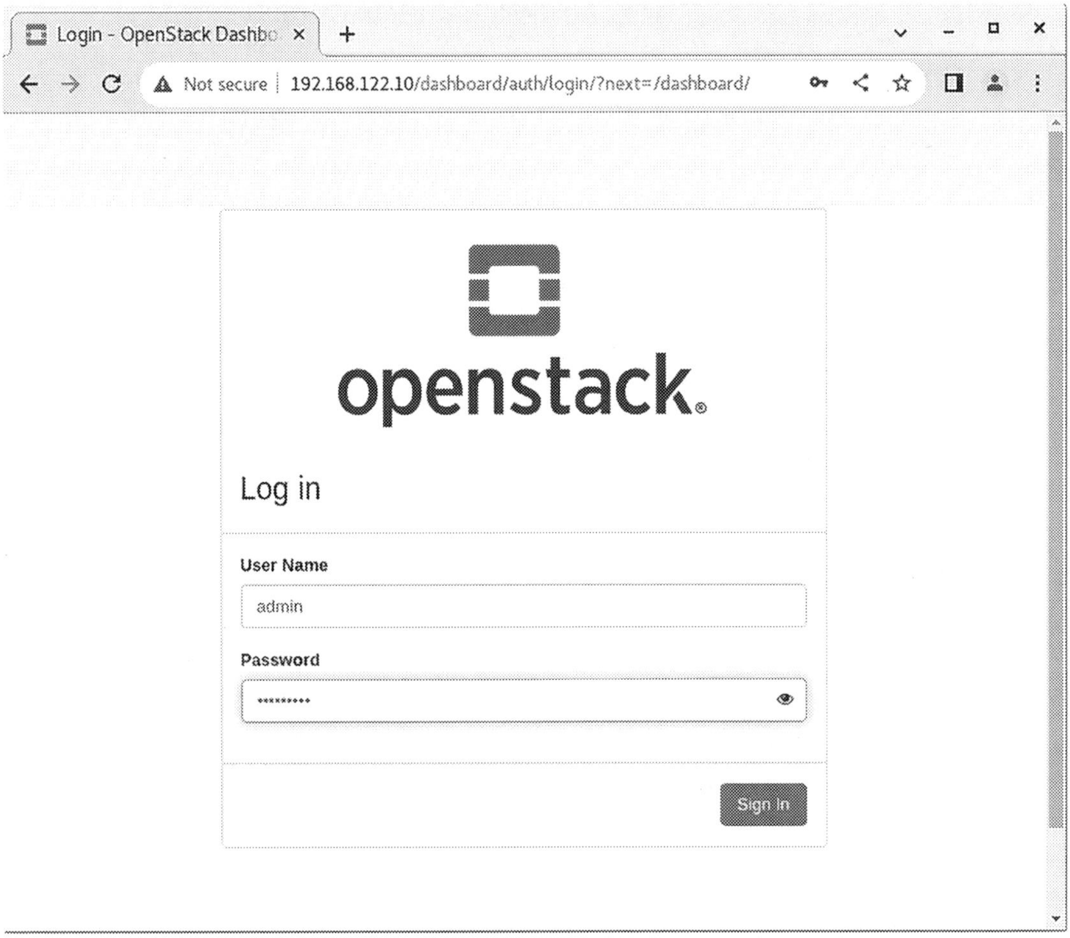

Figure 3-1. *OpenStack's dashboard login screen*

Horizon is a Python project that provides a complete dashboard and an extensible framework for building new dashboards. Horizon has the Django web framework as a dependency. The dashboard aims to support all core OpenStack projects. The minimum required set of running OpenStack services comprises Keystone, Nova, Neutron, and Glance. If the Keystone endpoint for a service is configured, Horizon detects it and enables support for optional services, such as Cinder, Swift, and Heat. Horizon can also work with services that are outside the scope of the Certified OpenStack Administrator exam and this book, such as Ceilometer, Sahara, and Trove.

OpenStack's Horizon dashboard runs under a web server, commonly Apache or NGINX. For large-scale deployments, it is recommended that you configure a caching layer in front of Horizon; for example, the memcached daemon.

You need to use a web browser with JavaScript and HTML5 support while working with Horizon, which is primarily tested and supported on the latest versions of Firefox, Chrome, and Microsoft Edge.

Tip   You can enable SSL support for the dashboard with the packstack installation tool. You need to provide the CONFIG_HORIZON_SSL=y option in the answer file for that.

Verifying the Operation of the Dashboard

When you start to work with Horizon, you should put your server IP or name in the web browser address bar and connect to port 80 or 443 in case you have SSL-enabled deployment of your Horizon server. It can be a separate server or one of the control nodes.

The dashboard's main configuration file is /etc/openstack-dashboard/local_settings. This configuration file has many options; however, the Keystone server URL is the most important.

```
OPENSTACK_KEYSTONE_URL = "http://192.168.122.10:5000/v3"
```

Another interesting option is a session timeout defined in seconds.

```
SESSION_TIMEOUT=3600
```

In some cases, it can be beneficial to increase this parameter. For example, if you plan to upload big virtual machine images via a slow connection.

The following is another option.

```
ALLOWED_HOSTS = ['*', ]
```

This lists the IP addresses or FQDNs on which Horizon accepts connections. The default star symbol means all server IPs accept it.

Tip   Some vendors supply their own themes with the Horizon dashboard installation. If your installation has a standard look, you can delete additional packages with branded themes. For Ubuntu, use `apt-get remove --auto-remove openstack-dashboard-ubuntu-theme`. For the Red Hat OpenStack platform, use `rpm -e openstack-dashboard-theme --nodeps`.

The Horizon log file is situated in the `/var/log/horizon/horizon.log` file.

Creating and Managing RC Files to Authenticate with Keystone for Command-Line Use

While working in the command line, it is recommended to use run control (RC) environment files, one for each user and project combination, to set authentication parameters. You are provided an RC file if you installed OpenStack using one of the deployment tools like PackStack or DevStack.

Another way to get the RC file is to download it from the Horizon dashboard. After successful login, click the username in the upper-right corner (see Figure 3-2), and then click OpenStack RC File. It is ready to use, with only one parameter missing inside. The file does not contain your password. Table 3-1 provides some RC file configuration options.

Table 3-1. *RC File Main Configuration Options*

Example of Config Options	Description
OS_AUTH_URL=http://192.168.122.10:5000/v3	The Keystone service URL
OS_REGION_NAME=RegionOne	The region name
OS_USERNAME=admin	The username
OS_PASSWORD=openstack	The password in clear text
OS_PROJECT_NAME=admin	The project name
OS_USER_DOMAIN_NAME=Default	The domain name
OS_IDENTITY_API_VERSION=3	The Keystone API version

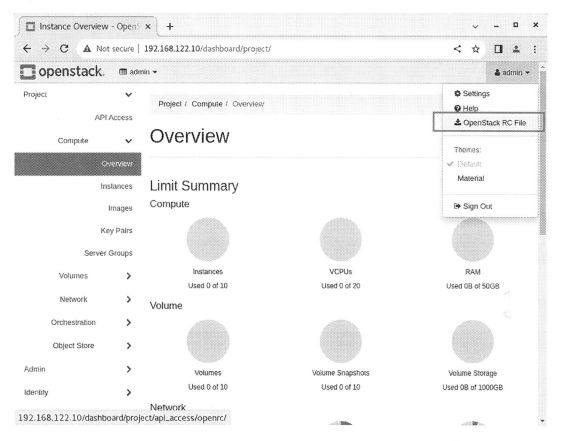

Figure 3-2. *How to download the RC file using the OpenStack dashboard*

Summary

This chapter described how to use OpenStack's CLI and dashboard, which are used in all the following chapters.

The next chapter explores identity management.

Review Questions

1. Which of the following is OpenStack dashboard's main configuration file?

   A. `/var/www/html/openstack-dashboard/local_settings`

   B. `/etc/openstack-dashboard/local_settings`

   C. `/etc/horizon/horizon.conf`

   D. `/etc/horizon/local_settings`

2. How do you set up a half-hour session timeout?

   A. `TIMEOUT=30`

   B. `SESSION_TIMEOUT=3600`

   C. `SESSION_TIMEOUT=1800`

   D. `TIMEOUT=300`

Answers

1. B

2. C

CHAPTER 4

Identity Management

Keystone, OpenStack's identity service, catalogs all its services. It provides the ability to authenticate and manage user accounts, regions, domains, projects, and role information for the cloud environment. If you are familiar with the Microsoft Windows Server environment, you can think of Keystone as the "Active Directory analog" for your OpenStack cloud. Usually, Keystone is the first component to be installed when starting an OpenStack cloud. Keystone supports multiple forms of authentication, including login name and password, token-based credentials, Amazon Web Services, REST API logins, and many others.

First, let's define some terms under which Keystone operates with.

- A **service** is an OpenStack cloud component listed in the Keystone catalog. These services include Nova, Neutron, Glance, and Keystone. Service provides one or more endpoints through which users can access the service's API.

- An **endpoint** is a URL from which the service is available. Service can have three endpoints: internal, public, and administration. They can have different subsets of API calls. An endpoint can look like this: `https://controller.my-domain.com:8776/v3`. Here, the service listens to incoming calls on port 8776, and the API is version 3. Common port numbers for OpenStack services are shown in Table 4-1. You can get a list of the endpoints for your OpenStack installation by executing the `openstack catalog list` command.

© Andrey Markelov 2022
A. Markelov, *Certified OpenStack Administrator Study Guide*,
https://doi.org/10.1007/978-1-4842-8804-7_4

Table 4-1. *Common Port Numbers for OpenStack Services*

Network Port Number	OpenStack Service
5000	Keystone's public API endpoint port
35357	Keystone's admin API endpoint port (can share 5000)
8776	Cinder block storage services
9292	Glance image services
8774	Nova compute services
8778	placement services
8080 and 6001–6003	Swift object storage services
9696	Neutron networking services
8042	aodh telemetry alarming services
8041	time series DB as a service
8004	Heat orchestration services

- A **project** represents the base unit of ownership in OpenStack. Networks, VMs, users, roles, and so forth belong to a particular project. An special project "admin" exists for administrative operations in OpenStack. The second utility project is the "services" project.

- A **domain** represents a collection of projects, groups, and users that defines administrative boundaries for managing OpenStack identity entities. In an initial OpenStack deployment, the only existing domain is the default domain.

- A **region** separates the OpenStack environment with dedicated API endpoints but with a common Keystone service. In an initial OpenStack deployment, the only existing region is RegionOne.

- A **token** is issued by Keystone service, then passed to API requests and used by OpenStack to verify that the client is authorized to run the requested operation. The token is issued for a limited time and, if necessary, may be withdrawn prior to the expiration. To get the user token, the user must either provide a name and password or the name and the key to access the API (API key). The token also contains a list of roles that defines the roles available to the user.

- A **user** is an individual API consumer. Users can be associated with roles, projects, or both. In an initial OpenStack deployment, the only existing user account is admin, which is assigned to the admin role in the default domain's admin project. The PackStack installation tool can create demo users with demo projects as well.

- A **role** is a specific set of operations associated with a user. A role includes a set of rights and privileges.

From an architectural point of view, Keystone is the simplest service in the cloud. As for many other OpenStack services, the identity service uses the MariaDB/MySQL database. Alternatively, storing information in the LDAP (Lightweight Directory Access Protocol) server or Microsoft Active Directory is possible. Starting from the Mitaka release, Keystone uses the Apache web server as the front end, so you no longer need to start `openstack-keystone.service`. Prior to the Mitaka release, Keystone worked under the built-in Eventlet Python service by default.

Tip   In modern documents, the OpenStack community prefers to use the word *project*. In older documents, you can still find the word *tenant*. Keep in mind that *project* and *tenant* are synonymous.

Let's quickly look through the Keystone main configuration file `/etc/keystone/keystone.conf`. Table 4-2 summarizes the main configuration options from config.

Table 4-2. *Main Configuration Options for /etc/keystone/keystone.conf*

Example of Config Options	Description
[DEFAULT] admin_token = ee224e8...	A "shared secret" that can be used to bootstrap and debug Keystone (This "token" does not represent a user.)
[DEFAULT] debug = True	Sets logging level to DEBUG instead of default INFO level in a journal
[DEFAULT] log_dir = /var/log/keystone	The base directory used for log files
[database] connection = mysql:// keystone_admin:password@ 192.168.122.10/keystone	The SQLAlchemy connection string to connect to the database
[token] expiration = 3600	Token validity timeframe (in seconds) (default–1 hour)
[ssl] Enable=False	Defines use of SSL connection

Managing Keystone Catalog Services and Endpoints

Before initiating something with OpenStack, you must go through the authorization and authentication processes. You can use the CLI commands options, but it is better and easier to create a file with global variables for GNU/Linux environment and to process this file with the source command. You need to create in any text editor something like the following code.

```
unset OS_SERVICE_TOKEN
export OS_AUTH_URL=http://192.168.122.10:5000/v3
export OS_TENANT_NAME=admin
export OS_REGION_NAME=RegionOne
export OS_USERNAME=admin
export OS_PASSWORD=openstack
export OS_PROJECT_NAME=admin
```

```
export OS_USER_DOMAIN_NAME=Default
export OS_PROJECT_DOMAIN_NAME=Default
export OS_IDENTITY_API_VERSION=3
```

If you used any of the installers described in Chapter 2, you would get this file automatically. You need to use your environment's correct IP address and admin password. Now you can execute the script.

```
$ source keystonerc_admin
```

Let's create a service record in Keystone for OpenStack's Glance image service (this service is described in Chapter 5).

```
$ openstack service create --name glance --description "OpenStack Image
service" image
+-------------+-----------------------------------+
| Field       | Value                             |
+-------------+-----------------------------------+
| description | OpenStack Image service           |
| enabled     | True                              |
| id          | 9d33c464f61749cd9f5811cda1ae5444  |
| name        | glance                            |
| type        | image                             |
+-------------+-----------------------------------+
```

Only two mandatory options exist in this command: the name of the service and the type of service. The name is glance, and the type is image. You can check the existing services with their types by using the openstack service list command.

```
$ openstack service list
+----------------------------------+-----------+---------------+
| ID                               | Name      | Type          |
+----------------------------------+-----------+---------------+
| 1512e88885c84cfa8a1d54ade990712b | placement | placement     |
| 44cb0eddaae5494f83d07bb48278eed6 | nova      | compute       |
| 5ae88c354230480e9b4e071d11587ee7 | glance    | image         |
| 5f094c2dcd964f2bbbc44172cc5a7840 | cinderv3  | volumev3      |
| 6435972a40544279944c7cc72edda939 | heat      | orchestration |
```

```
| 7c2aa7536caf43b5bf4ce51b96fea4a1 | keystone | identity       |
| a1b61cc227394eebbcd6198a3994185c | aodh     | alarming       |
| ad15ba2dcedb4f90ae0f8fc43511153e | heat-cfn | cloudformation |
| c355a9e2e6524d77afd8694d5ef326e0 | neutron  | network        |
| d7670dab054e43939c420c7c7f678a16 | gnocchi  | metric         |
| e0568d312dce42cc86b7ae25ac34d135 | swift    | object-store   |
+----------------------------------+----------+----------------+
```

If you made a mistake in service creation, you could easily delete it with the openstack service delete command. After creating the service record in the Keystone catalog, you need to create three endpoints for this service. This can be done with the next command.

```
$ openstack endpoint create image public  http://192.168.122.10:9292
--region RegionOne
+--------------+----------------------------------+
| Field        | Value                            |
+--------------+----------------------------------+
| enabled      | True                             |
| id           | 2bf154ca232640288fc36acff35a8997 |
| interface    | public                           |
| region       | RegionOne                        |
| region_id    | RegionOne                        |
| service_id   | 71595091f7df4feea97c9925bf181269 |
| service_name | glance                           |
| service_type | image                            |
| url          | http://192.168.122.10:9292       |
+--------------+----------------------------------+
```

You must repeat the command with two additional endpoints: internal and admin.

Note   The command's syntax changed in the Mitaka release. Do not be confused if you find examples where a single command created all three endpoints.

You can run a check on all the endpoints.

```
$ openstack endpoint list
+--------------------------------+-----------+-------------+------------------
-----------------+
| ID                             | Region    | Service Name | Service Type    |
Enabled | Interface | URL                                                     |
+--------------------------------+-----------+-------------+------------------
-----------------+
| 077925f6fc694aa78cd4ca84d6d24178 | RegionOne | glance      | image         |
True    | admin     | http://192.168.122.10:9292                              |
| 094235849d0a41ac87f087334fb39fdc | RegionOne | glance      | image         |
True    | internal  | http://192.168.122.10:9292                              |
| 0b36f879db4647568c29579f1347d386 | RegionOne | nova        | compute       |
True    | public    | http://192.168.122.10:8774/v2.1                         |
| 13cd54246edd4bc290442042734e2b8a | RegionOne | swift       | object-store  |
True    | public    | http://192.168.122.10:8080/v1/AUTH_%(tenant_id)s |
| 1c15ab54300a424c8697e42f69ad6f41 | RegionOne | swift       | object-store  |
True    | internal  | http://192.168.122.10:8080/v1/AUTH_%(tenant_id)s |
| 2ad9097a0ebc43c19e86001569b0c31f | RegionOne | heat-cfn    | cloudformation |
True    | admin     | http://192.168.122.10:8000/v1                           |
| 355e42ca7adf46b093ba86a401d04b55 | RegionOne | placement   | placement     |
True    | internal  | http://192.168.122.10:8778                              |
| 457ad6e5831645d0969af094ccf6be2a | RegionOne | heat-cfn    | cloudformation |
True    | internal  | http://192.168.122.10:8000/v1                           |
| 5435cb7957c142d89ed20123dd854eec | RegionOne | aodh        | alarming      |
True    | internal  | http://192.168.122.10:8042                              |
| 551894b71129448eb9efc934f7d1a374 | RegionOne | nova        | compute       |
True    | internal  | http://192.168.122.10:8774/v2.1                         |
| 56474f67106e42f49e7077f84af19d5e | RegionOne | keystone    | identity      |
True    | public    | http://192.168.122.10:5000                              |
| 57d55ed6bac14ca79ac9f0d843c92359 | RegionOne | heat        | orchestration |
True    | public    | http://192.168.122.10:8004/v1/%(tenant_id)s             |
| 62e904bfa98642c4a1b170881b95b01d | RegionOne | swift       | object-store  |
True    | admin     | http://192.168.122.10:8080/v1/AUTH_%(tenant_id)s |
| 6a59ce4050414804b727f36b021a1ed5 | RegionOne | glance      | image         |
True    | public    | http://192.168.122.10:9292                              |
| 6dda1a447ede47e38fbaabb68f012967 | RegionOne | gnocchi     | metric        |
True    | admin     | http://192.168.122.10:8041                              |
```

43

```
| 875f9b8d3ad74e8cbca45ab579e6ce6c | RegionOne | gnocchi     | metric          |
True   | internal | http://192.168.122.10:8041                                |
| 8b5aca21d1b343729f434aa47d902406 | RegionOne | heat-cfn    | cloudformation  |
True   | public   | http://192.168.122.10:8000/v1                             |
| 90ffbf140de6475c806725290ed7ed2b | RegionOne | cinderv3    | volumev3        |
True   | internal | http://192.168.122.10:8776/v3                             |
| 91822f8dbfed46a3a4b50d2c4c4b5e72 | RegionOne | cinderv3    | volumev3        |
True   | admin    | http://192.168.122.10:8776/v3                             |
| 978ae5905a0549e68d7050c4aba797d7 | RegionOne | gnocchi     | metric          |
True   | public   | http://192.168.122.10:8041                                |
| a4e0777b930e49a1b1d9736fed15d388 | RegionOne | keystone    | identity        |
True   | admin    | http://192.168.122.10:5000                                |
| afbd7fd5c23849ba95776349e613101e | RegionOne | placement   | placement       |
True   | public   | http://192.168.122.10:8778                                |
| b5ad13604eec4703aa4a2129ee286fd9 | RegionOne | placement   | placement       |
True   | admin    | http://192.168.122.10:8778                                |
| c1a044e51e794cf09e672a7ec29619fd | RegionOne | nova        | compute         |
True   | admin    | http://192.168.122.10:8774/v2.1                           |
| c4ec044916d74e1694f1ab54bc8706f3 | RegionOne | keystone    | identity        |
True   | internal | http://192.168.122.10:5000                                |
| cb2864864ba04da0935ab5a88fb34346 | RegionOne | cinderv3    | volumev3        |
True   | public   | http://192.168.122.10:8776/v3                             |
| d5c4c54e90c34f83bed5a8c45c69e7b2 | RegionOne | neutron     | network         |
True   | public   | http://192.168.122.10:9696                                |
| e0382c15ccd144f3baa3f2b1b62fe5f9 | RegionOne | neutron     | network         |
True   | admin    | http://192.168.122.10:9696                                |
| e42eaca2b18f4d3b923d2d14c5e97d81 | RegionOne | neutron     | network         |
True   | internal | http://192.168.122.10:9696                                |
| f3c12a3e48c04d9ba107859ad4302283 | RegionOne | aodh        | alarming        |
True   | public   | http://192.168.122.10:8042                                |
| f5d15ec7d0a04327b5d402c82a93799d | RegionOne | heat        | orchestration   |
True   | admin    | http://192.168.122.10:8004/v1/%(tenant_id)s               |
| f6e689e9a0c8452ea4a976bc591d6355 | RegionOne | heat        | orchestration   |
True   | internal | http://192.168.122.10:8004/v1/%(tenant_id)s               |
| fe476aade04f45feaaf98779dc79c60b | RegionOne | aodh        | alarming        |
True   | admin    | http://192.168.122.10:8042                                |
+----------------------------------+-----------+-------------+--------------------
------------------+
```

And if you want to show the details about a particular endpoint, you need to refer to it by ID.

```
$ openstack endpoint show f5d15ec7d0a04327b5d402c82a93799d
+--------------+-------------------------------------------+
| Field        | Value                                     |
+--------------+-------------------------------------------+
| enabled      | True                                      |
| id           | f5d15ec7d0a04327b5d402c82a93799d          |
| interface    | admin                                     |
| region       | RegionOne                                 |
| region_id    | RegionOne                                 |
| service_id   | 6435972a40544279944c7cc72edda939          |
| service_name | heat                                      |
| service_type | orchestration                             |
| url          | http://192.168.122.10:8004/v1/%(tenant_id)s |
+--------------+-------------------------------------------+
```

Horizon can handle approximately 70% of the overall available OpenStack functionality. So, you can't create services and endpoints through the web client, although you can check a list of services and their current statuses. Log in as an admin and go to Admin ➤ System ➤ System Information (see Figure 4-1).

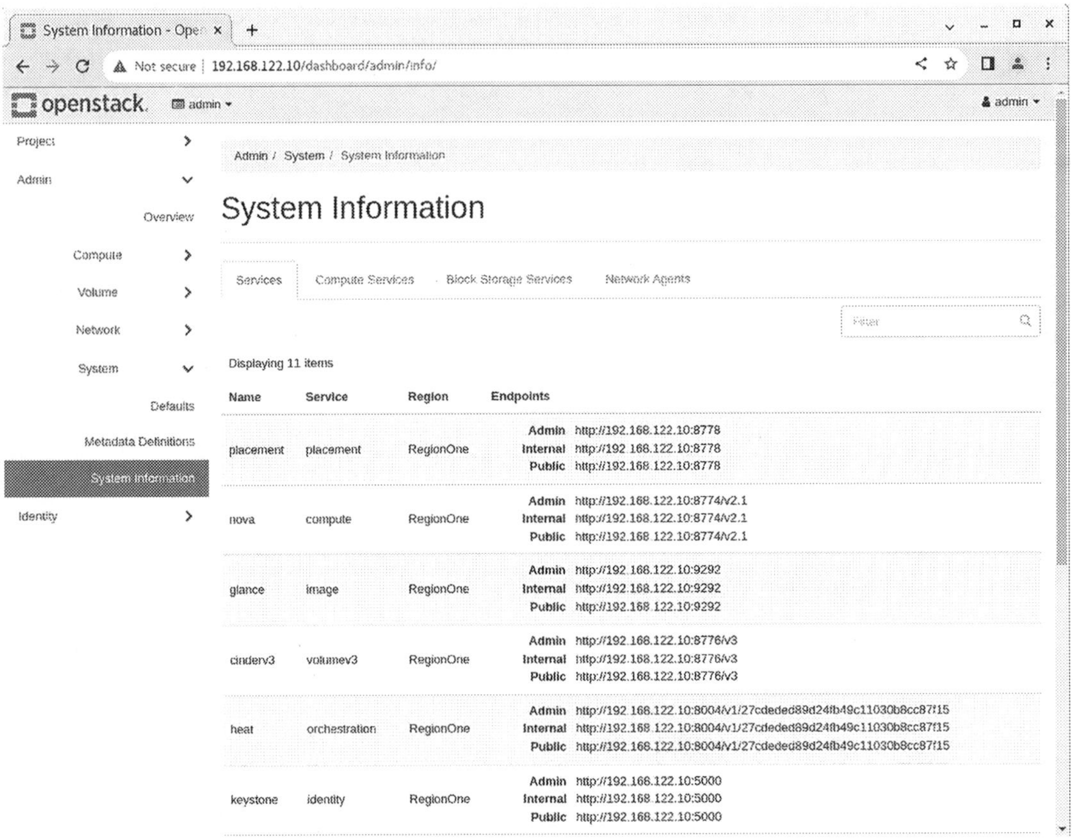

Figure 4-1. *List of services in Horizon*

Managing/Creating Domains, Projects, Users, and Roles

You can easily create projects, users, and roles with the help of the openstack CLI command. Let's start with a new domain. You need to use admin credentials for this operation.

```
$ source keystonerc_admin
$ openstack domain create --description "Test domain" newdomain
+-------------+----------------------------------+
| Field       | Value                            |
+-------------+----------------------------------+
| description | Test domain                      |
| enabled     | True                             |
| id          | 2eb7949c140f4c6f9da639fb4ff3b292 |
| name        | newdomain                        |
| options     | {}                               |
| tags        | []                               |
+-------------+----------------------------------+
```

Then, you can create a new project at the newdomain domain.

```
$ openstack project create --description "Test project" --domain
newdomain apress
+-------------+----------------------------------+
| Field       | Value                            |
+-------------+----------------------------------+
| description | Test project                     |
| domain_id   | 2eb7949c140f4c6f9da639fb4ff3b292 |
| enabled     | True                             |
| id          | 8850cf87ed6e463d91c6096687e236bf |
| is_domain   | False                            |
| name        | apress                           |
| options     | {}                               |
| parent_id   | 2eb7949c140f4c6f9da639fb4ff3b292 |
| tags        | []                               |
+-------------+----------------------------------+
```

You can get a list of all projects and details about each.

```
$ openstack project list
+----------------------------------+----------+
| ID                               | Name     |
+----------------------------------+----------+
| 27cdeded89d24fb49c11030b8cc87f15 | admin    |
| 53d4fd6c5b1d44e89e604957c4df4fc2 | services |
| 8850cf87ed6e463d91c6096687e236bf | apress   |
| 9e0c535c2240405b989afa450681df18 | demo     |
+----------------------------------+----------+
$ openstack project show apress
+-------------+----------------------------------+
| Field       | Value                            |
+-------------+----------------------------------+
| description | Test project                     |
| domain_id   | 2eb7949c140f4c6f9da639fb4ff3b292 |
| enabled     | True                             |
| id          | 8850cf87ed6e463d91c6096687e236bf |
| is_domain   | False                            |
| name        | apress                           |
| options     | {}                               |
| parent_id   | 2eb7949c140f4c6f9da639fb4ff3b292 |
| tags        | []                               |
+-------------+----------------------------------+
```

The first command provided three projects from the default domain and one from newdomain. You can create the second Apress project in another domain, the default domain. In this case, you see two Apress projects.

```
$ openstack project create --description "Test project" --domain
default apress
+-------------+----------------------------------+
| Field       | Value                            |
+-------------+----------------------------------+
| description | Test project                     |
| domain_id   | default                          |
| enabled     | True                             |
| id          | 3a9a59175cce4a74a72c882947e8bc86 |
```

48

```
| is_domain   | False                            |
| name        | apress                           |
| options     | {}                               |
| parent_id   | default                          |
| tags        | []                               |
+-------------+----------------------------------+
$ openstack project list
+----------------------------------+----------+
| ID                               | Name     |
+----------------------------------+----------+
| 27cdeded89d24fb49c11030b8cc87f15 | admin    |
| 3a9a59175cce4a74a72c882947e8bc86 | apress   |
| 53d4fd6c5b1d44e89e604957c4df4fc2 | services |
| 8850cf87ed6e463d91c6096687e236bf | apress   |
| 9e0c535c2240405b989afa450681df18 | demo     |
+----------------------------------+----------+
```

You can recognize projects by adding the --domain option.

```
$ openstack project list --domain default
+----------------------------------+----------+
| ID                               | Name     |
+----------------------------------+----------+
| 27cdeded89d24fb49c11030b8cc87f15 | admin    |
| 3a9a59175cce4a74a72c882947e8bc86 | apress   |
| 53d4fd6c5b1d44e89e604957c4df4fc2 | services |
| 9e0c535c2240405b989afa450681df18 | demo     |
+----------------------------------+----------+
$ openstack project list --domain newdomain
+----------------------------------+--------+
| ID                               | Name   |
+----------------------------------+--------+
| 8850cf87ed6e463d91c6096687e236bf | apress |
+----------------------------------+--------+
```

Now you can create a new user - apressadmin- granting _member_ a role in the Apress project.

```
$ openstack user create --password-prompt --domain newdomain apressuser
User Password:
Repeat User Password:
+---------------------+------------------------------------+
| Field               | Value                              |
+---------------------+------------------------------------+
| domain_id           | 2eb7949c140f4c6f9da639fb4ff3b292   |
| enabled             | True                               |
| id                  | b61d2670f55f425e9a8e5eabb8deeeda   |
| name                | apressuser                         |
| options             | {}                                 |
| password_expires_at | None                               |
+---------------------+------------------------------------+
$ openstack role add --project apress --user apressuser _member_
+-------+----------------------------------+
| Field | Value                            |
+-------+----------------------------------+
| id    | 9fe2ff9ee4384b1894a90878d3e92bab |
| name  | _member_                         |
+-------+----------------------------------+
```

Note   If you skip the --domain option, the user is created at the default domain. If more than one project exists with the name apress, the command fails. You must add the --domain option to specify the domain.

The admin role is global, not per project, so granting a user the admin role in any project gives the user administrative rights across the whole environment.

If you use the multi-domain model, then you must enable the OPENSTACK_ KEYSTONE_MULTIDOMAIN_SUPPORT = True option in the /etc/openstack-dashboard/ local_settings file; otherwise, users who are not from the default domain cannot log in to the Horizon dashboard. The screenshot on the left side of Figure 4-2 is disabled; the screenshot on the right side shows it enabled.

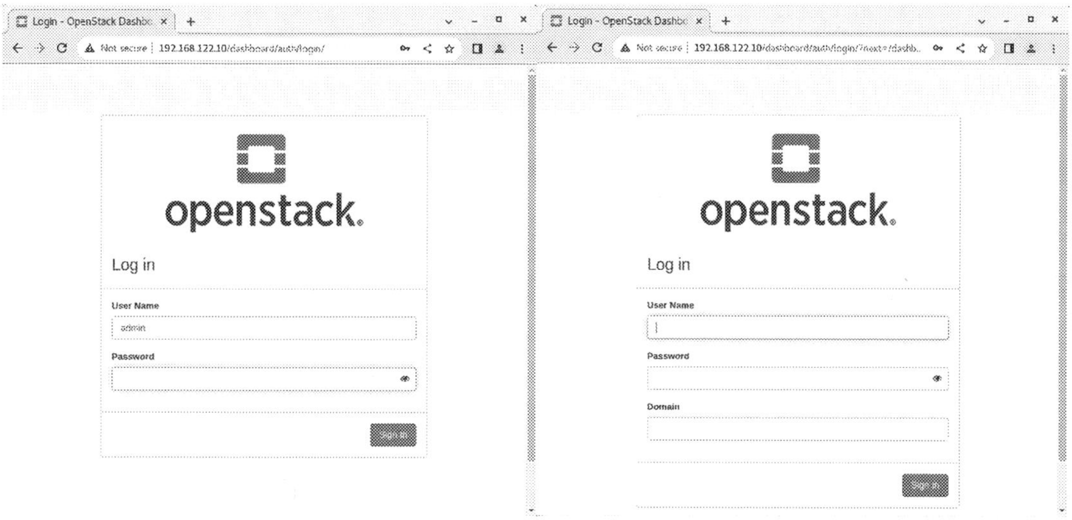

Figure 4-2. *Horizon dashboard login page*

If you want a list of all the roles in the OpenStack cloud, use the following command.

```
$ openstack role list
+----------------------------------+------------------+
| ID                               | Name             |
+----------------------------------+------------------+
| 1911ed7a60dd4747b1fa6acc5f92a043 | _member_         |
| 2fedf0797f424044bcab955aec0eab3d | ResellerAdmin    |
| 4954a6475ba9486db1a71d9a7c80678a | reader           |
| 5cee5adb606f46178d5afe98875d73b7 | heat_stack_user  |
| 90d2e65c22d44414a5f4426cc475be25 | heat_stack_owner |
| ac25b92ce9474945831685b249a4a07b | admin            |
| d88c81ae7b354abb9a2960115cff07a6 | SwiftOperator    |
| f7722f79327f40b7845899cef62c8b0a | member           |
+----------------------------------+------------------+
```

As you can see, to create a region or domain in the identity service, you need an admin role. You get an HTTP 403 error code if the current policy doesn't allow the command to be performed.

After creating a new user, you may want to create a new keystonerc file for it. You may use the keystonerc_admin file as a template. In this case, you need to change the OS_PROJECT_NAME, OS_USERNAME, and OS_PASSWORD variables.

51

If you need to delete a user or project, you can use the same `openstack` command but with the `delete` subcommand. The following is an example.

```
$ openstack user delete apressuser
$ openstack project delete apress
```

It is possible to create, delete, and edit users and projects in OpenStack in the web interface (Horizon). Go to Identity ➤ Users or Identity ➤ Projects. Examples of editing a project and creating a user are shown in Figures 4-3 and 4-4, respectively.

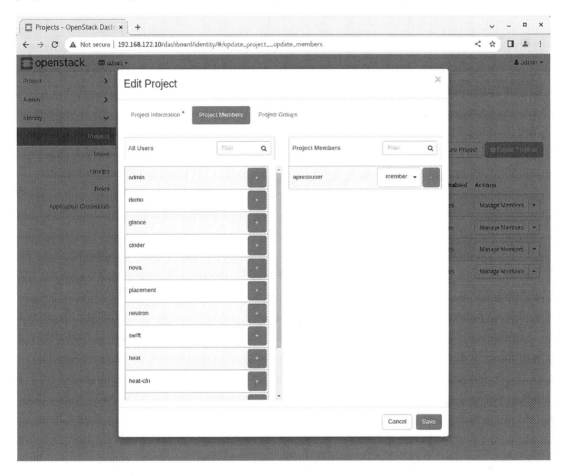

Figure 4-3. *Managing project members in Horizon*

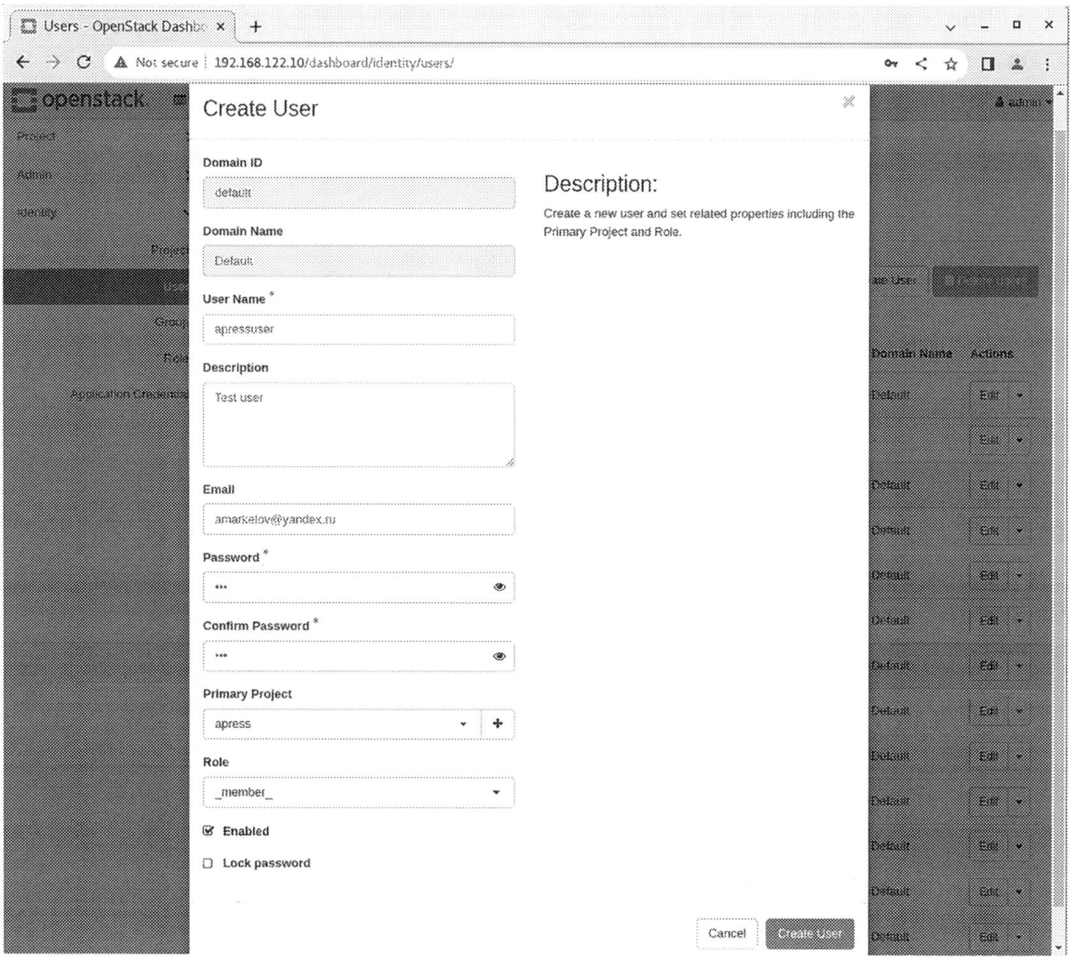

Figure 4-4. *Creating a new user in Horizon*

Managing and Verifying the Operation of the Identity Service

For performance, a modern OpenStack installation deploys the Apache HTTP server with the mod_wsgi package to handle requests and the Memcached front end to store tokens. CentOS, Scientific Linux, Oracle Linux, and other Red Hat Enterprise Linux derivatives use service management system distribution. You can check whether Memcached and Apache servers are started and active.

```
# systemctl status memcached.service
● memcached.service - Memcached
     Loaded: loaded (/usr/lib/systemd/system/memcached.service; enabled;
     vendor preset: disabled)
     Active: active (running) since Wed 2022-07-13 15:12:19 CEST; 20min ago
   Main PID: 1347 (memcached)
      Tasks: 14 (limit: 204820)
     Memory: 9.4M
        CPU: 192ms
     CGroup: /system.slice/memcached.service
             └─1347 /usr/bin/memcached -p 11211 -u memcached -m 3206 -c
8192 -l 0.0.0.0 -U 0 -t 8 ">>" /var/log/memcached.log "2>&1"

Jul 13 15:12:19 rdo.test.local systemd[1]: Started memcached daemon.
# systemctl status httpd.service
● httpd.service - The Apache HTTP Server
     Loaded: loaded (/usr/lib/systemd/system/httpd.service; enabled; vendor
     preset: disabled)
    Drop-In: /usr/lib/systemd/system/httpd.service.d
             └─openstack-dashboard.conf
     Active: active (running) since Wed 2022-07-13 15:12:49 CEST; 20min ago
...
```

Note   Keystone supports the three access tokens: PKI tokens (deprecated), UUID, and Fernet tokens. The first two are non-persistent, lightweight, and reduce the operational overhead required to run a cloud. Fernet tokens don't need to have the Memcached daemon run.

The standard GNU/Linux ps command can show you eight processes with names containing keystone.

```
# ps aux | grep keystone
keystone     4305  0.2  0.3 255984 111544 ?        Sl   15:12   0:03
keystone          -DFOREGROUND
keystone     4306  0.1  0.3 254192 109248 ?        Sl   15:12   0:02
keystone          -DFOREGROUND
...
```

There are daemon processes created for running through the WSGI module of the Apache HTTP server. You can find their configuration files in the /etc/httpd/conf.d/ directory.

```
# ls /etc/httpd/conf.d/*keystone*
/etc/httpd/conf.d/10-keystone_wsgi.conf
```

Here is a shortened example of the configuration file for the virtual host.

```
<VirtualHost *:5000>
  ServerName rdo.test.local
  ## Vhost docroot
  DocumentRoot "/var/www/cgi-bin/keystone"
  ## Directories, there should at least be a declaration for /var/www/cgi-
  bin/keystone
  <Directory "/var/www/cgi-bin/keystone">
    Options -Indexes +FollowSymLinks +MultiViews
    AllowOverride None
    Require all granted
  </Directory>
  ## Logging
  ErrorLog "/var/log/httpd/keystone_wsgi_error.log"
  ServerSignature Off
  CustomLog "/var/log/httpd/keystone_wsgi_access.log" combined
  SetEnvIf X-Forwarded-Proto https HTTPS=1
  ## WSGI configuration
  WSGIApplicationGroup %{GLOBAL}
  WSGIDaemonProcess keystone display-name=keystone group=keystone
  processes=8 threads=1 user=keystone
  WSGIProcessGroup keystone
  WSGIScriptAlias / "/var/www/cgi-bin/keystone/keystone"
  WSGIPassAuthorization On
</VirtualHost>
```

If troubleshooting is needed, you may also want to check the endpoints by ID.

```
$ openstack endpoint show <ID of endpoint>
```

When debugging, you may want to check the logins using /var/log/httpd/keystone_* and /var/log/keystone/keystone.log.

Summary

This chapter discussed Keystone's architecture and main components. You learned how to manage catalog services, endpoints, users, and domains.

The next chapter delves into image management.

Review Questions

1. Which of the following adds user apressuser with a member role to the only Apress project?

   A. openstack role add --project apress --user apressuser _member_

   B. openstack role add --project apress --user apressuser member

   C. openstack role add --project apress --user _member_ apressuser

   D. openstack role add --project apress --user member apressuser

2. Which system service should be started for proper Keystone functioning?

   A. httpd

   B. keystone-admin

   C. memcached

   D. keystone

3. How do you define a new role in the OpenStack cloud? (Choose all that are applicable.)

   A. Enter the openstack role create newrole command.

   B. Restart the httpd service.

   C. Create a new keystonerc file.

   D. Add a definition to the policy.json file.

4. How do you separate two or more cloud instances but manage them with one Keystone instance?

   A. Use the Domains feature.

   B. Use the Regions feature.

   C. Use availability zones.

   D. Each cloud instance should use its own Keystone instance feature.

5. Which HTTP error code do you get if the Keystone token has expired?

   A. ERROR 404

   B. ERROR 403

   C. ERROR 401

   D. All of them

Answers

1. A

2. D

3. A

4. A

5. C

CHAPTER 5

Image Management

This chapter covers 5% of the Certified OpenStack Administrator exam requirements. It describes how to work with the image management service. Any OpenStack installation has this service. It is essential for running virtual machines.

Glance's Architecture and Main Components

Chapter 4 touched on the Keystone service that acts as a catalog of other OpenStack services. This chapter covers one of the services in almost all OpenStack installations. The name of this service is Glance, and its purpose is to act as an images-as-a-service provider. First, let's deconstruct Glance to its components, as shown in Figure 5-1.

© Andrey Markelov 2022
A. Markelov, *Certified OpenStack Administrator Study Guide*,
https://doi.org/10.1007/978-1-4842-8804-7_5

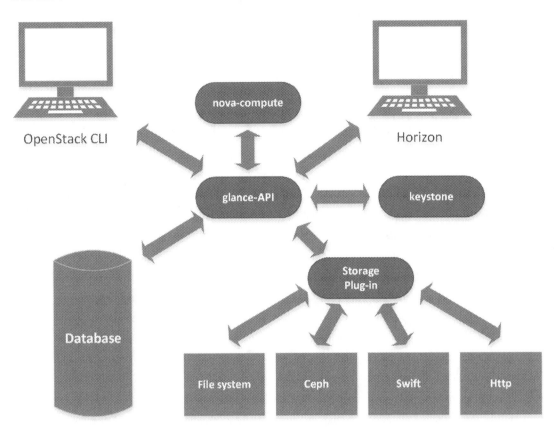

Figure 5-1. *Glance architecture (Cinder and Glance integration is not shown to avoid complexity)*

Glance consists of two main components.

- **glance-api** is a service implemented as GNU/Linux daemon. It accepts Image REST API calls for image discovery, retrieval, and storage.

- **Storage plug-ins** for accessing various types of storage.

Take note that the old **glance-registry** service was deprecated. It stored, processed, and retrieved image metadata.

As shown in Figure 5-1, Glance does not store images. It uses plug-ins for storage, which can be your local file system, Swift object storage, Ceph storage, NFS (Network File System), or other back ends. Image metadata is usually stored in the Glance database as a MariaDB instance.

Glance supports many disk formats. Table 5-1 describes some of them.

Table 5-1. *Disk Formats Supported by Glance*

Type of Disk	Description
aki	An Amazon kernel image
ami	An Amazon machine image
ari	An Amazon RAM disk image
iso	An archive format for the data contents of an optical disk, such as CD-ROM
qcow2	Supported by the QEMU emulator that can expand dynamically and supports Copy on Write
raw	An unstructured disk image format (If you have a file without an extension, it is possibly a raw format.)
vdi	Supported by VirtualBox virtual machine monitor and the QEMU emulator
vhd	A common disk format used by virtual machine monitors, such as VMware, Xen, Microsoft, and VirtualBox
vmdk	A common disk format supported by many common virtual machine monitors

Let's check the Glance service on the OpenStack controller.

```
# systemctl | grep glance
  openstack-glance-api.serviceloaded active running    OpenStack Image
  Service (code-named Glance) API server
```

As you can see, the service is up and running.

When Nova, the compute service, is trying to spawn a new virtual machine, it usu-ally sends a GET request to the URL `http://path_to_Glance_service/images/pat-icular_image_ID`. If glance-api finds the requested image, the service returns the URL where the image is located. After that, Nova sends the link to the hypervisor's driver, and the hypervisor downloads the image directly.

Then you need to look through the glance-api main configuration file, `/etc/glance/glance-api.conf`.

Tip   Default config files come with many comments and are a very good source
of information. But sometimes, you need to closely examine the configs. You
can use RegEx magic to remove all comments and make the configs shorter.
For example, the `grep -o '^[^#]*'` `/etc/glance/glance-api.conf`
command lets you cut the default file from 1200 lines to 29. It can make your
life easier.

Glance uses the database for storing metadata. In both config files, you can find
something like the following.

```
[database]
...
connection=mysql+pymysql://glance:password@192.168.122.10/glance
```

This is the connection URL for the Glance database. Next, you need the authentication parameters for Keystone. As with other services, you need to define the basic authentication credentials.

```
[keystone_authtoken]
www_authenticate_uri=http://192.168.122.10:5000/v3
auth_url=http://192.168.122.10:5000
username=glance
password=password
project_name=services
project_domain_name=Default
user_domain_name=Default
[paste_deploy]
flavor=keystone
```

In our setup, the Keystone server has the 192.168.122.10 IP address, and you can
see the public Identity API endpoint and Admins Identity API endpoint definitions. The
Glance username, service tenant, and password are in clear text in the config files. It is
very important to keep the right permissions for all config files because many of them
contain the password in clear text.

The back end of this installation uses the following files.

```
[glance_store]
default_backend=file
[file]
filesystem_store_datadir=/var/lib/glance/images/
```

Deploying a New Image to an OpenStack Instance

You can download various cloud-ready images from the Internet. Most major Linux distributions already have prepared images for OpenStack. Table 5-2 lists several examples.

Table 5-2. *Cloud-ready Images*

Linux Distro or OS	URL
CirrOS	http://download.cirros-cloud.net/
Ubuntu	http://cloud-images.ubuntu.com/
Debian	http://cdimage.debian.org/images/cloud/
Fedora	https://getfedora.org/cloud/download/
CentOS Linux and Stream	http://cloud.centos.org/centos/
Windows Server 2012 R2 Evaluation for OpenStack	https://cloudbase.it/windows-cloud-images/

For testing purposes, you can use CirrOS, a minimal Linux distro designed for testing images on the cloud. First, you need to download the image from

```
$ wget -P /tmp http://download.cirros-cloud.net/0.5.2/cirros-0.5.2-x86_64-disk.img.
```

Tip   In a CirrOS image, the username of the existing account is cirros. The password is cubswin.

It's good to know an image's information before onboarding it to OpenStack. Use the qemu-img command from the package with the same name.

```
$ qemu-img info /tmp/cirros-0.5.2-x86_64-disk.img
image: /tmp/cirros-0.5.2-x86_64-disk.img
file format: qcow2
virtual size: 112 MiB (117440512 bytes)
disk size: 15.5 MiB
cluster_size: 65536
Format specific information:
    compat: 1.1
    compression type: zlib
    lazy refcounts: false
    refcount bits: 16
    corrupt: false
    extended l2: false
```

You can get the following information from the output.

- **file format** is the disk format.

- **virtual size** is the disk size of a virtual machine

- **disk size** is the size of the file

- **cluster_size** is the block size for qcow2

- Format-specific information means that when using qcow2 in our example, compat: 1.1 is specified; specifically, a new version of the qcow2 image, which is supported by QEMU version 1.1.

Then you can deploy the image in the cloud.

```
$ openstack image create --file /tmp/cirros-0.5.2-x86_64-disk.img --disk-format
qcow2 --container-format bare --public cirros-0.5.2-x86_64
+-----------------+------------------------------------------------------------+
| Field           | Value                                                      |
+-----------------+------------------------------------------------------------+
| container_format | bare                                                      |
| created_at      | 2022-07-14T13:46:20Z                                       |
| disk_format     | qcow2                                                      |
```

```
| file              | /v2/images/7ffe1b43-7e86-4ad0-86b6-9fffa38b3c20/file               |
| id                | 7ffe1b43-7e86-4ad0-86b6-9fffa38b3c20                               |
| min_disk          | 0                                                                  |
| min_ram           | 0                                                                  |
| name              | cirros-0.5.2-x86_64                                                |
| owner             | 27cdeded89d24fb49c11030b8cc87f15                                   |
| properties        | os_hidden='False', owner_specified.openstack.md5='',              |
|                   |  owner_specified.openstack.object='images/cirros-0.5.2-x86_64',   |
|                   |  owner_specified.openstack.sha256=''                              |
| protected         | False                                                              |
| schema            | /v2/schemas/image                                                  |
| status            | queued                                                             |
| tags              |                                                                    |
| updated_at        | 2022-07-14T13:46:20Z                                               |
| visibility        | public                                                             |
+-------------------+--------------------------------------------------------------------+
```

In the preceding command, `--public` means that the image can be used across projects/tenants for every user in the OpenStack cloud. To get information about the image, you can use the `openstack image show` command followed by the ID of the image or name. In this case, the ID is `7ffe1b43-7e86-4ad0-86b6-9fffa38b3c20`, and the name is `cirros-0.5.2-x86_64`.

To get a list of all available images for the current user, use the following.

```
$ openstack image list
+--------------------------------------+---------------------+--------+
| ID                                   | Name                | Status |
+--------------------------------------+---------------------+--------+
| cb14ee7c-02e4-4274-bd3f-8d81cd139593 | CentOS9             | active |
| ff8ebfb3-7a6e-446c-8fe7-2466b8ebd29b | Ubuntu2210          | active |
| 7ffe1b43-7e86-4ad0-86b6-9fffa38b3c20 | cirros-0.5.2-x86_64 | active |
+--------------------------------------+---------------------+--------+
```

As an admin, you can see all the images in the cloud.

You can create an image in OpenStack in a web interface (Horizon). Go to Project ➤ Compute ➤ Images. Click the Create Image button (see Figure 5-2). Only the image name, format, and file are mandatory.

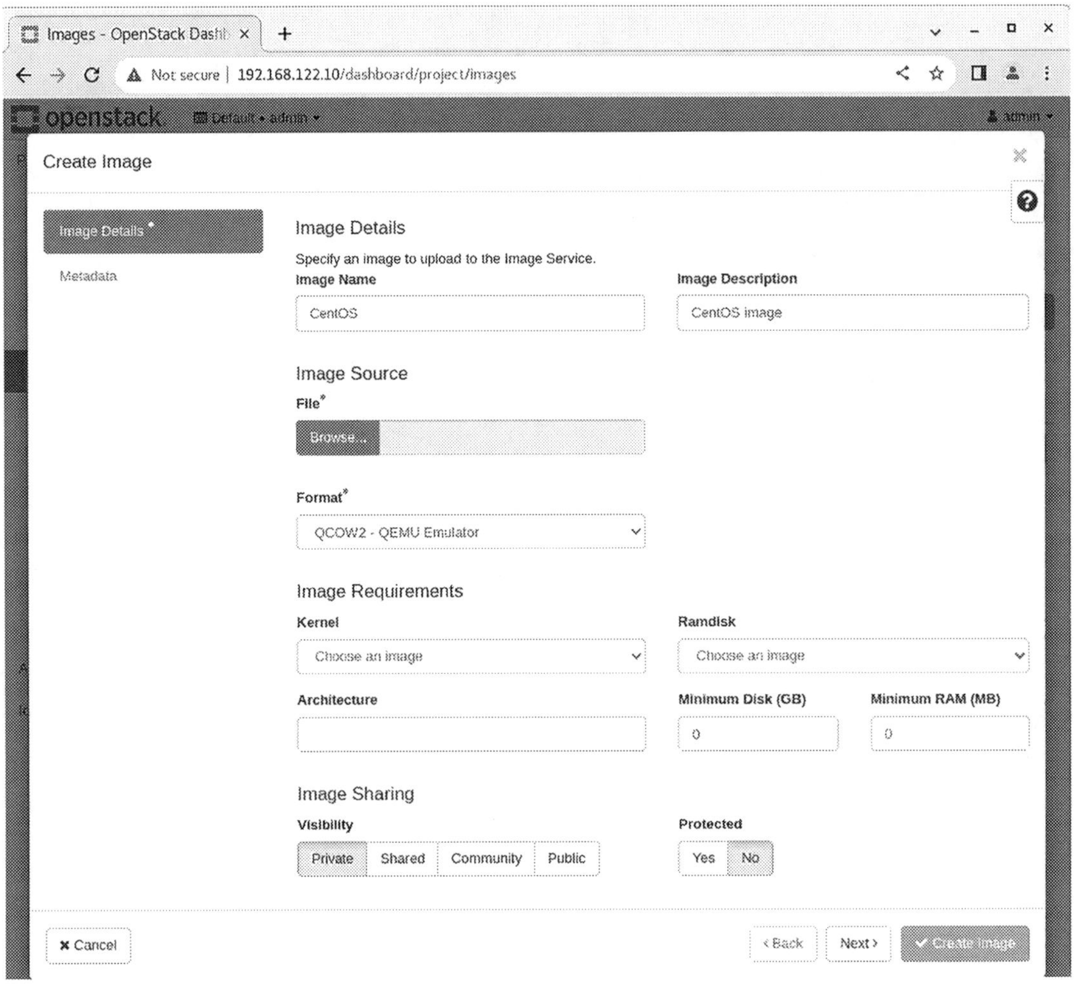

Figure 5-2. *Creating an image in the Horizon web interface*

As a user admin, you can also see all images on the Admin ➤ Compute ➤ Images page. It is possible to edit or add some of the metadata from this point. Figure 5-3 shows the Project view of the images (Project ➤ Compute ➤ Images).

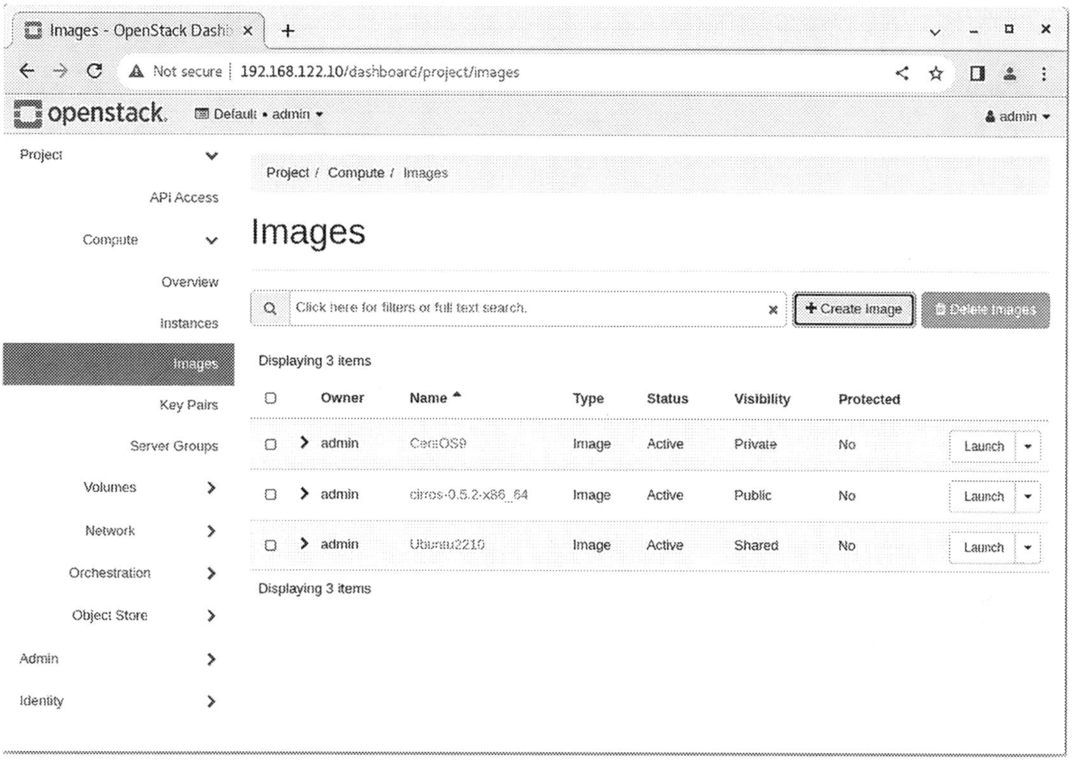

Figure 5-3. *Project view of images in the Horizon web interface*

Managing Images

Table 5-3 lists the most common commands for Glance management. In old versions of OpenStack, you can use only the glance command. This command will probably become obsolete in the future. To search options and command descriptions, add --h to the end of your subcommand.

Table 5-3. *CLI Commands for Glance Management*

Command	Purpose of Command
openstack image create or glance image-create	Create/upload an image
openstack image delete or glance image-delete	Delete image(s)
openstack image add project or glance member-create	Associate project with an image
openstack image remove project or glance member-delete	Disassociate project with an image
openstack image list or glance image-list	List available images
openstack image save or glance image-download	Save an image locally on disk
openstack image show or glance image-show	Display image details
openstack image set	Set image properties
glance image-update	Set image metadata

```
$ openstack image add project -h
usage: openstack image add project [-h]
                                   [-f {html,json,json,shell,table,value,ya
                                   ml,yaml}]
                                   [-c COLUMN] [--max-width <integer>]
                                   [--noindent] [--prefix PREFIX]
                                   [--project-domain <project-domain>]
                                   <image> <project>
Associate project with image
positional arguments:
  <image>              Image to share (name or ID)
  <project>            Project to associate with image (name or ID)
...
```

Table 5-3 shows how some commands work.

Once you have your image set up, you can download it. A simple example looks something like the following.

```
$ openstack image save Ubuntu2210 > local_image.img
$ ls -l local_image.img
-rw-rw-r-- 1 andrey andrey 658309120 Jul 14 16:44 local_image.img
```

You can add your own metadata to an image. For instance, the following command adds two new properties to the existing image.

```
$ glance image-update ff8ebfb3-7a6e-446c-8fe7-2466b8ebd29b --property os_
name=linux --property contact_person="andrey.markelov@ericsson.com"
+------------------+------------------------------------+
| Property         | Value                              |
+------------------+------------------------------------+
| checksum         | e605f3167a2a63e4e7562c6f4b80c28d   |
| contact_person   | andrey.markelov@ericsson.com       |
| container_format | bare                               |
| created_at       | 2022-07-14T14:29:54Z               |
| description      | Ubuntu Server 22.10 (Kinetic Kudu) |
| disk_format      | qcow2                              |
| id               | ff8ebfb3-7a6e-446c-8fe7-2466b8ebd29b |
| min_disk         | 0                                  |
| min_ram          | 0                                  |
| name             | Ubuntu2210                         |
| os_hash_algo     | sha512                             |
| os_hash_value    | 118a3bb84e31e91ad9d957fc07b94e39f... |
| os_hidden        | False                              |
| os_name          | linux                              |
| owner            | 27cdeded89d24fb49c11030b8cc87f15   |
| protected        | False                              |
| size             | 658309120                          |
| status           | active                             |
| stores           | file                               |
| tags             | []                                 |
```

```
| updated_at       | 2022-07-14T14:48:00Z                 |
| virtual_size     | 2361393152                           |
| visibility       | shared                               |
+------------------+--------------------------------------+
```

To delete a property, use the following command.

```
$ glance image-update ff8ebfb3-7a6e-446c-8fe7-2466b8ebd29b --remove-
property contact_person
```

And if you want, you can delete the image.

```
$ openstack image delete Ubuntu2210
$ openstack image list
+--------------------------------------+--------------------+--------+
| ID                                   | Name               | Status |
+--------------------------------------+--------------------+--------+
| cb14ee7c-02e4-4274-bd3f-8d81cd139593 | CentOS9            | active |
| 7ffe1b43-7e86-4ad0-86b6-9fffa38b3c20 | cirros-0.5.2-x86_64 | active |
+--------------------------------------+--------------------+--------+
```

For almost all commands, you may use either the name of the image or the ID. The glance and openstack utilities have the --debug option to show what is behind the CLI. It might be useful for troubleshooting or learning more about the API.

```
$ openstack image list --debug
START with options: ['image', 'list', '--debug']
...
REQ: curl -g -i -X GET http://192.168.122.10:9292/v2/images -H "Accept:
application/json" -H "User-Agent: openstacksdk/0.61.0 keystoneauth1/4.5.0
python-requests/2.25.1 CPython/3.9.13" -H "X-Auth-Token: {SHA256}b9043a5b26
1b01359dc91e6585209c89cdcfaa73ff7139ed9feb0826b83f8b2f"
http://192.168.122.10:9292 "GET /v2/images HTTP/1.1" 200 1876
RESP: [200] Connection: keep-alive Content-Length: 1876 Content-Type: ap-
plication/json Date: Thu, 14 Jul 2022 14:55:40 GMT X-Openstack-Request-Id:
req-85c98971-36db-4e58-810f-9fc862e43a1a
...
```

```
GET call to image for http://192.168.122.10:9292/v2/images used request id
req-85c98971-36db-4e58-810f-9fc862e43a1a
+------------------------------------+--------------------+--------+
| ID                                 | Name               | Status |
+------------------------------------+--------------------+--------+
| cb14ee7c-02e4-4274-bd3f-8d81cd139593 | CentOS9          | active |
| 7ffe1b43-7e86-4ad0-86b6-9fffa38b3c20 | cirros-0.5.2-x86_64 | active |
+------------------------------------+--------------------+--------+
clean_up ListImage:
END return value: 0
```

Managing Image Back Ends

Glance can support various data store back ends, such as Swift, Ceph, NFS, the local file system, and others. Storage vendors like EMC or NetApp produce plug-ins for their hardware. You can define each back end in the [glance_store] section of the /etc/glance/glance-api.conf configuration file.

The following is the simplest example of the local file system.

```
[glance_store]
...
default_store = file
filesystem_store_datadir = /var/lib/glance/images/
```

If you look at this directory, you can find files with names equal to the image's ID.

```
# ls -l /var/lib/glance/images/
total 871552
-rw-r-----. 1 glance glance  16300544 Jul 14 15:46
7ffe1b43-7e86-4ad0-86b6-9fffa38b3c20
-rw-r-----. 1 glance glance 876164096 Jul 14 16:29 cb14ee7c-02e4-4274-
bd3f-8d81cd139593
```

Glance can serve multiple back ends at the same time. In this case, Glance chooses a particular back end depending on the free space and priority. For example, if you have two mounted disks in /var/lib/glance/images/, you can add something like the following.

```
[glance_store]
filesystem_store_datadirs = /var/lib/glance/images/mountA/:10
filesystem_store_datadirs = /var/lib/glance/images/mountB/:20
...
```

To limit the size of images, you need to add the image_size_cap parameter and maximum size in bytes to the glance-api configuration file and restart the glance-api service.

Here is an example of adding a 1 GB parameter.

```
[default]
image_size_cap = 1073741824
...
# systemctl restart openstack-glance-api
```

If you need to limit the storage amount per user in Glance, use another option.

```
[default]
user_storage_quota = 500MB
...
# systemctl restart openstack-glance-api
```

Verifying Operation of the Image Service

Let's check the presence of Glance service in the Keystone services catalog. You can do that with the old-fashioned command keystone or the new openstack command. It's better to use the openstack CLI when possible because it will likely become the only command-line client available.

```
$ source keystonerc_admin
$ openstack service show glance
+-------------+---------------------------------+
| Field       | Value                           |
+-------------+---------------------------------+
| description | OpenStack Image Service         |
| enabled     | True                            |
| id          | 5ae88c354230480e9b4e071d11587ee7 |
| name        | glance                          |
| type        | image                           |
+-------------+---------------------------------+
```

Looks like everything is fine with that. For troubleshooting, you may also need to know where the glance-api endpoint is.

```
$ openstack endpoint list | grep glance
| 077925f6fc694aa78cd4ca84d6d24178 | RegionOne | glance      | image
| True      | admin     | http://192.168.122.10:9292
| 094235849d0a41ac87f087334fb39fdc | RegionOne | glance      | image
| True      | internal  | http://192.168.122.10:9292
| 6a59ce4050414804b727f36b021a1ed5 | RegionOne | glance      | image
| True      | public    | http://192.168.122.10:9292
```

In this environment, the Glance service listens for incoming connections at IP addresses 192.168.122.10 and port 9292. All communications are happening through HTTP. In real life, it can also be done through the HTTPS protocol. URLs for the admin interface, public interface, and internal interface can also differ.

You may also want to check Glance's /var/log/glance/api.log log file. To adjust how the logs are detailed, you can add the option to Glance's configuration files.

```
[DEFAULT]
...
verbose = True
debug = True
```

Summary

This chapter discussed how to work with the image management service. Although this topic weighs 5% from an exam point of view, this knowledge is essential for other topics like compute management.

In the next chapter, you learn about OpenStack networking.

Review Questions

1. Where are images stored when using the local file system by default?

   A. `/var/cache/glance/`

   B. `/var/lib/glance/store/`

   C. `/var/log/glance/`

   D. `/var/lib/glance/images/`

2. Which main daemon is in charge of Glance?

   A. `glance-endpoint`

   B. `glance-registry`

   C. `glance-backend`

   D. `glance-api`

3. Which parameter in Glance's configuration files defines the back end for storing files?

   A. `default_store`

   B. `default_backend`

   C. `preferred_store`

   D. `preferred_backend`

4. How can an image in the OpenStack cloud be stored with CLI?

    A. `openstack image create --file image.img --disk-format qcow2 --container-format bare --public image`

    B. `openstack image add --file image.img --disk-format qcow2 --container-format bare --public image`

    C. `openstack image create --file image.img --disk qcow2 --container-format bare --public image`

    D. `openstack image add --file image.img --disk qcow2 --container-format bare --public image`

5. How can the storage volume per user be limited in Glance?

    A. Put image_size_cap option to /etc/glance/glance-api.conf

    B. Put image_size_cap option to /etc/glance/glance.conf

    C. Put user_storage_quota option to /etc/glance/glance-api.conf

    D. Put user_storage_quota option to /etc/glance/glance.conf

Answers

1. D

2. D

3. B

4. A

5. C

CHAPTER 6

OpenStack Networking

This chapter covers 30% of the Certified OpenStack Administrator exam requirements. It is one of the most impotent topics in the book. Without a solid knowledge of the network components, you will be unable to perform most exam tasks.

Neutron's Architecture and Components

Neutron is one of the most complicated OpenStack services. Let's start by looking at its architecture and general concepts. Figure 6-1 shows the objects in OpenStack's networking service.

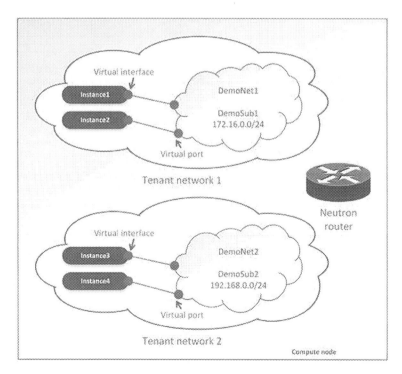

Figure 6-1. *Logical objects in OpenStack's networking service*

© Andrey Markelov 2022
A. Markelov, *Certified OpenStack Administrator Study Guide*,
https://doi.org/10.1007/978-1-4842-8804-7_6

The following describes the most important components.

- A **tenant network** is a virtual network that provides connectivity between entities. The network consists of subnets, and each subnet is a logical subdivision of an IP network. A subnet can be private or public. Virtual machines can get access to an external world through the public subnet. If a virtual machine is connected only to the private subnet, then only other virtual machines from this network can access it. Only a user with an admin role can create a public network.

- A **router** is a virtual network device that passes network traffic between different networks. A router can have one gateway and many connected subnets.

- A **security group** is a set of ingress and egress firewall rules that can be applied to one or many virtual machines. It is possible to change a Security Group at runtime.

- A **floating IP address** is an IP address that can be associated with a virtual machine so that the instance has the same IP from the public network each time it boots.

- A **port** is a virtual network port within OpenStack's networking service. It is a connection between the subnet and vNIC or virtual router.

- A **vNIC (virtual network interface card)** or **VIF (virtual network interface)** is an interface plugged into a port in a network.

Let's continue this discussion by learning more about Neutron architecture (see Figure 6-2).

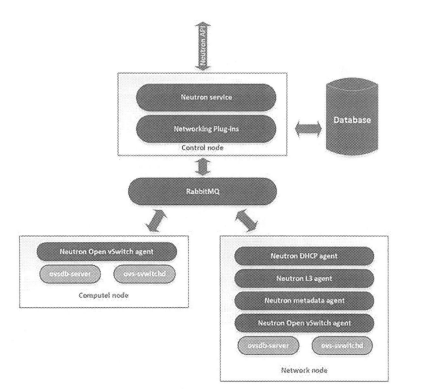

Figure 6-2. *Neutron's architecture (OVS example)*

Upstream documentation from `docs.openstack.org` defines several types of OpenStack nodes. Neutron is usually spread across three of them. API service usually exists at the control node. Open vSwitch and client-side Neutron agents are usually started at the hypervisor or compute node. And all server-side components of OpenStack's networking service work on network nodes, which can be gateways to an external network.

Neutron consists of several services that are implemented as standard GNU/Linux daemons.

- **neutron-server** is the main service of Neutron. Accepts and routes API requests through message bus to the OpenStack networking plug-ins for action.

- **neutron-openvswitch-agent** receives commands from neutron-server and sends them to Open vSwitch (OVS) for execution. The neutron-openvswitch-agent uses the local GNU/Linux commands for OVS management.

79

- **neutron-l3-agent** provides routing and network address translation (NAT) using standard GNU/Linux technologies like Linux Routing and Network Namespaces.

- **neutron-dhcp-agent** manages dnsmasq services, which is a lightweight Dynamic Host Configuration Protocol (DHCP) and caching DNS server. Also, neutron-dhcp-agent starts proxies for the metadata server.

- **neutron-metadata-agent** allows instances to get information such as hostname, SSH keys, and so on. Virtual machines can request HTTP protocol information such as `http://169.254.169.254` at boot time. Usually, this happens with scripts like cloud-init (`https://launchpad.net/cloud-init`). An agent acts as a proxy to nova-api for retrieving metadata.

Neutron also uses Open vSwitch. Its configuration is discussed in the next section of this chapter. Some modern OpenStack distributions migrated to Open Virtual Networking (OVN) instead of OVS. OVN includes a DHCP service, L3 routing, and NAT. It replaces the OVS ML2 driver and the Neutron agent with the OVN ML2 driver. OVN does not use the Neutron agents at all. In OVN-enabled OpenStack, the ovn-controller service implements all functionality. Some gaps from ML2/OVS are still present (see `https://docs.openstack.org/neutron/yoga/ovn/gaps.html`). Note that the current OpenStack installation guide refers to OVS, but if you install the last version of DevStack or Pack-Stack, you get OVN.

You will not be tested on this knowledge on the exam. You may directly jump to the "Manage Network Resources" section. From an exam point of view, your experience should be the same.

Table 6-1 lists what type of node (compute, network, or control) services are started and the location of their configs.

Table 6-1. *OpenStack Neutron Services and Their Placement*

Service	Node Type	Configuration Files
neutron-service	Control	`/etc/neutron/neutron.conf`
neutron-openvswitch-agent	Network and Compute	`/etc/neutron/plugins/ml2/openvswitch_agent.ini`
neutron-l3-agent	Network	`/etc/neutron/l3_agent.ini`
neutron-dhcp-agent	Network	`/etc/neutron/dhcp_agent.ini`
neutron-metadata-agent	Network	`/etc/neutron/metadata_agent.ini`
Modular Layer 2 agent (it is not run as a daemon)	Network	`/etc/neutron/plugins/ml2/ml2_conf.ini` and `/etc/neutron/plugin.ini` (symbolic link to `ml2_conf.ini`)

Opening vSwitch's Architecture

OVS is an important part of networking in the OpenStack cloud. The website for OVS with documentation and source code is `https://www.openvswitch.org/`. Open vSwitch is not a part of the OpenStack project. However, OVS is used in most implementations of OpenStack clouds. It has also been integrated into many other virtual management systems, including OpenQRM, OpenNebula, and oVirt. Open vSwitch can support protocols such as OpenFlow, GRE, VLAN, VXLAN, NetFlow, sFlow, SPAN, RSPAN, and LACP. It can operate in distributed configurations with a central controller.

Open vSwitch by itself consists of several components.

- **openswitch_mod.ko** is a GNU/Linux kernel module that plays the role of ASIC (application-specific integrated circuit) in hardware switches. This module is an engine of traffic processing.

- **ovs-vswitchd** is a daemon in charge of management and logic for data transmitting.

- **ovsdb-server** is a daemon used for the internal database. It also provides RPC (remote procedure call) interfaces to one or more Open vSwitch databases (OVSDBs).

You will likely not need to manage Open vSwitch at the exam time, but commands can be useful. Let's look at examples of using the `ovs-vsctl` management utility for interacting with OVS. First, let's check for the version of Open vSwitch.

```
# ovs-vsctl -V
ovs-vsctl (Open vSwitch) 2.4.0
   Compiled Oct  7 2015 18:01:06
   DB Schema 7.12.1
```

You can create a new bridge and delete it with the help of the following commands.

```
# ovs-vsctl add-br br-new
# ovs-vsctl del-br br-new
```

The same with adding or removing a physical interface to or from the bridge.

```
# ovs-vsctl add-port br-ex enp0s3
# ovs-vsctl del-port br-ex enp0s3
```

The most interesting command is `ovs-vsctl show`. The output of this command is printed from the lab environment with three nodes.

```
# ovs-vsctl show
22a0e0a2-7ac2-493a-9398-65e5683835e9
    Bridge br-int
        fail_mode: secure
        Port br-int
            Interface br-int
                type: internal
        Port "tap7fd27c60-32"
            tag: 1
            Interface "tap7fd27c60-32"
                type: internal
        Port patch-tun
            Interface patch-tun
                type: patch
                options: {peer=patch-int}
```

```
      Port int-br-ex
          Interface int-br-ex
              type: patch
              options: {peer=phy-br-ex}
      Port "qr-8d2a382b-01"
          tag: 1
          Interface "qr-8d2a382b-01"
              type: internal
Bridge br-ex
    Port "eth1"
        Interface "eth1"
    Port br-ex
        Interface br-ex
            type: internal
    Port "qg-dbd535f0-05"
        Interface "qg-dbd535f0-05"
            type: internal
    Port phy-br-ex
        Interface phy-br-ex
            type: patch
            options: {peer=int-br-ex}
Bridge br-tun
    fail_mode: secure
    Port "gre-c0a87ad2"
        Interface "gre-c0a87ad2"
            type: gre
            options: {df_default="true", in_key=flow, local_
            ip="10.0.2.15", out_key=flow, remote_ip="10.0.2.20"}
    Port br-tun
        Interface br-tun
            type: internal
    Port patch-int
        Interface patch-int
            type: patch
            options: {peer=patch-tun}
```

```
        Port "gre-c0a87ad7"
            Interface "gre-c0a87ad7"
                type: gre
                options: {df_default="true", in_key=flow, local_
                ip="10.0.2.15", out_key=flow, remote_ip="10.0.2.30"}
    ovs_version: "2.4.0"
```

As you can see, three bridges exist.

- br-int is the **integration bridge**. There is one on each node. This bridge acts as a virtual switch where all virtual network cards from all virtual machines are connected. OVS Neutron agent automatically creates the integration bridge.

- br-ex is the **external bridge** for interconnection with external networks. In our example, the eth1 physical interface is connected to this bridge.

- br-tun is the **tunnel bridge**. It is a virtual switch like br-int. It connects the GRE and VXLAN tunnel endpoints. As you can see in our example, it connects the node with the IP address 10.0.2.15 and two others with IP 10.0.2.20 and 10.0.2.30. In our example, a GRE tunnel was used.

Here is an example of the code from a config file for neutron-openvswitch-agent.

```
# grep -o '^[^#]*' /etc/neutron/plugins/ml2/openvswitch_agent.ini
[DEFAULT]
[agent]
tunnel_types =vxlan,gre
vxlan_udp_port = 4789
l2_population = False
drop_flows_on_start = False
[ovs]
integration_bridge = br-int
tunnel_bridge = br-tun
local_ip = 10.0.2.15
enable_tunneling=True
```

```
[securitygroup]
firewall_driver = neutron.agent.linux.iptables_firewall.
OVSHybridIptablesFirewallDriver
```

The Tip in Chapter 5 explains how RegEx can be used in the grep command.

Opening Virtual Networking (OVN)

OVN is an open source project launched by the Open vSwitch team. Open vSwitch (OVS) includes OVN starting with version 2.5. OVN has been released as a separate project since version 2.13.

Instead of the Neutron agents, it uses ovn-controller and OVS flows to support all functions.

The OVN northbound (NB) database stores the logical configuration, which it gets from the OVN ML2 plug-in. The plug-in runs on the controller nodes and listens on port 6641/TCP.

The northbound service converts the logical network configuration from the northbound database to the logical path flows. The ovn-northd service populates the OVN southbound database with the logical path flows. The service runs on the controller nodes.

The southbound (SB) database listens on port 6642/TCP. The ovn-controller connects to the Southbound database to control and monitor network traffic. This service runs on all compute nodes.

The OVN metadata agent runs the HAProxy instances. These instances manage the HAProxy instances, OVS interfaces, and namespaces. It runs on all compute nodes.

The OpenFlow protocol configures Open vSwitch and defines how network traffic will flow. OpenFlow can dynamically rewrite flow tables, allowing it to add and remove network functions as required.

Table 6-2 contrasts some differences between ML2 using OVS and OVN.

Table 6-2. *Differences Between OVS and OVN*

Area	OVS	OVN
DHCP Service	Provided by dnsmasq service per dhcp-xxx namespaces	OpenFlow rules by ovn-controller
High availability of dataplane	Implemented via creating qrourer namespace	OpenFlow rules by ovn-controller
Communication	RabbitMQ broker	Ovsdb protocol
Components of data plane	Veth, iptables, namespaces	OpenFlow rules
Metadata service	DHCP namespaces on controller nodes	Ovnmeta-xxx namespace on compute nodes

```
$ openstack network agent list
+-------------------------------------+---------------------+
----------------+-------+-------+-----------------------------+
| ID                                  | Agent Type          |
  Host            | Alive | State | Binary                      |
+-------------------------------------+---------------------+
----------------+-------+-------+-----------------------------+
| dff0df04-e035-42cc-98a6-d2aee745b9bf | OVN Controller agent |
  rdo.test.local | :-)   | UP    | ovn-controller              |
| 238f88a3-f9c6-5d22-89bb-6b9b8f369d25 | OVN Metadata agent   |
  rdo.test.local | :-)   | UP    | neutron-ovn-metadata-agent  |
+-------------------------------------+---------------------+
----------------+-------+-------+-----------------------------+
```

```
$ openstack network agent list
+------+-------------------+-------------------------+---------+-------+
-------+-------------------------+
| ID   | Agent Type        | Host                    | Av Zone | Alive |
  State | Binary              |
+------+-------------------+-------------------------+---------+-------+
-------+-------------------------+
| 02.. | Metadata agent    | network.test.local      | None    | :-)   |
  UP   | neutron-metadata-agent    |
| 25.. | Open vSwitch agent | network.test.local     | None    | :-)   |
  UP   | neutron-openvswitch-agent |
| 40.. | L3 agent          | network.test.local      | nova    | :-)   |
  UP   | neutron-l3-agent          |
| 59.. | DHCP agent        | network.test.local      | nova    | :-)   |
  UP   | neutron-dhcp-agent        |
+------+-------------------+-------------------------+---------+-------+
-------+-------------------------+
```

Managing Network Resources

Now let's go through the process of creating all the necessary network resources for connecting an instance to the external world. For that, you can use the openstack or neutron
command. Both commands have built-in help. Keep in mind that the Neutron CLI is
deprecated and will be removed in the coming versions of OpenStack. This book only
uses the OpenStack CLI. First, let's create a flat external network. You should have an
admin role before doing that.

```
$ source keystonerc_demo
$ openstack network create  --share --external --provider-physical-network
provider --provider-network-type flat ext-net
+-----------------------------+-------------------------------------+
| Field                       | Value                               |
+-----------------------------+-------------------------------------+
| admin_state_up              | UP                                  |
| availability_zone_hints     |                                     |
```

availability_zones	
created_at	2022-07-17T17:43:17Z
description	
dns_domain	None
id	5f18929b-70f6-4729-ac05-7bea494b9c5a
ipv4_address_scope	None
ipv6_address_scope	None
is_default	False
is_vlan_transparent	None
mtu	1500
name	ext-net
port_security_enabled	True
project_id	27cdeded89d24fb49c11030b8cc87f15
provider:network_type	flat
provider:physical_network	provider
provider:segmentation_id	None
qos_policy_id	None
revision_number	1
router:external	External
segments	None
shared	True
status	ACTIVE
subnets	
tags	
updated_at	2022-07-17T17:43:17Z

Tip   If you can't create a network with type `flat`, add `flat` to the `type_drivers` option in the `/etc/neutron/plugins/ml2/ml2_conf.ini` config file. After changes, you need to restart the Neutron service.

The next step is to create a subnet for this network. It is an existing external network. You need to disable DHCP for this network.

```
$ openstack subnet create --network ext-net --no-dhcp --allocation-pool st
art=192.168.122.200,end=192.168.122.220 --gateway 192.168.122.1 --subnet-
range 192.168.122.0/24 ext-subnet
+---------------------+-------------------------------------+
| Field               | Value                               |
+---------------------+-------------------------------------+
| allocation_pools    | 192.168.122.200-192.168.122.220     |
| cidr                | 192.168.122.0/24                    |
| created_at          | 2022-07-17T17:56:32Z                |
| description         |                                     |
| dns_nameservers     |                                     |
| dns_publish_fixed_ip | None                               |
| enable_dhcp         | False                               |
| gateway_ip          | 192.168.122.1                       |
| host_routes         |                                     |
| id                  | d065c027-bb60-4464-9619-7d9754535c5c |
| ip_version          | 4                                   |
| ipv6_address_mode   | None                                |
| ipv6_ra_mode        | None                                |
| name                | ext-subnet                          |
| network_id          | 5f18929b-70f6-4729-ac05-7bea494b9c5a |
| project_id          | 27cdeded89d24fb49c11030b8cc87f15    |
| revision_number     | 0                                   |
| segment_id          | None                                |
| service_types       |                                     |
| subnetpool_id       | None                                |
| tags                |                                     |
| updated_at          | 2022-07-17T17:56:32Z                |
+---------------------+-------------------------------------+
```

If you use Horizon for net and subnet creation, go to Project ➤ Network ➤ Networks, and click the Create Network button. You then see the window shown in Figure 6-3. Click the Next button to go to the Subnet tab.

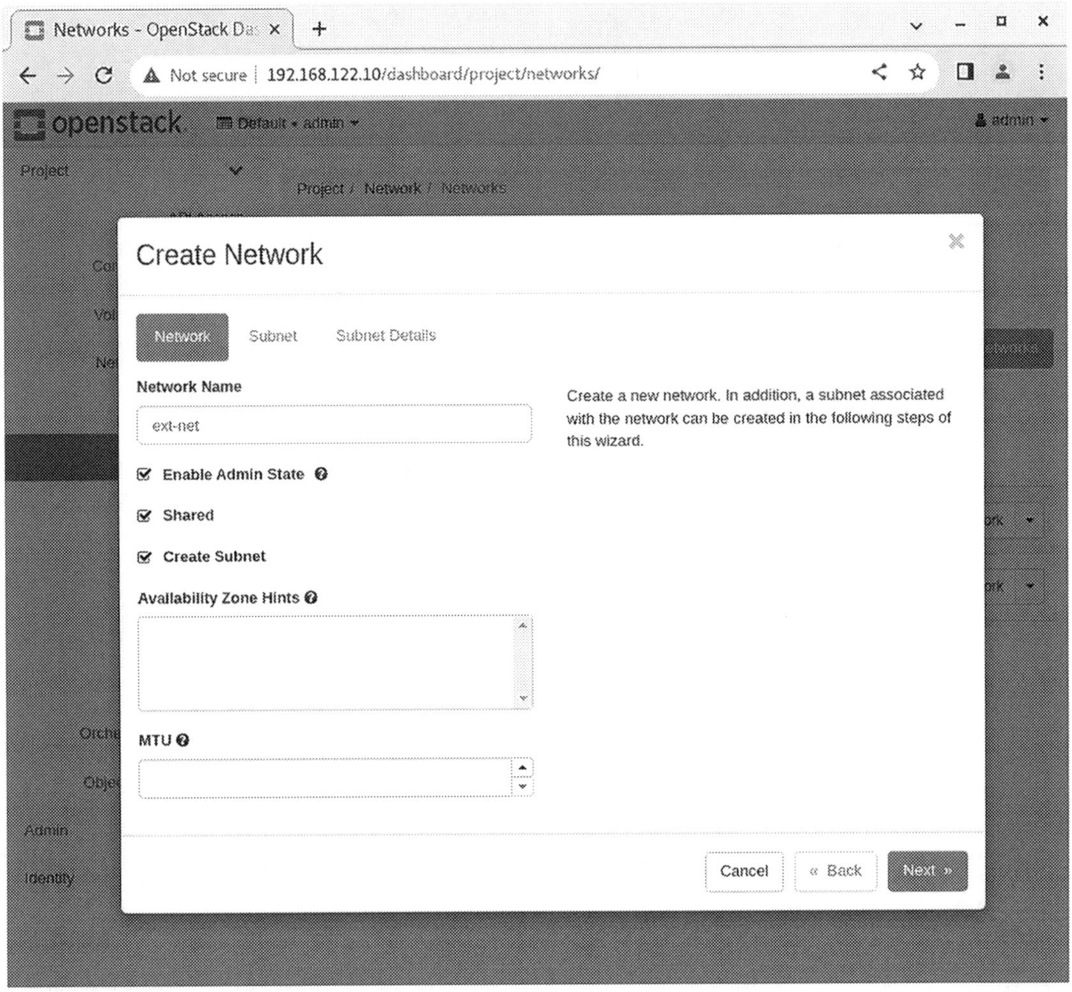

Figure 6-3. *Net creating dialog in Horizon*

Now it is possible to check the work that has already been done. First, let's check the list of all networks.

```
$ openstack network list
+--------------------------------------+---------+--------------------------------------+
| ID                                   | Name    | Subnets                              |
+--------------------------------------+---------+--------------------------------------+
| 5f18929b-70f6-4729-ac05-7bea494b9c5a | ext-net | d065c027-bb60-4464-9619-7d9754535c5c |
+--------------------------------------+---------+--------------------------------------+
```

Then you may want to check the details of ext-net.

```
$ openstack network show ext-net
+---------------------------+------------------------------------------+
| Field                     | Value                                    |
+---------------------------+------------------------------------------+
| admin_state_up            | UP                                       |
| availability_zone_hints   |                                          |
| availability_zones        |                                          |
| created_at                | 2022-07-17T17:43:17Z                     |
| description               |                                          |
| dns_domain                | None                                     |
| id                        | 5f18929b-70f6-4729-ac05-7bea494b9c5a     |
| ipv4_address_scope        | None                                     |
| ipv6_address_scope        | None                                     |
| is_default                | False                                    |
| is_vlan_transparent       | None                                     |
| mtu                       | 1500                                     |
| name                      | ext-net                                  |
| port_security_enabled     | True                                     |
| project_id                | 27cdeded89d24fb49c11030b8cc87f15         |
| provider:network_type     | flat                                     |
| provider:physical_network | provider                                 |
| provider:segmentation_id  | None                                     |
| qos_policy_id             | None                                     |
| revision_number           | 2                                        |
| router:external           | External                                 |
| segments                  | None                                     |
| shared                    | True                                     |
| status                    | ACTIVE                                   |
| subnets                   | d065c027-bb60-4464-9619-7d9754535c5c     |
| tags                      |                                          |
| updated_at                | 2022-07-17T17:56:32Z                     |
+---------------------------+------------------------------------------+
```

The corresponding Networks screen from Horizon is shown in Figure 6-4.

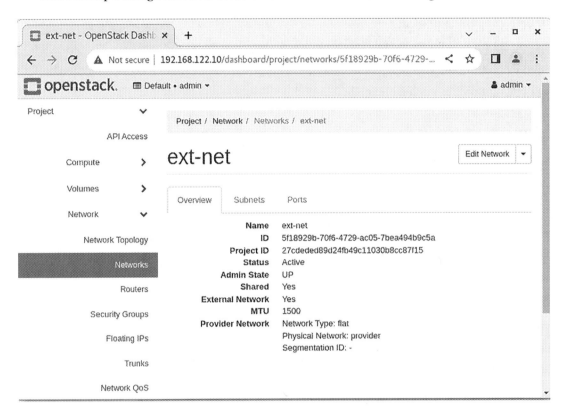

Figure 6-4. *Properties of the chosen network in Horizon*

You can do the rest of the work as a demo user from the demo project. The only action where you need an admin role is when you name the network as external. Now let's create the tenant network.

```
$ source keystonerc_demo
$ openstack network create demo-net
+---------------------------+------------------------------------+
| Field                     | Value                              |
+---------------------------+------------------------------------+
| admin_state_up            | UP                                 |
| availability_zone_hints   |                                    |
| availability_zones        |                                    |
| created_at                | 2022-07-17T18:12:02Z               |
| description               |                                    |
```

```
| dns_domain                  | None                                  |
| id                          | 5ee4e933-de9b-4bcb-9422-83cc0d276d33  |
| ipv4_address_scope          | None                                  |
| ipv6_address_scope          | None                                  |
| is_default                  | False                                 |
| is_vlan_transparent         | None                                  |
| mtu                         | 1442                                  |
| name                        | demo-net                              |
| port_security_enabled       | True                                  |
| project_id                  | 9e0c535c2240405b989afa450681df18      |
| provider:network_type       | None                                  |
| provider:physical_network   | None                                  |
| provider:segmentation_id    | None                                  |
| qos_policy_id               | None                                  |
| revision_number             | 1                                     |
| router:external             | Internal                              |
| segments                    | None                                  |
| shared                      | False                                 |
| status                      | ACTIVE                                |
| subnets                     |                                       |
| tags                        |                                       |
| updated_at                  | 2022-07-17T18:12:02Z                  |
+-----------------------------+---------------------------------------+
```

You also need a subnet for your network.

```
$ openstack subnet create --network demo-net --gateway 172.16.0.1 --subnet-
range 172.16.0.0/24 demo-subnet
+---------------------+---------------------------------------+
| Field               | Value                                 |
+---------------------+---------------------------------------+
| allocation_pools    | 172.16.0.2-172.16.0.254               |
| cidr                | 172.16.0.0/24                         |
| created_at          | 2022-07-17T18:14:52Z                  |
| description         |                                       |
| dns_nameservers     |                                       |
```

```
| dns_publish_fixed_ip | None                                 |
| enable_dhcp          | True                                 |
| gateway_ip           | 172.16.0.1                           |
| host_routes          |                                      |
| id                   | 18736455-80f6-4513-9d81-6cedbfe271fe |
| ip_version           | 4                                    |
| ipv6_address_mode    | None                                 |
| ipv6_ra_mode         | None                                 |
| name                 | demo-subnet                          |
| network_id           | 5ee4e933-de9b-4bcb-9422-83cc0d276d33 |
| project_id           | 9e0c535c2240405b989afa450681df18     |
| revision_number      | 0                                    |
| segment_id           | None                                 |
| service_types        |                                      |
| subnetpool_id        | None                                 |
| tags                 |                                      |
| updated_at           | 2022-07-17T18:14:52Z                 |
+----------------------+--------------------------------------+
```

You then need to create a virtual router for routing traffic.

```
$ openstack router create demo-router
+-------------------------+--------------------------------------+
| Field                   | Value                                |
+-------------------------+--------------------------------------+
| admin_state_up          | UP                                   |
| availability_zone_hints |                                      |
| availability_zones      |                                      |
| created_at              | 2022-07-17T18:16:19Z                 |
| description             |                                      |
| external_gateway_info   | null                                 |
| flavor_id               | None                                 |
| id                      | 3daad728-4075-49a4-ad05-3b279de738fa |
| name                    | demo-router                          |
| project_id              | 9e0c535c2240405b989afa450681df18     |
| revision_number         | 0                                    |
```

```
| routes                 |                                    |
| status                 | ACTIVE                             |
| tags                   |                                    |
| updated_at             | 2022-07-17T18:16:19Z               |
+------------------------+------------------------------------+
```

Now connect the router with the tenant subnet from one side.

```
$ openstack router add subnet demo-router demo-subnet
```

And from the other side, you need to set ext-net as a gateway for the router.

```
$ openstack router set --external-gateway ext-net demo-router
```

You can create a virtual router in Horizon by going to Project ➤ Network ➤ Router tab. An example of the router properties is shown in Figure 6-5.

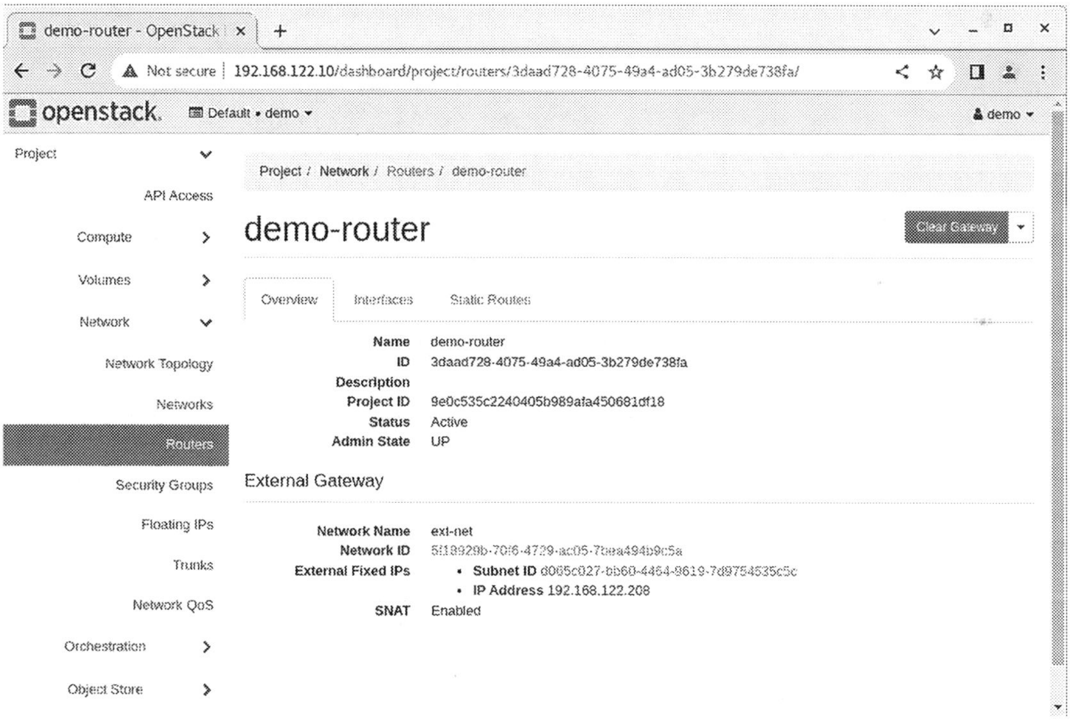

Figure 6-5. *Properties of a virtual router in Horizon*

Now you can check all of the ports. Remember, it is the connection between a subnet and vNIC (or a virtual router).

```
$ source keystonerc_admin
$ openstack port list
+----------------------------------------+------+------------------+
----------------------------------------+--------+
| ID                                     | Name | MAC Address      |
 Fixed IP Addresses                      | Status |
+----------------------------------------+------+------------------+
----------------------------------------+--------+
| 29b05750-0c52-4fb2-88c0-f6fc7a87ecb4   |      | fa:16:3e:b6:88:ea |
 ip_address='172.16.0.2', subnet_id='18736455-80f6-4513-9d81-6cedbfe-
271fe'                                   | DOWN   |
| 2f0ef8d7-0219-46f8-b874-19b308dc29dd   |      | fa:16:3e:24:49:cc |
                                         | DOWN   |
| 5bcc90fc-9a54-4c91-9e6a-988ac0a4a4a8   |      | fa:16:3e:2d:7b:4d |
 ip_address='172.16.0.1', subnet_id='18736455-80f6-4513-9d81-6cedbfe-
271fe'                                   | ACTIVE |
| d3838abc-14ec-4025-b808-3fe6e5ace51b   |      | fa:16:3e:53:11:2c |
 ip_address='192.168.122.208', subnet_id='d065c027-
bb60-4464-9619-7d9754535c5c'            | ACTIVE |
+----------------------------------------+------+------------------+
----------------------------------------+--------+
```

Then you can get information about any chosen port.

```
$ openstack port show 5bcc90fc-9a54-4c91-9e6a-988ac0a4a4a8
+-------------------------+---------------------------------------------+
| Field                   | Value                                       |
+-------------------------+---------------------------------------------+
| admin_state_up          | UP                                          |
| allowed_address_pairs   |                                             |
| binding_host_id         |                                             |
| binding_profile         |                                             |
| binding_vif_details     |                                             |
| binding_vif_type        | unbound                                     |
| binding_vnic_type       | normal                                      |
| created_at              | 2022-07-17T18:17:36Z                        |
| data_plane_status       | None                                        |
| description             |                                             |
| device_id               | 3daad728-4075-49a4-ad05-3b279de738fa        |
| device_owner            | network:router_interface                    |
| device_profile          | None                                        |
| dns_assignment          | None                                        |
| dns_domain              | None                                        |
| dns_name                | None                                        |
| extra_dhcp_opts         |                                             |
| fixed_ips               | ip_address='172.16.0.1', subnet_id=         |
|                         | '18736455-80f6-4513-9d81-6cedbfe271fe'      |
| id                      | 5bcc90fc-9a54-4c91-9e6a-988ac0a4a4a8        |
| ip_allocation           | None                                        |
| mac_address             | fa:16:3e:2d:7b:4d                           |
| name                    |                                             |
| network_id              | 5ee4e933-de9b-4bcb-9422-83cc0d276d33        |
| numa_affinity_policy    | None                                        |
```

```
| port_security_enabled  | False                              |
| project_id             | 9e0c535c2240405b989afa450681df18   |
| propagate_uplink_status | None                              |
| qos_network_policy_id  | None                               |
| qos_policy_id          | None                               |
| resource_request       | None                               |
| revision_number        | 3                                  |
| security_group_ids     |                                    |
| status                 | ACTIVE                             |
| tags                   |                                    |
| trunk_details          | None                               |
| updated_at             | 2022-07-17T18:17:37Z               |
+------------------------+------------------------------------+
```

At this stage, you can start the instance and get an overall picture of a configured network by going to Project ➤ Network ➤ Network Topology. It is shown in Figure 6-6.

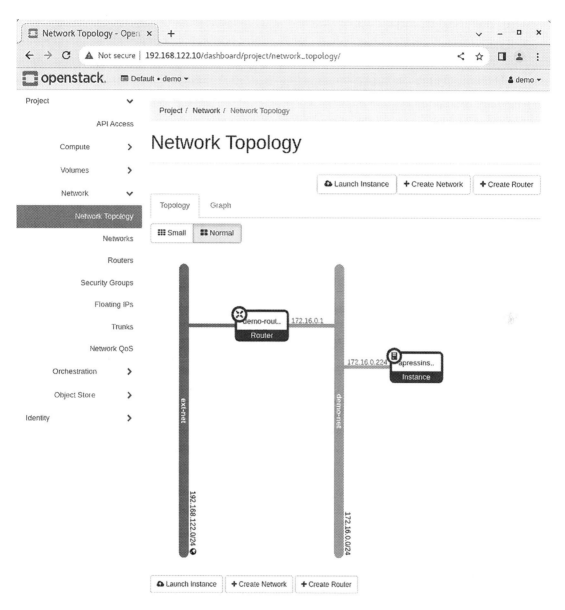

Figure 6-6. *Network Topology tab in Horizon*

At this point, you have only one missing part. Your instances within the tenant network can connect to each other, but none of the instances can reach out to an external network. You need to add a floating IP from ext-net to the virtual machine.

First, let's create the floating IP. The default quota for the number of floating IPs is 10, which can be adjusted by anyone with admin capacity.

```
$ openstack floating ip create ext-net
+---------------------+------------------------------------------+
| Field               | Value                                    |
+---------------------+------------------------------------------+
| created_at          | 2022-07-17T18:35:34Z                     |
| description         |                                          |
| dns_domain          |                                          |
| dns_name            |                                          |
| fixed_ip_address    | None                                     |
| floating_ip_address | 192.168.122.215                          |
| floating_network_id | 5f18929b-70f6-4729-ac05-7bea494b9c5a     |
| id                  | e41419bf-7642-4cc5-9569-cd7d546e0f62     |
| name                | 192.168.122.215                          |
| port_details        | None                                     |
| port_id             | None                                     |
| project_id          | 9e0c535c2240405b989afa450681df18         |
| qos_policy_id       | None                                     |
| revision_number     | 0                                        |
| router_id           | None                                     |
| status              | DOWN                                     |
| subnet_id           | None                                     |
| tags                | []                                       |
| updated_at          | 2022-07-17T18:35:34Z                     |
+---------------------+------------------------------------------+
```

Take a moment to locate the IP of the new floating IP from the output. You will need this IP soon. Next, determine which current IP is associated with the virtual machine.

```
$ openstack server list
+------------------------------------+-------------+--------+
--------------------+------------------------+---------+
| ID                                 | Name        | Status |
  Networks              | Image                  | Flavor  |
+------------------------------------+-------------+--------+
--------------------+------------------------+---------+
| f6fda94b-a6d2-43cc-8e93-18a538759a22 | apressinst1 | ACTIVE |
  demo-net=172.16.0.224 | N/A (booted from volume) | m1.tiny |
+------------------------------------+-------------+--------+
--------------------+------------------------+---------+
```

Now you can associate the floating IP with the server.

```
$ openstack server add floating ip apressinst1 192.168.122.215
```

Let's confirm that the VM got the new IP. The following shows the second external IP and the virtual machine properties.

```
$ openstack server list
+------------------------------------+-------------+--------+
------------------------------------+------------------------+---------+
| ID                                 | Name        | Status |
  Networks                         | Image                  | Flavor  |
+------------------------------------+-------------+--------+
------------------------------------+------------------------+---------+
| f6fda94b-a6d2-43cc-8e93-18a538759a22 | apressinst1 | ACTIVE |
  demo-net=172.16.0.224, 192.168.122.215 | N/A (booted from volume) | m1.tiny |
+------------------------------------+-------------+--------+
------------------------------------+------------------------+---------+
```

You can find information about floating IPs in Horizon by going to Project ➤ Network ➤ Floating IPs (see Figure 6-7).

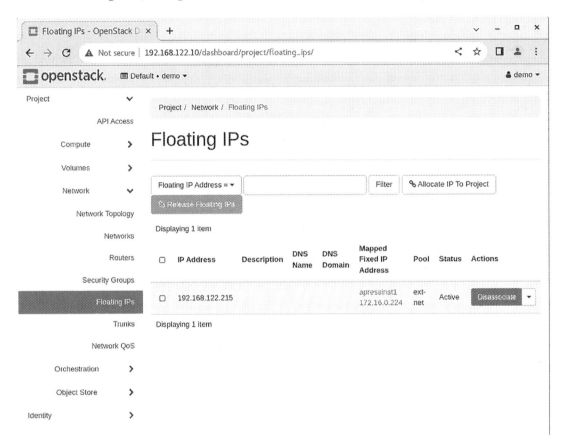

Figure 6-7. *Floating IPs tab in Horizon*

Managing Project Security Group Rules

Security groups are firewall rules that can filter ingress and egress traffic for virtual machines. In OVS, they are implemented by ML2 with iptables rules. The iptables rules could only be applied using a Linux bridge and were connected to the kernel using a tap device. OVN uses the conntrack module to implement them. Again, there are no differences between the user's point of view and the exam's point of view. To create the security group, use the following command.

```
$ openstack security group create apress-sgroup
+------------------+-----------------------------------------------------------+
| Field            | Value                                                     |
+------------------+-----------------------------------------------------------+
| created_at       | 2022-07-18T09:05:16Z                                      |
| description      | apress-sgroup                                             |
| id               | 7ec1083a-05c9-4df9-8b8e-941f0718e7b8                      |
|                  |                                                           |
| name             | apress-sgroup                                             |
| project_id       | 27cdeded89d24fb49c11030b8cc87f15                          |
|                  |                                                           |
| revision_number  | 1                                            |            |
| rules            | created_at='2022-07-18T09:05:16Z', direction='egress',    |
|                  | ethertype='IPv4', id='4a5c9c50-e8f2-4196-8d20-            |
|                  | bf66435de42e', standard_attr_id='47', tenant_id='27cde    |
|                  | ded89d24fb49c11030b8cc87f15', updated_at='2022-07-18T0    |
|                  | 9:05:16Z'                                             |    |
|                  | created_at='2022-07-18T09:05:16Z',                        |
|                  | direction='egress', ethertype='IPv6', id='7481b436-       |
|                  | eabb-4358-8b72-968290929722', standard_attr_id='48',      |
|                  | tenant_id='27cdeded89d24fb49c11030b8cc87f15',             |
|                  | updated_at='2022-07-18T09:05:16Z'                    |    |
| stateful         | True                                                      |
| tags             | []                                                        |
| updated_at       | 2022-07-18T09:05:16Z                                      |
+------------------+-----------------------------------------------------------+
```

Then you can add a rule. It provides SSH access (TCP port 22).

```
$ openstack security group rule create --protocol tcp --dst-port 22
apress-sgroup
+-------------------------+--------------------------------------+
| Field                   | Value                                |
+-------------------------+--------------------------------------+
| created_at              | 2022-07-18T09:55:23Z                 |
| description             |                                      |
| direction               | ingress                              |
| ether_type              | IPv4                                 |
| id                      | 87291f07-420d-4b99-8eb2-edc3f8fd5082 |
| name                    | None                                 |
| port_range_max          | 22                                   |
| port_range_min          | 22                                   |
| project_id              | 27cdeded89d24fb49c11030b8cc87f15     |
| protocol                | tcp                                  |
| remote_address_group_id | None                                 |
| remote_group_id         | None                                 |
| remote_ip_prefix        | 0.0.0.0/0                            |
| revision_number         | 0                                    |
| security_group_id       | 7ec1083a-05c9-4df9-8b8e-941f0718e7b8 |
| tags                    | []                                   |
| tenant_id               | 27cdeded89d24fb49c11030b8cc87f15     |
| updated_at              | 2022-07-18T09:55:23Z                 |
+-------------------------+--------------------------------------+
```

And you can also apply security groups to instances at boot time.

```
$ openstack server create --image cirros-0.5.2-x86_64 --flavor
m1.tiny --network demo-net --security-group apress-sgroup apressinst2
```

Field	Value
OS-DCF:diskConfig	MANUAL
OS-EXT-AZ:availability_zone	
OS-EXT-STS:power_state	NOSTATE
OS-EXT-STS:task_state	scheduling
OS-EXT-STS:vm_state	building
OS-SRV-USG:launched_at	None
OS-SRV-USG:terminated_at	None
accessIPv4	
accessIPv6	
addresses	
adminPass	47Fcbt3ZiCxv
config_drive	
created	2022-07-18T10:13:02Z
flavor	m1.tiny (1)
hostId	
id	b031aa84-ca26-4a17-b302-8929bb18f647
image	cirros-0.5.2-x86_64 (7ffe1b43-7e86-4ad0-86b6-9fffa38b3c20)
key_name	None
name	apressinst2
progress	0
project_id	9e0c535c2240405b989afa450681df18
properties	
security_groups	name='7748dc9f-1573-4225-a51e-8fc6328aafc0'
status	BUILD
updated	2022-07-18T10:13:02Z
user_id	a20b5a5995b740ff90034297335b330a
volumes_attached	

You can add or remove a security group on the fly.

```
$ openstack server add security group apressinst1 apress-sgroup
$ openstack server remove security group apressinst1 apress-sgroup
```

The following command lists the rules.

```
$ openstack security group rule list apress-sgroup
+--------------------------------------+-------------+-----------+
-----------+------------+----------+----------------------+
--------------------+
| ID                                   | IP Protocol | Ethertype |
 IP Range  | Port Range | Direction | Remote Security Group |
 Remote Address Group |
+--------------------------------------+-------------+-----------+
-----------+------------+----------+----------------------+
--------------------+
| 73ed6fac-0cc4-4a30-8fe6-a113d7c84b03 | None        | IPv6      |
 ::/0       |            | egress    | None                  |
None                 |
| 94c8ba4c-e9e0-49e4-8e9f-b1fef14d030e | None        | IPv4      |
 0.0.0.0/0 |            | egress    | None                  |
None                 |
| fa9b7ece-2370-4060-9c2d-649dd3b13064 | tcp         | IPv4      |
 0.0.0.0/0 | 22:22      | ingress   | None                  |
None                 |
+--------------------------------------+-------------+-----------+
-----------+------------+----------+----------------------+
--------------------+
```

You can find information about security groups in Horizon by going to Project ➤ Network ➤ Security Groups, as shown in Figure 6-8.

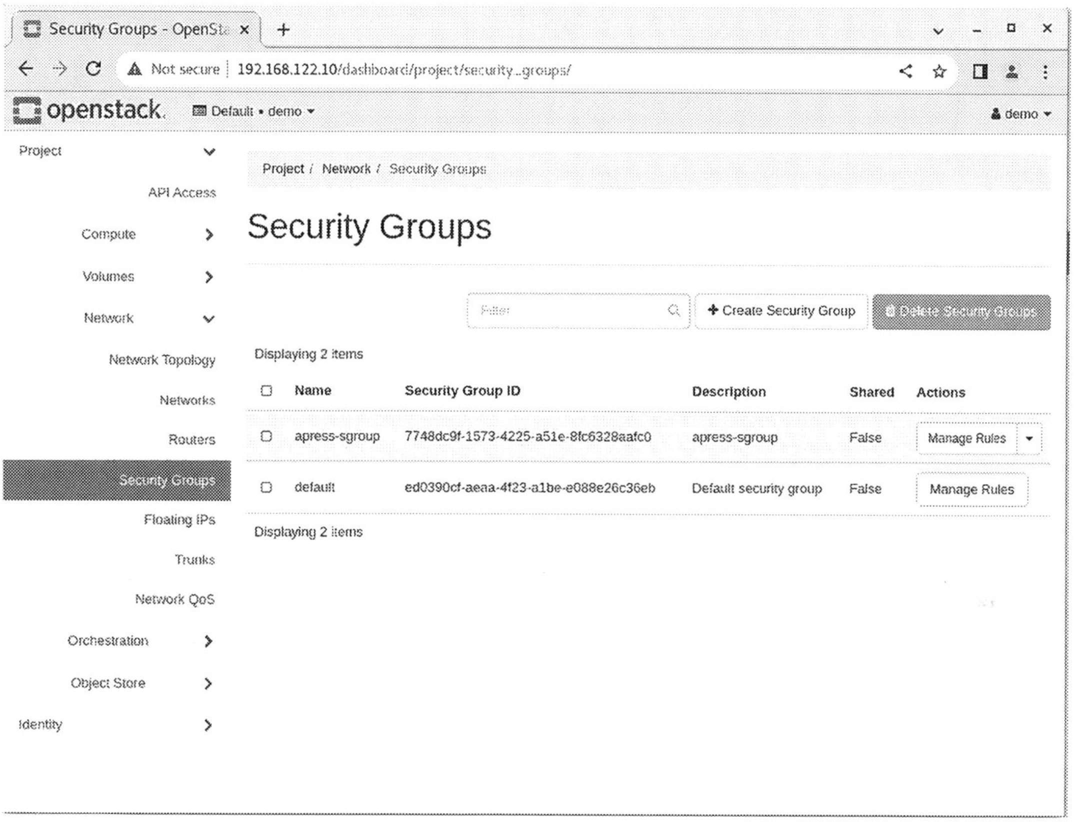

Figure 6-8. *Security Groups tab in Horizon*

Managing Quotas

A quota limits the number of available resources. The default number of resources allowed per project can be retrieved by an admin using the `openstack quota list` command. Here is an example.

```
$ openstack quota list --network --detail
+----------------------+--------+----------+-------+
| Resource             | In Use | Reserved | Limit |
+----------------------+--------+----------+-------+
| floating_ips         |      1 |        0 |    50 |
| networks             |      1 |        0 |   100 |
| ports                |      1 |        0 |   500 |
| rbac_policies        |      2 |        0 |    10 |
| routers              |      0 |        0 |    10 |
| subnets              |      1 |        0 |   100 |
| subnet_pools         |      0 |        0 |    -1 |
| security_group_rules |      7 |        0 |   100 |
| security_groups      |      2 |        0 |    10 |
+----------------------+--------+----------+-------+
```

The corresponding section of the Horizon interface is presented in Figure 6-9. You can find it by clicking Admin ➤ System ➤ Defaults and then selecting the Network Quotas tab.

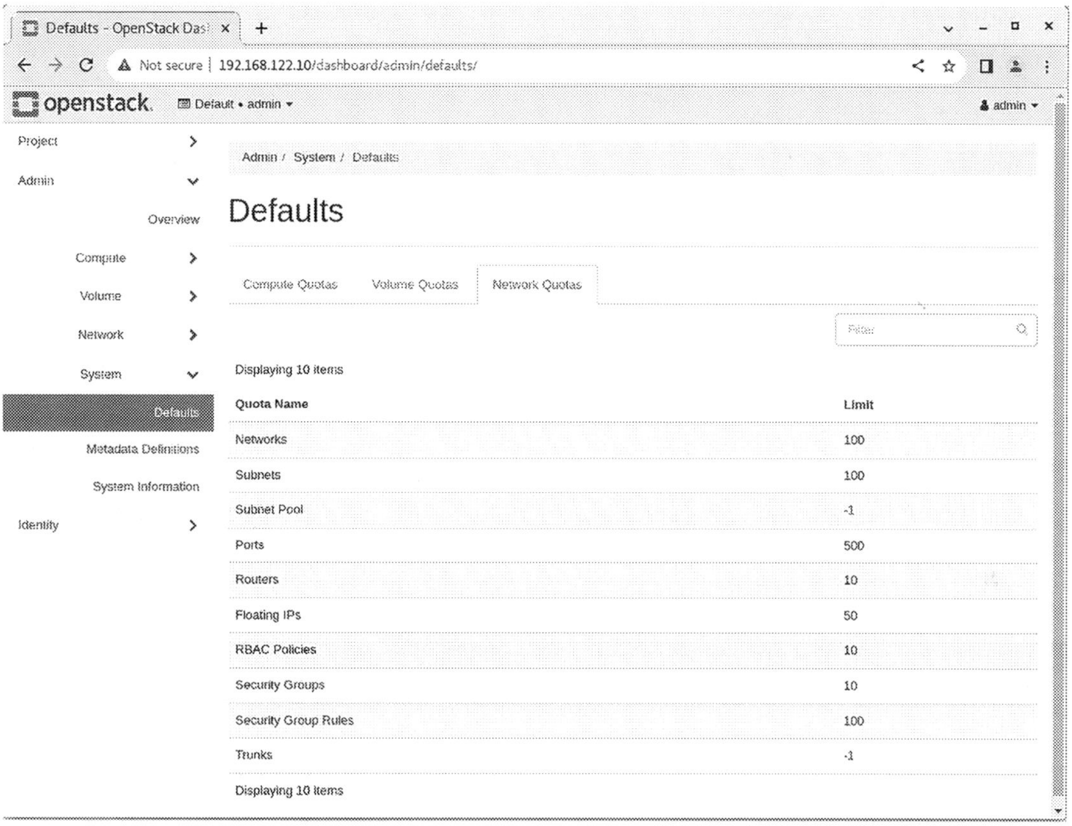

Figure 6-9. *Default network quotas*

Regular users can get their project quotas with the openstack quota show and openstack quota show --default commands.

```
$ openstack quota show
+----------------------+------------------------------------------------+
| Field                | Value                                          |
+----------------------+------------------------------------------------+
| backup-gigabytes     | 1000                                           |
| backups              | 10                                             |
| cores                | 20                                             |
| fixed-ips            | -1                                             |
| floating-ips         | 50                                             |
| gigabytes            | 1000                                           |
| gigabytes___DEFAULT__ | -1                                            |
```

```
| gigabytes_iscsi        | -1                                              |
| groups                 | 10                                              |
| injected-file-size     | 10240                                           |
| injected-files         | 5                                               |
| injected-path-size     | 255                                             |
| instances              | 10                                              |
| key-pairs              | 100                                             |
| location               | Munch({'cloud': '', 'region_name': 'Region-    |
|                        | One', 'zone': None, 'project': Munch({'id':     |
|                        | '9e0c535c2240405b989afa450681df18', 'name':     |
|                        | 'demo', 'domain_id': None, 'domain_name':       |
|                        | 'Default'})})                                   |
| networks               | 100                                             |
| per-volume-gigabytes   | -1                                              |
| ports                  | 500                                             |
| project                | 9e0c535c2240405b989afa450681df18                |
| project_name           | demo                                            |
| properties             | 128                                             |
| ram                    | 51200                                           |
| rbac_policies          | 10                                              |
| routers                | 10                                              |
| secgroup-rules         | 100                                             |
| secgroups              | 10                                              |
| server-group-members   | 10                                              |
| server-groups          | 10                                              |
| snapshots              | 10                                              |
| snapshots__DEFAULT__   | -1                                              |
| snapshots_iscsi        | -1                                              |
| subnet_pools           | -1                                              |
| subnets                | 100                                             |
| volumes                | 10                                              |
| volumes__DEFAULT__     | -1                                              |
| volumes_iscsi          | -1                                              |
+------------------------+-------------------------------------------------+
```

Admins can do the same, but only for any project by adding the project's name. If an admin needs to change the quotas for a particular project, the openstack quota set command is used.

```
$ openstack quota set
usage: openstack quota set [-h] [--class] [--cores <cores>] [--fixed-ips
<fixed-ips>] [--injected-file-size <injected-file-size>]
                            [--injected-path-size <injected-path-size>]
                            [--injected-files <injected-files>] [--instances
                            <instances>]
                            [--key-pairs <key-pairs>] [--properties <proper-
                            ties>] [--ram <ram>] [--server-groups <server-
                            groups>]
                            [--server-group-members <server-group-members>]
                            [--backups <backups>] [--backup-gigabytes <back-
                            up-gigabytes>]
                            [--gigabytes <gigabytes>] [--per-volume-gi-
                            gabytes <per-volume-gigabytes>] [--snapshots
                            <snapshots>] [--volumes <volumes>]
                            [--floating-ips <floating-ips>] [--secgroup-
                            rules <secgroup-rules>] [--secgroups <sec-
                            groups>] [--networks <networks>]
                            [--subnets <subnets>] [--ports <ports>] [--rout-
                            ers <routers>] [--rbac-policies <rbac-policies>]
                            [--subnetpools <subnetpools>] [--volume-type
                            <volume-type>] [--force] [--check-limit]
                            <project/class>
```

```
$ openstack quota set --secgroups 99 apress
```

Admins can manage quotas on a per-project basis in Horizon by going to Identity ➤ Projects ➤ Modify Quotas through the drop-down menu to the right of the project's name. Part of the network's Edit Quotas page is shown in Figure 6-10. A user can check the overall limits, including Neutron quotas, in Horizon by going to Project ➤ Compute ➤ Overview tab.

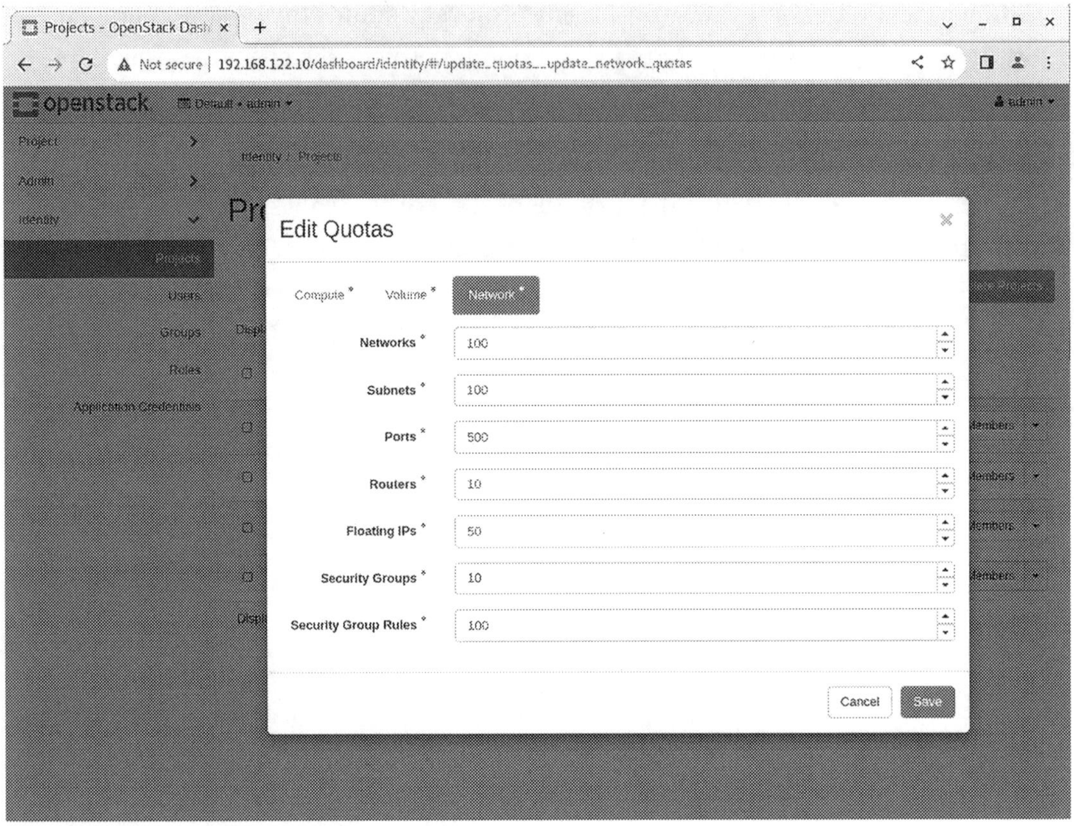

Figure 6-10. *Checking quotas in Horizon*

Verifying the Operation of the Network Service

Neutron consists of several components. Its configuration files were listed at the beginning of this chapter. The Neutron API service is bound to port 9696. The log file for the Neutron server is available at /var/log/neutron/server.log.

You can check the supported extension for Neutron with the following command.

```
$ openstack extension list --network
+-------------------------------------------------------------------------------+
-------------------------------------------+
-------------------------------------------------------------------------------+
| Name                                                                          |
    Alias                                  |
 Description                                                                    |
+-------------------------------------------------------------------------------+
-------------------------------------------+
-------------------------------------------------------------------------------+
| Address group                                                                 |
    address-group                          |
 Support address group                                                          |
| Address scope                                                                 |
    address-scope                          |
 Address scopes extension.                                                      |
| agent                                                                         |
    agent                                  |
 The agent management extension.                                                |
| Allowed Address Pairs                                                         |
    allowed-address-pairs                  |
 Provides allowed address pairs                                                 |
| Auto Allocated Topology Services                                              |
    auto-allocated-topology                |
 Auto Allocated Topology Services.                                              |
| Availability Zone                                                             |
    availability_zone                      |
 The availability zone extension.                                               |
| Default Subnetpools                                                           |
    default-subnetpools                    |
 Provides ability to mark and use a subnetpool as the default.                  |
| DNS Integration                                                               |
    dns-integration                        |
 Provides integration with DNS.                                                 |
```

| dns_domain for ports |
    dns-domain-ports |
Allows the DNS domain to be specified for a network port. |
| DNS domain names with keywords allowed |
    dns-integration-domain-keywords |
Allows to use keywords like <project_id>, <project_name>, <user_id> and
<user_name> as DNS domain name |
| Neutron external network |
    external-net |
Adds external network attribute to network resource. |
| Neutron Extra DHCP options |
    extra_dhcp_opt |
Extra options configuration for DHCP. For example PXE boot options to DHCP
clients can be specified (e.g. tftp-server, server-ip-address, bootfile-name) |
| Neutron Extra Route |
    extraroute |
Extra routes configuration for L3 router |
| Filter parameters validation |
    filter-validation |
Provides validation on filter parameters. |
| Floating IP Port Details Extension |
    fip-port-details |
Add port_details attribute to Floating IP resource |
| Neutron Service Flavors |
    flavors |
Flavor specification for Neutron advanced services. |
| Floating IP Pools Extension |
    floatingip-pools |
Provides a floating IP pools API. |
| Neutron L3 Router |
    router |
Router abstraction for basic L3 forwarding between L2 Neutron networks and
access to external networks via a NAT gateway. |

| Neutron L3 Configurable external gateway mode |
    ext-gw-mode |
Extension of the router abstraction for specifying whether SNAT should occur on
the external gateway |
| Multi Provider Network |
    multi-provider |
Expose mapping of virtual networks to multiple physical networks |
| Network MTU |
    net-mtu |
Provides MTU attribute for a network resource. |
| Network MTU (writable) |
    net-mtu-writable |
Provides a writable MTU attribute for a network resource. |
| Network Availability Zone |
    network_availability_zone |
Availability zone support for network. |
| Network IP Availability |
    network-ip-availability |
Provides IP availability data for each network and subnet. |
| Pagination support |
    pagination |
Extension that indicates that pagination is enabled. |
| Port device profile |
    port-device-profile |
Expose the port device profile (Cyborg) |
| Neutron Port MAC address regenerate |
    port-mac-address-regenerate |
Network port MAC address regenerate |
| Port NUMA affinity policy |
    port-numa-affinity-policy |
Expose the port NUMA affinity policy |
| Port Resource Request |
    port-resource-request |
Expose resource request to Port |

| Port Resource Request Groups |
  port-resource-request-groups |
Support requesting multiple groups of resources and traits from the same
RP subtree in resource_request |
| Port Binding |
  binding |
Expose port bindings of a virtual port to external application |
| Port Bindings Extended |
  binding-extended |
Expose port bindings of a virtual port to external application |
| Port Security |
  port-security |
Provides port security |
| project_id field enabled |
  project-id |
Extension that indicates that project_id field is enabled. |
| Provider Network |
  provider |
Expose mapping of virtual networks to physical networks |
| Quality of Service |
  qos |
The Quality of Service extension. |
| Direction for QoS bandwidth limit rule |
  qos-bw-limit-direction |
Allow to configure QoS bandwidth limit rule with specific direction: ingress
or egress |
| Ingress direction for QoS minimum bandwidth rule |
  qos-bw-minimum-ingress |
Allow to configure QoS minumum bandwidth rule with ingress direction. |
| QoS default policy |
  qos-default |
Expose the QoS default policy per project |
| Floating IP QoS |
  qos-fip |
The floating IP Quality of Service extension |

| QoS port network policy ID |
    qos-port-network-policy |
Adds a the QoS network ID to the port definition |
| QoS minimum packet rate rule |
    qos-pps-minimum |
Allow to configure QoS minimum packet rate rule. |
| QoS minimum packet rate rule alias |
    qos-pps-minimum-rule-alias |
API to enable GET, PUT and DELETE operations on QoS minimum packet rate rule
without specifying policy ID |
| QoS Rule Type Packet per Second Extension |
    qos-pps |
Add QoS Rule Type Packet per Second |
| Details of QoS rule types |
    qos-rule-type-details |
Expose details about QoS rule types supported by loaded backend drivers |
| Quality of Service rules alias API |
    qos-rules-alias |
API to enable GET, PUT and DELETE operations on QoS policy rules without
specifying policy ID |
| Quota engine limit check |
    quota-check-limit |
Support for checking the resource usage before applying a new quota limit |
| Quota management support |
    quotas |
Expose functions for quotas management per project |
| Quota details management support |
    quota_details |
Expose functions for quotas usage statistics per project |
| RBAC Policies |
    rbac-policies |
Allows creation and modification of policies that control tenant access to
resources. |

| Add address_scope type to RBAC |
| rbac-address-scope |
 Add address_scope type to RBAC |
| Add security_group type to network RBAC |
| rbac-security-groups |
 Add security_group type to network RBAC |
| If-Match constraints based on revision_number |
| revision-if-match |
 Extension indicating that If-Match based on revision_number is supported. |
| Resource revision numbers |
| standard-attr-revisions |
 This extension will display the revision number of neutron resources. |
| Router Availability Zone |
| router_availability_zone |
 Availability zone support for router. |
| Normalized CIDR field for security group rules |
| security-groups-normalized-cidr |
 Add new field with normalized remote_ip_prefix cidr in SG rule |
| Remote address group id field for security group rules |
| security-groups-remote-address-group |
 Add new field of remote address group id in SG rules |
| Security group filtering on the shared field |
| security-groups-shared-filtering |
 Support filtering security groups on the shared field |
| security-group |
| security-group |
 The security groups extension. |
| Neutron Service Type Management |
| service-type |
 API for retrieving service providers for Neutron advanced services |
| Sorting support |
| sorting |
 Extension that indicates that sorting is enabled. |

```
| standard-attr-description                                                |
     standard-attr-description              |
  Extension to add descriptions to standard attributes                     |
| Stateful security group                                                  |
     stateful-security-group                |
  Indicates if the security group is stateful or not                       |
| Subnet DNS publish fixed IP                                              |
     subnet-dns-publish-fixed-ip            |
  Support choosing to publish DNS records for IPs from a subnet            |
| Subnet service types                                                     |
     subnet-service-types                   |
  Provides ability to set the subnet service_types field                   |
| Subnet Allocation                                                        |
          subnet_allocation                 |
  Enables allocation of subnets from a subnet pool                         |
| Tag support for resources with standard attribute: port, subnet, subnetpool,
   network, security_group, router, floatingip, policy, trunk, network_segment_range |
     standard-attr-tag                      |
  Enables to set tag on resources with standard attribute.                 |
| Resource timestamps                                                      |
     standard-attr-timestamp                |
  Adds created_at and updated_at fields to all Neutron resources that have
  Neutron standard attributes.                                            |
| Trunk Extension                                                          |
     trunk                                  |
  Provides support for trunk ports                                         |
| Trunk port details                                                       |
     trunk-details                          |
  Expose trunk port details                                               |
+--------------------------------------------------------------------------+
----------------------------------------------+
--------------------------------------------------------------------------+
```

And you can check the state of the running agents with the following command.

```
$ openstack network agent list
+----------------------------------------+----------------------+----------------+
------------------+-------+-------+---------------------------+
| ID                                     | Agent Type           | Host           |
 Availability Zone | Alive | State | Binary                    |
+----------------------------------------+----------------------+----------------+
------------------+-------+-------+---------------------------+
| dff0df04-e035-42cc-98a6-d2aee745b9bf   | OVN Controller agent | rdo.test.local |
                  | :-)   | UP    | ovn-controller            |
| 238f88a3-f9c6-5d22-89bb-6b9b8f369d25   | OVN Metadata agent   | rdo.test.local |
                  | :-)   | UP    | neutron-ovn-metadata-agent |
+----------------------------------------+----------------------+----------------+
------------------+-------+-------+---------------------------+
```

Summary

It is essential to study this chapter's material to pass the exam. You may not need to dig into the differences between OVS and OVN, but you must know the practical aspects of using a network in OpenStack.

The next chapter covers OpenStack's compute services.

Review Questions

1. Which service provides routing and NAT in OVS-enabled OpenStack?

   A. neutron-server

   B. neutron-openvswitch-agent

   C. neutron-l3-agent

   D. neutron-metadata-agent

2. Which checks the status of running Neutron agents?

   A. neutron agent-list

   B. openstack network agent show

    C. openstack network agent list

    D. neutron agents-list

3. Which is the Neutron API service config?

    A. /etc/neutron/neutron.conf

    B. /etc/neutron.conf

    C. /etc/neutron/plugin.ini

    D. /etc/neutron/api-server.conf

4. Which correctly adds a new rule to an existing security group?

    A. openstack security group rule create --protocol tcp --dst-port 22 apress-sgroup

    B. openstack sgroup rule create --protocol tcp --dst-port 22 apress-sgroup

    C. openstack sgroup rule create apress-sgroup --protocol tcp --dst-port 22

    D. openstack security-group rule create --protocol tcp --dst-port 22 apress-sgroup

5. Where is the Neutron API log file located?

    A. /var/log/neutron/neutron.log

    B. /var/log/neutron/server.log

    C. /var/log/neutron/api.log

    D. /var/log/neutron/api-server.log

Answers

1. B

2. B

3. A

4. A

5. B

## CHAPTER 7

OpenStack Compute

This chapter covers 35% of the Certified OpenStack Administrator exam requirements. OpenStack Compute is the heart of OpenStack, so you must study this chapter to pass the exam without excuses.

Nova's Architecture and Components

Nova, OpenStack's compute service, is the heart of the OpenStack cloud. Its main goal is to manage basic virtual machines functions like creating, starting, stopping, and so on. Let's look at the architecture and general parts of Nova. As with other services, Nova uses a message broker and database. By default the database is MariaDB, and the message broker is RabbitMQ. The main services that support Nova are.

- **nova-api** is a service that receives REST API calls from other services and clients and responds to them.

- **nova-scheduler** is Nova's scheduling service. It takes requests for starting instances from the queue and selects a compute node for running a virtual machine on it. The selection of a hypervisor is based on its weight and filters. Filters can include an amount of memory, a requested availability zone, and a set of group hosts. The rules apply each time the instance is started or when migrating to another hypervisor.

- **nova-conductor** is the proxy service between the database and the nova-compute services. It helps with horizontal scalability.

© Andrey Markelov 2022
A. Markelov, *Certified OpenStack Administrator Study Guide*,
https://doi.org/10.1007/978-1-4842-8804-7_7

- **nova-compute** is the main part of an IaaS system. This daemon usually runs only on compute nodes. Its role is to rule a hypervisor through its specific API. It is designed to manage pools of computer resources and can work with widely available virtualization technologies.

- **placement-api** is a REST API stack and data model used to track resource provider inventories, usages, and different classes of resources. It was introduced in the Newton release of OpenStack.

- **nova-nonvncproxy** and **nova-spicehtml5proxy** are services providing access to the instances console through remote access VNC and SPICE protocols.

Figures 7-1 and 7-2 illustrate the process of starting an instance.

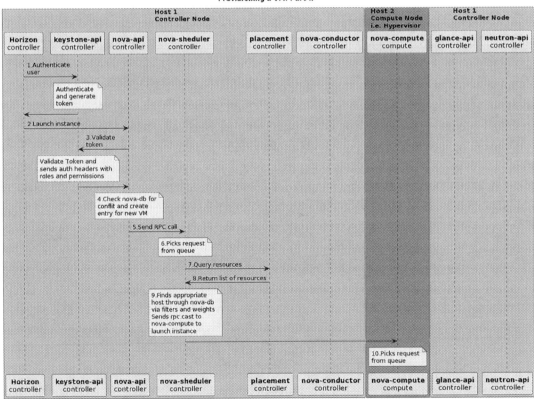

Figure 7-1. *Instance provision workflow—Part I*

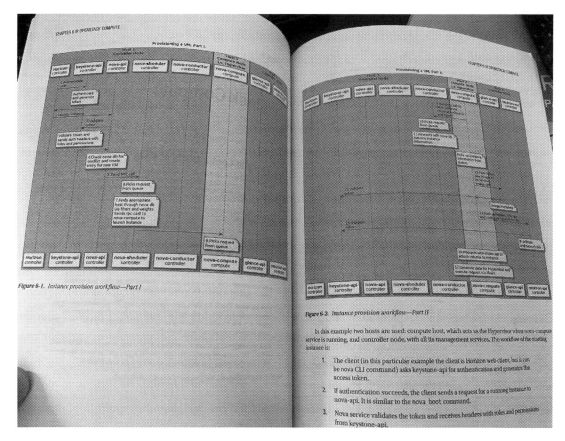

Figure 7-2. *Instance provision workflow—Part II*

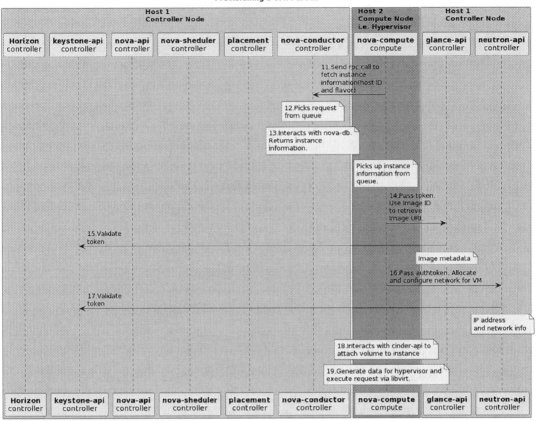

Provisioning a VM. Part II.

Figure 7.2 (*continued*)

In this example, two hosts are used: compute host, which acts as the hypervisor when the nova-compute service is running, and controller node, with all its management services. The following describes the workflow for starting the instance.

1. The client (in this particular example, the client is a Horizon web client, but it can be the openstack CLI command) asks keystone-api for authentication and generates the access token.

2. If authentication succeeds, the client sends a request for a running instance to nova-api. It is similar to the openstack server create command.

3. Nova validates the token and receives headers with roles and permissions from keystone-api.

4. Nova checks the database for conflicts with existing names of objects and creates a new entry for this instance in its database.

5. nova-api sends the RPC for a scheduling instance to the nova-scheduler service.

6. The nova-scheduler service picks up the request from the message queue.

7. The nova-scheduler service queries resources from the placement service.

8. Placement returns a list of available resources to nova-scheduler.

9. nova-scheduler uses filters and weights to build a list of nodes to target. Then scheduler sends the RPC call to the nova-compute service to launch the virtual machine.

10. The nova-compute service picks up the request from the message queue.

11. The nova-compute service asks nova-conductor to fetch information about the instance, for example, host ID and flavor.

12. The nova-conductor service picks up the request from the message queue.

13. The nova-conductor service gets information about an instance from the database.

14. The nova-compute takes the instance information from the queue. The compute host now knows which image is used to start the instance. nova-compute asks the glance-api service for a particular image URL.

15. glance-api validates the token and returns the image's metadata, including the URL.

16. The nova-compute service passes a token to neutron-api and asks it to configure the network for the instance.

17. Neutron validates the token and configures the network.

18. nova-compute interacts with cinder-api to attach the volume to the instance.

19. nova-compute generates data for the hypervisor and executes the request via libvirt.

Now let's look at Nova's main configuration file, /etc/nova/nova.conf. Table 7-1 lists the options available.

127

Table 7-1. *Main Configuration Options in* /etc/nova/nova.conf

Examples of Config Options	Description
[DEFAULT] my_ip = 192.168.122.10	Management interface IP address of the controller node
[DEFAULT] enabled_apis = osapi_ compute,metadata	Enables support for the compute service and metadata APIs
[api] auth_strategy = keystone [keystone_authtoken] www_authenticate_uri = http://192.168.122.10:5000/ auth_url = http://192.168.122.10:5000/ memcached_servers = 192.168.122.10:11211 auth_type = password project_domain_name = Default user_domain_name = Default project_name = service username = nova password = password	Authentication parameters: endpoints and other parameters like default project name, domain name, project name for services, and account information for Nova user
[api_database] connection=mysql+pymysql:// nova_api:password@192.168.122.10/ nova_api [database] connection=mysql+pymysql:// nova:password@192.168.122.10/nova	Connection strings used to connect to Nova's databases

(*continued*)

Table 7-1. (*continued*)

Examples of Config Options	Description
[DEFAULT] transport_url = rabbit://openstac k:password@192.168.122.10:5672/	RabbitMQ broker address, port, user name, and password
[vnc] enabled = true vncserver_listen = $my_ip vncserver_proxyclient_address = $my_ip	Management interface IP address of the VNC proxy
[glance] api_servers=192.168.122.10:9292 [placement] region_name = RegionOne project_domain_name = Default project_name = service auth_type = password user_domain_name = Default auth_url = http://192.168.122.10:5000/v3 username = placement password = password	Location of the Image Service API Configuration for access to the Placement service

Managing Flavors

Instance flavor is a virtual machine template that describes the main parameters. It is also known as an instance type. Immediately after installing the OpenStack cloud, you can choose several predefined flavors. You can also add new flavors and delete existing ones. Use the following command to list the flavors.

```
$ openstack flavor list
+----+-----------+-------+------+-----------+-------+-----------+
| ID | Name      |   RAM | Disk | Ephemeral | VCPUs | Is Public |
+----+-----------+-------+------+-----------+-------+-----------+
| 1  | m1.tiny   |   512 |    1 |         0 |     1 | True      |
| 2  | m1.small  |  2048 |   20 |         0 |     1 | True      |
| 3  | m1.medium |  4096 |   40 |         0 |     2 | True      |
| 4  | m1.large  |  8192 |   80 |         0 |     4 | True      |
| 5  | m1.xlarge | 16384 |  160 |         0 |     8 | True      |
+----+-----------+-------+------+-----------+-------+-----------+
```

As you can see in the listing, some flavors were created during OpenStack's installation. In some of distributions list will be empty out of box. To list the details of the flavor use next command. As you can see m1.tiny has one vCPU and 512 Mb of memory.

```
$ openstack flavor show m1.tiny
+----------------------------+---------+
| Field                      | Value   |
+----------------------------+---------+
| OS-FLV-DISABLED:disabled   | False   |
| OS-FLV-EXT-DATA:ephemeral  | 0       |
| access_project_ids         | None    |
| description                | None    |
| disk                       | 1       |
| id                         | 1       |
| name                       | m1.tiny |
| os-flavor-access:is_public | True    |
| properties                 |         |
| ram                        | 512     |
| rxtx_factor                | 1.0     |
| swap                       |         |
| vcpus                      | 1       |
+----------------------------+---------+
```

By default, only the admin can list all the flavors and create new ones. Here is an example of the creation of a new publicly available flavor.

```
$ source keystonerc_admin
$ openstack flavor create --public --ram 400 --disk 3 --vcpus 1 m10.tiny
+----------------------------+---------+
| Field                      | Value   |
+----------------------------+---------+
| OS-FLV-DISABLED:disabled   | False   |
| OS-FLV-EXT-DATA:ephemeral  | 0       |
| access_project_ids         | None    |
| description                | None    |
| disk                       | 1       |
| id                         | 1       |
| name                       | m1.tiny |
| os-flavor-access:is_public | True    |
| properties                 |         |
| ram                        | 512     |
| rxtx_factor                | 1.0     |
| swap                       |         |
| vcpus                      | 1       |
+----------------------------+---------+
```

In this example, a new flavor was created with the name m10.tiny that has a 3 GB disk, 400 MB RAM, and 1 vCPU. You can delete the flavor with the following command.

```
$ openstack flavor delete m10.tiny
```

For managing flavors in Horizon, go to Admin ➤ Compute ➤ Flavors (see Figure 7-3).

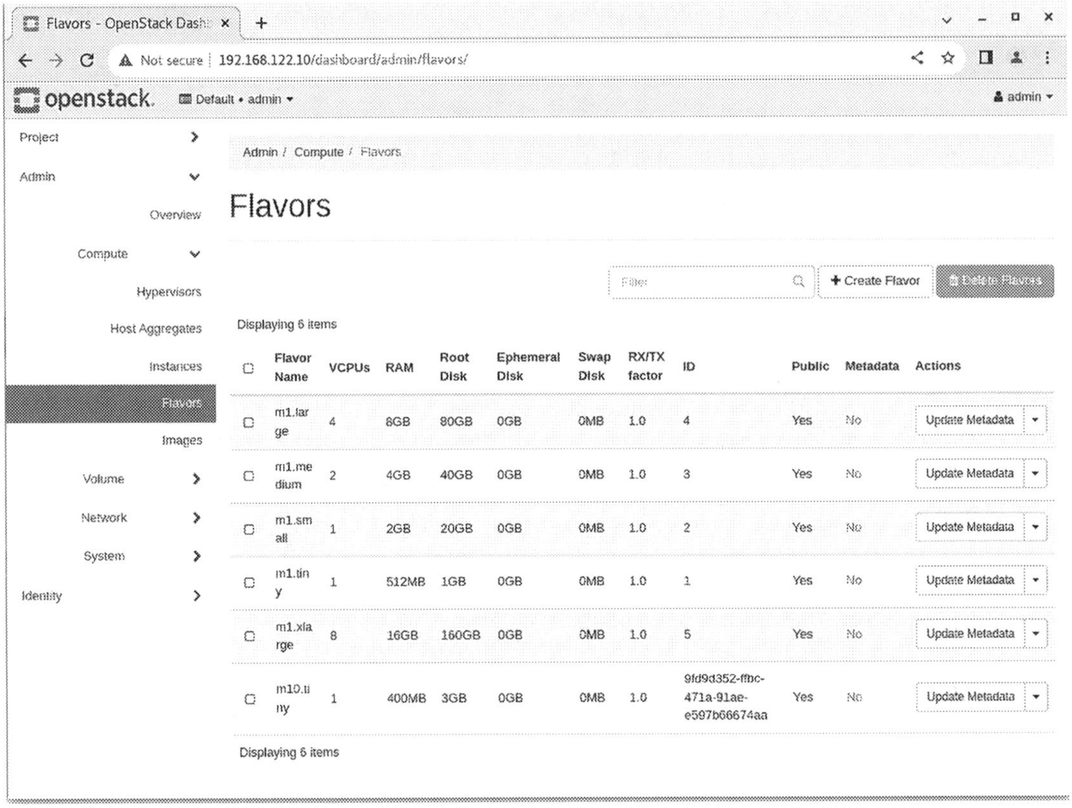

Figure 7-3. *Managing flavors in Horizon*

Managing and Accessing an Instance Using a Key Pair

Before launching instances, you should know how to work with OpenSSH key pairs. Access to virtual machines with OpenSSH key-based authentication is essential for using GNU/Linux in the cloud computing environment.

SSH (Secure Shell) allows you to authenticate users by using the private-public key pair. You should generate two linked cryptographic keys: public and private. The public key can be given to anyone. Your private key should be kept in a secure place—it is only yours. An instance running the OpenSSH server with your public key can issue a challenge that can only be answered by the system holding your private key. As a result, it can be authenticated through the presence of your key. This allows you to access a virtual machine in a way that does not require passwords.

OpenStack can store public keys and put them inside the instance when it is started. It is your responsibility to keep the private key secured. If you lose the key, you can't recover it. In that case, you should remove the public key from your OpenStack cloud and generate a new key pair. If somebody steals a private key, they can get access to your instances.

Tip In a GNU/Linux system, public keys are stored in the ~/.ssh/ authorized_keys file.

Let's start by creating a key pair. The corresponding command is.

```
$ openstack keypair create apresskey1 > key1
```

You create a key pair with this command. The private key is stored in the key1 file in your workstation.

```
$ cat key1
-----BEGIN RSA PRIVATE KEY-----
FliElAoNnAoKvQaELyeHnPaLwb8KlpnIC65PunAsRz5FsoBZ8VbnYhD76DON/BDVT
...
gdYjBM1CqqmUw54HkMJp8DLcYmBP+CRTwia9iSyY42Zw7eAi/QTIbQ574d8=
-----END RSA PRIVATE KEY-----
```

A public key is stored in your OpenStack cloud and is ready to use. You can check the list of public keys accessible to you with the following command.

```
$ openstack keypair list
+------------+-------------------------------------------------+------+
| Name       | Fingerprint                                     | Type |
+------------+-------------------------------------------------+------+
| apresskey1 | 1a:29:52:3c:19:cc:9d:61:c4:f1:98:03:02:85:b3:40 | ssh  |
+------------+-------------------------------------------------+------+
```

Before an SSH client can use a private key, you should make sure that the file has the correct GNU/Linux permissions.

```
$ chmod 600 key1
$ ls -l key1
-rw------- 1 andrey andrey 1676 Jul 20 15:44 key1
```

133

If you want to create and delete key pairs in Horizon, go to Project ➤ Compute ➤ Key Pairs (see Figure 7-4).

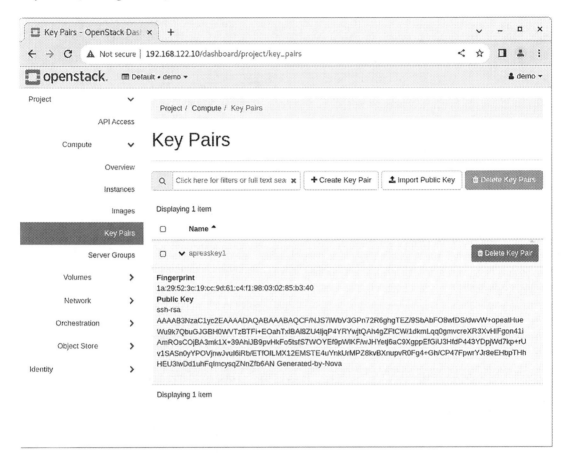

Figure 7-4. *Managing key pairs in Horizon*

When your instance runs and has a floating IP, you can connect to it with a similar command.

```
$ ssh -i key1 cirros@10.100.1.103
```

Option -i points to your private key. The next section explains how to run an instance and inject a public key into it.

Launching, Shutting Down, and Terminating the Instance

If you have only one network in the project, you need at least three parameters to start an instance: the name of an instance, the flavor, and the source of an instance. The instance source can be an image, snapshot, or block storage volume. At boot time, you can specify optional parameters, like key pairs, security groups, user data files, and volume for persistent storage. There are two networks.

```
$ openstack network list
+--------------------------------------+----------+--------------------------------------+
| ID                                   | Name     | Subnets                              |
+--------------------------------------+----------+--------------------------------------+
| 5ee4e933-de9b-4bcb-9422-83cc0d276d33 | demo-net | 18736455-80f6-4513-9d81-6cedbfe271fe |
| 5f18929b-70f6-4729-ac05-7bea494b9c5a | ext-net  | d065c027-bb60-4464-9619-7d9754535c5c |
+--------------------------------------+----------+--------------------------------------+
```

In this case, you need to specify the network. You can try the following example.

```
$ openstack server create --image cirros-0.5.2-x86_64 --flavor m1.tiny
--network demo-net --security-group apress-sgroup --key-name apresskey1
apressinst3
+-----------------------------+--------------------------------------+
| Field                       | Value                                |
+-----------------------------+--------------------------------------+
| OS-DCF:diskConfig           | MANUAL                               |
| OS-EXT-AZ:availability_zone |                                      |
| OS-EXT-STS:power_state      | NOSTATE                              |
| OS-EXT-STS:task_state       | scheduling                           |
| OS-EXT-STS:vm_state         | building                             |
| OS-SRV-USG:launched_at      | None                                 |
| OS-SRV-USG:terminated_at    | None                                 |
| accessIPv4                  |                                      |
| accessIPv6                  |                                      |
| addresses                   |                                      |
| adminPass                   | Gp4VWJ7ZYpk7                         |
| config_drive                |                                      |
| created                     | 2022-07-20T14:50:34Z                 |
```

```
| flavor                | m1.tiny (1)                              |
| hostId                |                                          |
| id                    | e69b0560-0441-4ee4-b97c-35a05bc833c2     |
| image                 | cirros-0.5.2-x86_64                      |
|                       | (7ffe1b43-7e86-4ad0-86b6-9fffa38b3c20)   |
| key_name              | apresskey1                               |
| name                  | apressinst3                              |
| progress              | 0                                        |
| project_id            | 9e0c535c2240405b989afa450681df18         |
| properties            |                                          |
| security_groups       | name='7748dc9f-1573-4225-a51e-8fc6328a   |
|                       | afc0'                                    |
| status                | BUILD                                    |
| updated               | 2022-07-20T14:50:34Z                     |
| user_id               | a20b5a5995b740ff90034297335b330a         |
| volumes_attached      |                                          |
+----------------------+------------------------------------------+
```

This example tried to run the instance with the name apressinst3 by the flavor m1.tiny from an image named cirros-0.5.2-x86_64. You also specified the security group named apress-sgroup and the keypair apresskey1. To check the current state of the instances available, use the following command.

```
$ openstack server list
+--------------------------------------+-------------+--------+----------------------+
----------------------+---------+
| ID                                   | Name        | Status | Networks             |
Image                 | Flavor  |
+--------------------------------------+-------------+--------+----------------------+
----------------------+---------+
| e69b0560-0441-4ee4-b97c-35a05bc833c2 | apressinst3 | ACTIVE | demo-net=172.16.0.125 |
cirros-0.5.2-x86_64   | m1.tiny |
+---------+-------------+--------+----------------------+----------------------+---------+
```

You may want to connect to the instance console in your browser by the noVNC client, which is the VNC client using HTML5 with encryption support. To get the URL, use the following command.

```
$ openstack console url show apressinst3
+----------+-------------------------------------------------------------+
| Field    | Value                                                       |
+----------+-------------------------------------------------------------+
| protocol | vnc                                                         |
| type     | novnc                                                       |
| url      | http://192.168.122.10:6080/vnc_auto.                       |
|            html?path=%3Ftoken%3D622f9d39-e362-4a1f-b280-467eac740155 |
+----------+-------------------------------------------------------------+
```

If you put the URL in your browser's address bar, you can connect to the machine, as shown in Figure 7-5.

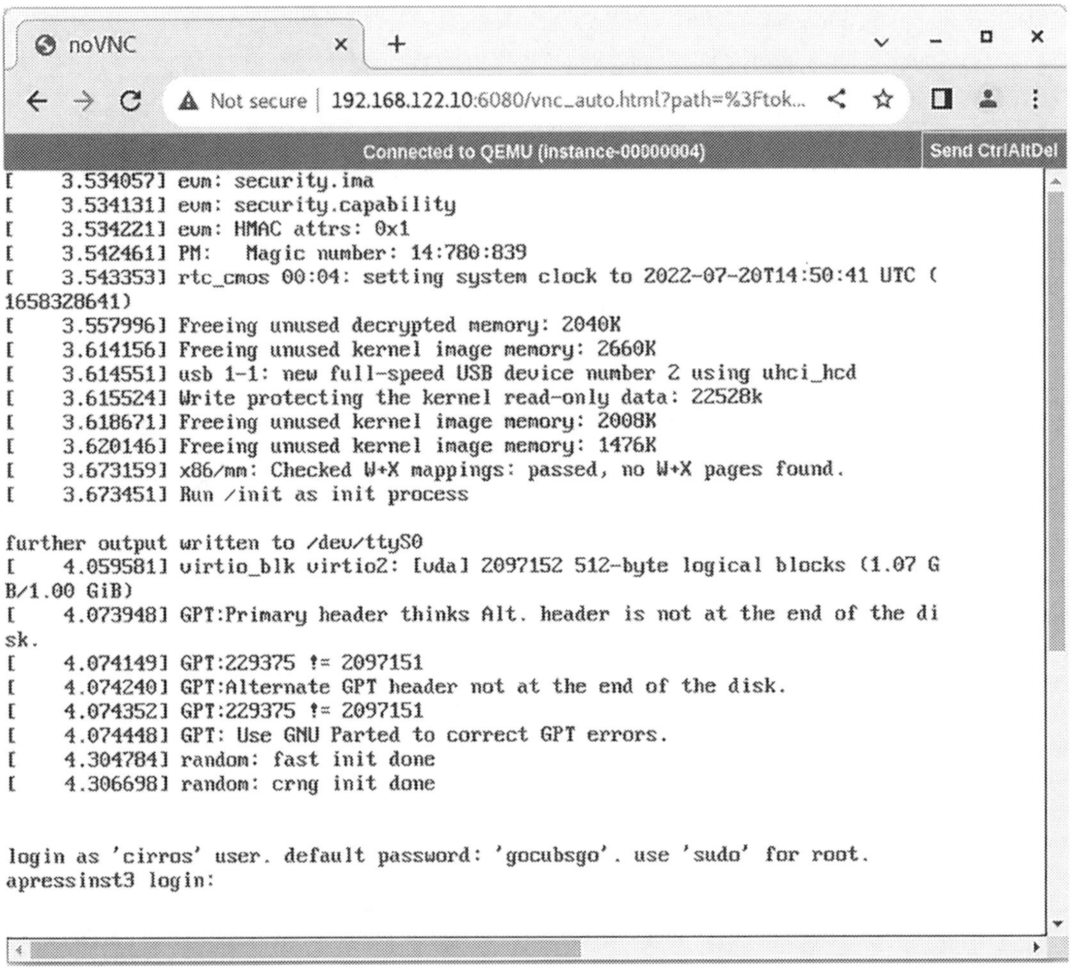

Figure 7-5. *Example of the console of running instance in a browser*

Tip   If you got an error by using PackStack installation, check that the hostname of your OpenStack server is present in /etc/hosts.

If you prefer to work with instances in GUI, you can use the Horizon web interface. For that, go to Project ➤ Compute ➤ Instances. An example of the series of launch dialogs is shown in Figure 7-6. Walk through them by using the Next button.

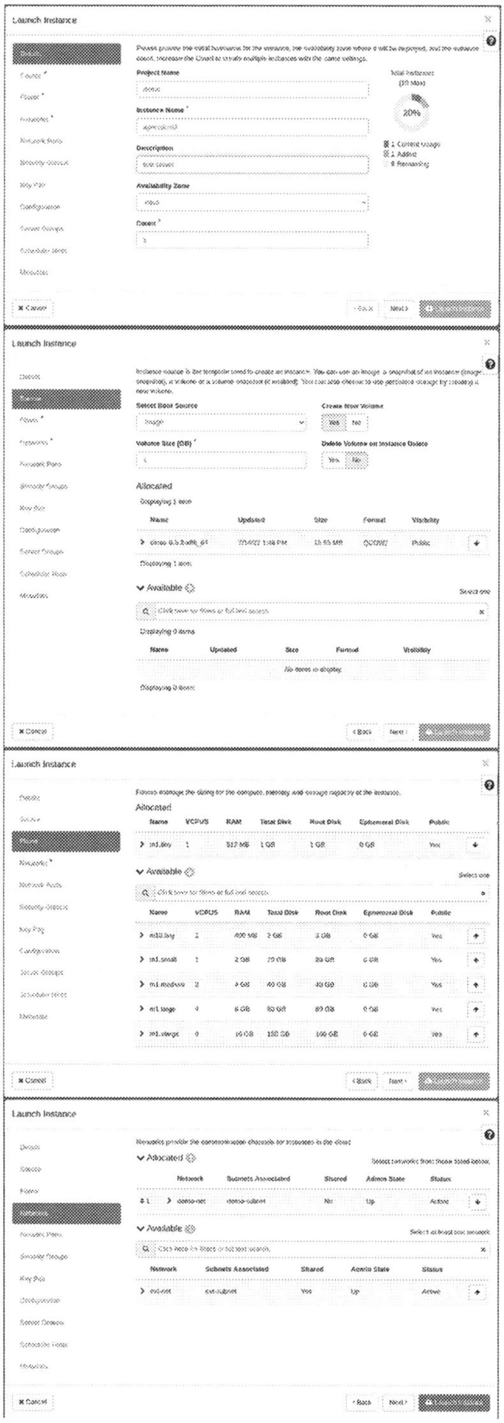

Figure 7-6. *Example of a launch instance dialog window*

If there is an error, you may see something like the following.

```
$ openstack server list
+--------------------------------------+------------+--------+
--------------------+--------+-----------+
| ID                                   | Name       | Status |
Networks | Image          | Flavor    |
+--------------------------------------+------------+--------+
--------------------+--------+-----------+
| c9831978-a84c-4df4-8c45-005c533fbf8b | apressinst3 | ERROR  |
        | cirros-0.5.2-x86_64 | m1.xlarge |
+--------------------------------------+------------+--------+
--------------------+--------+-----------+
```

To get detailed information about the instance, you can run the following command.

```
$ openstack server show apressinst3
+-----------------------------+-------------------------------------------+
| Field                       | Value                                     |
+-----------------------------+-------------------------------------------+
| OS-DCF:diskConfig           | MANUAL                                    |
| OS-EXT-AZ:availability_zone |                                           |
| OS-EXT-STS:power_state      | NOSTATE                                   |
| OS-EXT-STS:task_state       | None                                      |
| OS-EXT-STS:vm_state         | error                                     |
| OS-SRV-USG:launched_at      | None                                      |
| OS-SRV-USG:terminated_at    | None                                      |
| accessIPv4                  |                                           |
| accessIPv6                  |                                           |
| addresses                   |                                           |
| config_drive                |                                           |
| created                     | 2022-07-21T12:20:43Z                      |
| fault                       | {'code': 500, 'created':                  |
|                             | '2022-07-21T12:20:43Z', 'message': 'No    |
|                             | valid host was found. '}                  |
| flavor                      | m1.xlarge (5)                             |
| hostId                      |                                           |
| id                          | c9831978-a84c-4df4-8c45-005c533fbf8b      |
```

```
| image                        | cirros-0.5.2-x86_64 (7ffe1b43-7e86-   |
|                              | 4ad0-86b6-9fffa38b3c20)               |
| key_name                     | apresskey1                            |
| name                         | apressinst3                           |
| project_id                   | 9e0c535c2240405b989afa450681df18      |
| properties                   |                                       |
| status                       | ERROR                                 |
| updated                      | 2022-07-21T12:20:43Z                  |
| user_id                      | a20b5a5995b740ff90034297335b330a      |
| volumes_attached             |                                       |
+------------------------------+---------------------------------------+
```

The following is the command to start this instance.

```
$ openstack server create --image cirros-0.5.2-x86_64 --flavor m1.xlarge
--network demo-net --security-group apress-sgroup --key-name apresskey1
apressinst3
```

From the output, it is easy to see that there is no room to put such a big instance within flavor m1.xlarge. Flavor m1.xlarge requires 16 GB of RAM.

The next command completely deletes this instance.

```
$ openstack server delete apressinst3
```

If you need to reboot your virtual machine, use the following command.

```
$ openstack server reboot apressinst3
```

For a hard reset of the server, you can add the --hard option. You may stop and start an instance if needed.

```
$ openstack server stop apressinst3
$ openstack server list
```

```
+----------------------------------------------+--------------+----------+
---------------------+--------------------+---------+
| ID                                           | Name         | Status   |
Networks            | Image               | Flavor  |
+----------------------------------------------+--------------+----------+
---------------------+--------------------+---------+
| b360f5a5-b528-4f77-bdc7-3676ffcf0dff | apressinst3 | SHUTOFF |
demo-net=172.16.0.48 | cirros-0.5.2-x86_64 | m1.tiny |
+----------------------------------------------+--------------+----------+
---------------------+--------------------+---------+
$ openstack server start apressinst3
$ openstack server list
+----------------------------------------------+--------------+----------+
---------------------+--------------------+---------+
| ID                                           | Name         | Status   |
Networks            | Image               | Flavor  |
+----------------------------------------------+--------------+----------+
---------------------+--------------------+---------+
| b360f5a5-b528-4f77-bdc7-3676ffcf0dff | apressinst3 | ACTIVE |
demo-net=172.16.0.48 | cirros-0.5.2-x86_64 | m1.tiny |
+----------------------------------------------+--------------+----------+
---------------------+--------------------+---------+
```

Managing Instance Snapshots

OpenStack can create snapshots of instances, even if a virtual machine is running. In this case, the user must keep the data consistent. It is important to know that snapshot is not an instance recovery point. Snapshot is the same as a regular Glance image. You can start a new virtual machine from the snapshot of another virtual machine.

Let's check whether there is at least one image in Glance and one instance.

```
$ openstack image list
+----------------------------------------------+---------------------+--------+
| ID                                           | Name                | Status |
+----------------------------------------------+---------------------+--------+
| 7ffe1b43-7e86-4ad0-86b6-9fffa38b3c20 | cirros-0.5.2-x86_64 | active |
+----------------------------------------------+---------------------+--------+
```

And there is at least one running server.

```
$ openstack server list
+------------------------------------+------------+--------+
--------------------+--------------------+---------+
| ID                                 | Name       | Status |
Networks            | Image              | Flavor  |
+------------------------------------+------------+--------+
--------------------+--------------------+---------+
| b360f5a5-b528-4f77-bdc7-3676ffcf0dff | apressinst3 | ACTIVE |
demo-net=172.16.0.48 | cirros-0.5.2-x86_64 | m1.tiny |
+------------------------------------+------------+--------+
--------------------+--------------------+---------+
```

Now you can create a snapshot from a running instance.

```
$ openstack server image create --name apressinst3_snap apressinst3
```

And after that, you can list the available images.

```
$ openstack image list
+------------------------------------+--------------------+--------+
| ID                                 | Name               | Status |
+------------------------------------+--------------------+--------+
| 81d0b487-6384-4759-82b2-f0cfff075897 | apressinst3_snap   | active |
| 7ffe1b43-7e86-4ad0-86b6-9fffa38b3c20 | cirros-0.5.2-x86_64 | active |
+------------------------------------+--------------------+--------+
```

As you can see, a snapshot was added to the list. You are free to create a new instance from this snapshot.

```
$ openstack server create --image apressinst3_snap --flavor m1.tiny
--network demo-net --security-group apress-sgroup --key-name apresskey1
apressinst_snap
+-----------------------------+-------------------------------------------+
| Field                       | Value                                     |
+-----------------------------+-------------------------------------------+
| OS-DCF:diskConfig           | MANUAL                                    |
| OS-EXT-AZ:availability_zone |                                           |
```

```
| OS-EXT-STS:power_state    | NOSTATE                                      |
| OS-EXT-STS:task_state     | scheduling                                   |
| OS-EXT-STS:vm_state       | building                                     |
| OS-SRV-USG:launched_at    | None                                         |
| OS-SRV-USG:terminated_at  | None                                         |
| accessIPv4                |                                              |
| accessIPv6                |                                              |
| addresses                 |                                              |
| adminPass                 | 6ZtJ2okTBG28                                 |
| config_drive              |                                              |
| created                   | 2022-07-21T13:22:29Z                         |
| flavor                    | m1.tiny (1)                                  |
| hostId                    |                                              |
| id                        | 51ee0c05-242f-41a5-ba20-b10dc4621fdb         |
| image                     | apressinst3_snap (81d0b487-6384-4759-        |
|                           | 82b2-f0cfff075897)                           |
| key_name                  | apresskey1                                   |
| name                      | apressinst_snap                              |
| progress                  | 0                                            |
| project_id                | 9e0c535c2240405b989afa450681df18             |
| properties                |                                              |
| security_groups           | name='7748dc9f-1573-4225-a51e-8fc6328aafc0'  |
| status                    | BUILD                                        |
| updated                   | 2022-07-21T13:22:29Z                         |
| user_id                   | a20b5a5995b740ff90034297335b330a             |
| volumes_attached          |                                              |
+---------------------------+----------------------------------------------+
```

You can use Horizon to create snapshots of instances, as shown in the dialog in Figure 7-7.

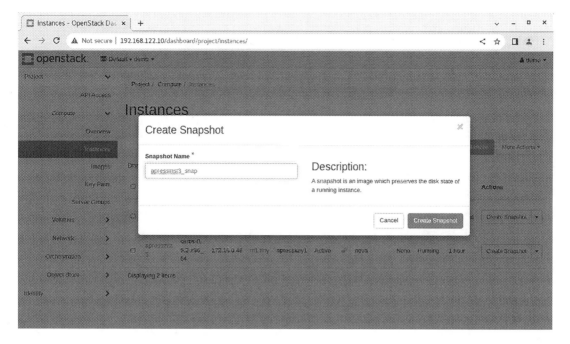

Figure 7-7. *Example of snapshot creation*

Managing Quotas

A quota limits the number of available resources. The default number of resources allowed per tenant is defined in the main configuration file: /etc/nova/nova.conf. Here is an example.

```
[quota]
# Quota options allow to manage quotas in openstack deployment.

# The number of instances allowed per project.
# Minimum value: -1
instances=10

# The number of instance cores or vCPUs allowed per project.
# Minimum value: -1
cores=20

# The number of megabytes of instance RAM allowed per project.
# Minimum value: -1
ram=51200
```

145

```
# The number of metadata items allowed per instance.
# Minimum value: -1
metadata_items=128

# The number of injected files allowed.
# Minimum value: -1
injected_files=5

# The number of bytes allowed per injected file.
# Minimum value: -1
injected_file_content_bytes=10240

# The maximum allowed injected file path length.
# Minimum value: -1
injected_file_path_length=255

# The maximum number of key pairs allowed per user.
# Minimum value: -1
key_pairs=100

# The maximum number of server groups per project.
# Minimum value: -1
server_groups=10

# The maximum number of servers per server group.
# Minimum value: -1
server_group_members=10
```

The admin can retrieve the default number of resources allowed per project with the openstack quota list command. Here is an example.

```
$ openstack quota list --compute --detail
+----------------------------+--------+----------+-------+
| Resource                   | In Use | Reserved | Limit |
+----------------------------+--------+----------+-------+
| cores                      |      0 |        0 |    20 |
| fixed_ips                  |      0 |        0 |    -1 |
| floating_ips               |      0 |        0 |    -1 |
| injected_file_content_bytes|      0 |        0 | 10240 |
```

```
| injected_file_path_bytes  |      0 |        0 |   255 |
| injected_files            |      0 |        0 |     5 |
| instances                 |      0 |        0 |    10 |
| key_pairs                 |      0 |        0 |   100 |
| metadata_items            |      0 |        0 |   128 |
| ram                       |      0 |        0 | 51200 |
| security_group_rules      |      0 |        0 |    -1 |
| security_groups           |      0 |        0 |    -1 |
| server_group_members      |      0 |        0 |    10 |
| server_groups             |      0 |        0 |    10 |
+---------------------------+--------+----------+-------+
```

Users can see a part of the current quotas in a graphical view on the project's Overview page, as shown in Figure 7-8.

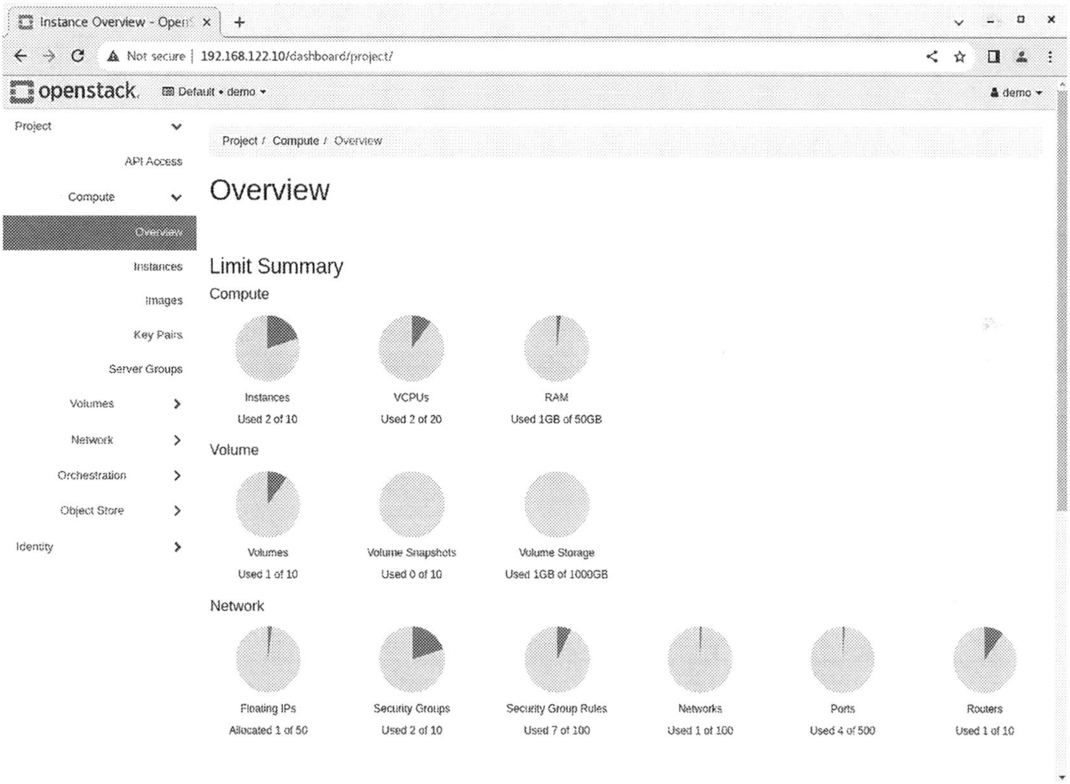

Figure 7-8. *User's overview of the current quota status*

Admins can manage quotas on a per-project basis in Horizon by going to Identity ➤ Projects ➤ Modify Quotas and accessing the drop-down menu to the right of the project's name.

Getting Nova Stats

First, let's grab the list of all hypervisors.

```
$ openstack hypervisor list
+----+---------------------+-----------------+-----------------+-------+
| ID | Hypervisor Hostname | Hypervisor Type | Host IP         | State |
+----+---------------------+-----------------+-----------------+-------+
| 1  | rdo.test.local      | QEMU            | 192.168.122.10  | up    |
+----+---------------------+-----------------+-----------------+-------
```

To get a summary of resource usage of all instances running on the host, use the following command.

```
$ openstack hypervisor show rdo.test.local
+---------------------+------------------------------------+
| Field               | Value                              |
+---------------------+------------------------------------+
| current_workload    | 0                                  |
| aggregates          | []                                 |
| cpu_info            | arch='x86_64', features='['smep',.. |
| disk_available_least | 49                                |
| free_disk_gb        | 57                                 |
| free_ram_mb         | 30527                              |
| host_ip             | 192.168.122.10                     |
| host_time           | 16:02:08                           |
| hypervisor_hostname | rdo.test.local                     |
| hypervisor_type     | QEMU                               |
| hypervisor_version  | 7000000                            |
| id                  | 1                                  |
| load_average        | 0.69, 0.57, 0.45                   |
| local_gb            | 59                                 |
```

```
| local_gb_used         | 2                    |
| memory_mb             | 32063                |
| memory_mb_used        | 1536                 |
| running_vms           | 2                    |
| service_host          | rdo.test.local       |
| service_id            | 8                    |
| state                 | up                   |
| status                | enabled              |
| uptime                | 1:50                 |
| users                 | 1                    |
| vcpus                 | 8                    |
| vcpus_used            | 2                    |
+-----------------------+----------------------------------------+
```

You can use the --all-projects option to search as admin for all virtual machines in all projects.

```
$ openstack server list --all-projects
+--------------------------------------+----------------+--------+
---------------------+---------------------+---------+
| ID                                   | Name           | Status |
Networks             | Image               | Flavor  |
+--------------------------------------+----------------+--------+
---------------------+---------------------+---------+
| 51ee0c05-242f-41a5-ba20-b10dc4621fdb | apressinst_snap | ACTIVE |
demo-net=172.16.0.25 | apressinst3_snap    | m1.tiny |
| b360f5a5-b528-4f77-bdc7-3676ffcf0dff | apressinst3    | ACTIVE |
demo-net=172.16.0.48 | cirros-0.5.2-x86_64 | m1.tiny |
+--------------------------------------+----------------+--------+
---------------------+---------------------+---------+
```

And as admin, you can see an overall picture of all the hypervisors in Horizon, as shown in Figure 7-9.

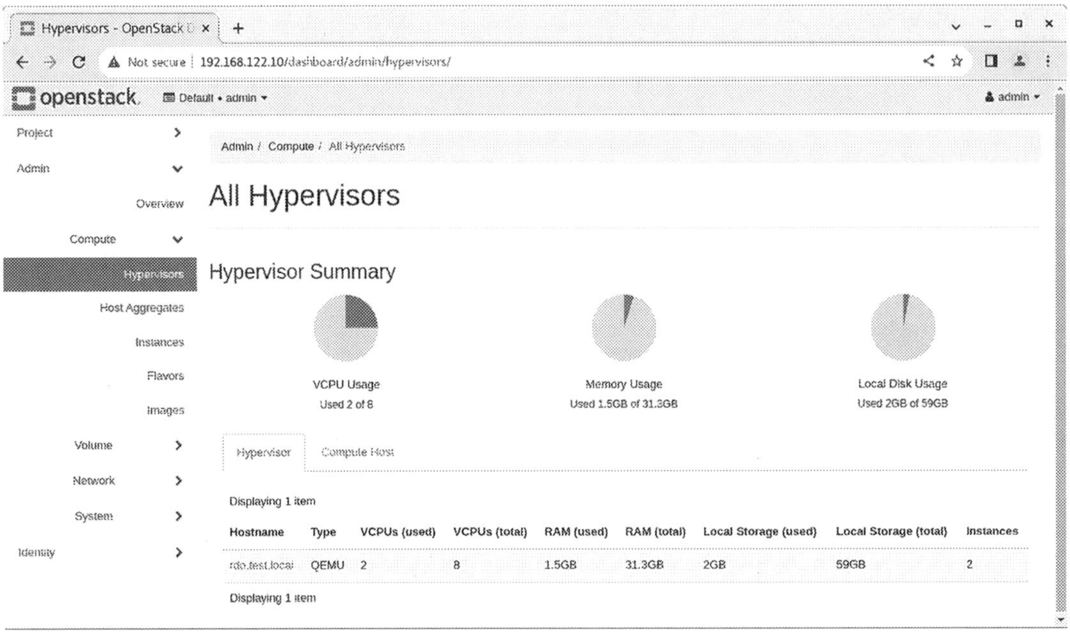

Figure 7-9. *Example of the hypervisors' summary picture*

For some low-level operations, you may want to use the old nova command. If needed, you can easily get diagnostic information about any instance.

```
$ nova diagnostics 51ee0c05-242f-41a5-ba20-b10dc4621fdb
+----------------+-----------------------------------------+
| Property       | Value                                   |
+----------------+-----------------------------------------+
| config_drive   | False                                   |
| cpu_details    | [{"id": 0, "time": 13890000000,         |
|                |    "utilisation": null}]                |
| disk_details   | [{"read_bytes": 29513728, "read_requests":|
|                |    5022, "write_bytes": 450560,         |
|                | | "write_requests": 56, "errors_count": -1}]|
| driver         | libvirt                                 |
| hypervisor     | qemu                                    |
| hypervisor_os  | linux                                   |
| memory_details | {"maximum": 0, "used": 0}               |
```

```
| nic_details    | [{"mac_address": "fa:16:3e:19:3d:f9",        |
|                | "rx_octets": 11097, "rx_errors": 0,          |
|                | "rx_drop": 0, "rx_packets": 123, "rx_rate":  |
|                | null, "tx_octets": 9746,                     |
|                | "tx_errors": 0, "tx_drop": 0, "tx_packets":  |
|                | 83, "tx_rate": null}]                        |
| num_cpus       | 1                                            |
| num_disks      | 1                                            |
| num_nics       | 1                                            |
| state          | running                                      |
| uptime         | 66626                                        |
+----------------+----------------------------------------------+
```

And at the end, you can get a summary of the statistics for each tenant.

```
$ nova usage-list
Usage from 2022-06-24 to 2022-07-23:
+-----------+---------+---------------+-----------+---------------+
| Tenant ID                        | Servers | RAM MiB-Hours | CPU Hours |
Disk GiB-Hours |
+-----------+---------+---------------+-----------+---------------+
| 9e0c535c2240405b989afa450681df18 | 3       | 30456.67      | 59.49     |
59.49          |
+-----------+---------+---------------+-----------+---------------+
```

Verifying the Operation and Managing Nova Compute Servers

You can check whether all Nova servers are started and active by using the systemctl command.

```
# systemctl status *nova* -n 0
● openstack-nova-conductor.service - OpenStack Nova Conductor Server
    Loaded: loaded (/usr/lib/systemd/system/openstack-nova-conductor.
    service; enabled; vendor preset: disabled)
```

```
      Active: active (running) since Fri 2022-07-22 08:52:33 CEST; 1h
      2min ago
    Main PID: 4085 (nova-conductor)
       Tasks: 19 (limit: 204820)
      Memory: 385.9M
         CPU: 56.945s
      CGroup: /system.slice/openstack-nova-conductor.service
              ├─4085 /usr/bin/python3 /usr/bin/nova-conductor
              ├─4790 /usr/bin/python3 /usr/bin/nova-conductor
              ├─4791 /usr/bin/python3 /usr/bin/nova-conductor
              ├─4792 /usr/bin/python3 /usr/bin/nova-conductor
              ├─4793 /usr/bin/python3 /usr/bin/nova-conductor
              ├─4794 /usr/bin/python3 /usr/bin/nova-conductor
              ├─4796 /usr/bin/python3 /usr/bin/nova-conductor
              ├─4797 /usr/bin/python3 /usr/bin/nova-conductor
              └─4798 /usr/bin/python3 /usr/bin/nova-conductor

● openstack-nova-scheduler.service - OpenStack Nova Scheduler Server
      Loaded: loaded (/usr/lib/systemd/system/openstack-nova-scheduler.
      service; enabled; vendor preset: disabled)
      Active: active (running) since Fri 2022-07-22 08:52:33 CEST; 1h
      2min ago
    Main PID: 4086 (nova-scheduler)
       Tasks: 5 (limit: 204820)
      Memory: 197.1M
         CPU: 37.323s
      CGroup: /system.slice/openstack-nova-scheduler.service
              ├─4086 /usr/bin/python3 /usr/bin/nova-scheduler
              ├─4773 /usr/bin/python3 /usr/bin/nova-scheduler
              ├─4774 /usr/bin/python3 /usr/bin/nova-scheduler
              ├─4775 /usr/bin/python3 /usr/bin/nova-scheduler
              └─4776 /usr/bin/python3 /usr/bin/nova-scheduler

● openstack-nova-compute.service - OpenStack Nova Compute Server
      Loaded: loaded (/usr/lib/systemd/system/openstack-nova-compute.
      service; enabled; vendor preset: disabled)
```

```
   Active: active (running) since Fri 2022-07-22 08:52:45 CEST; 1h
   4min ago
 Main PID: 1408 (nova-compute)
    Tasks: 25 (limit: 204820)
   Memory: 151.3M
      CPU: 35.221s
   CGroup: /system.slice/openstack-nova-compute.service
           └─1408 /usr/bin/python3 /usr/bin/nova-compute

● openstack-nova-novncproxy.service - OpenStack Nova NoVNC Proxy Server
   Loaded: loaded (/usr/lib/systemd/system/openstack-nova-novncproxy.
   service; enabled; vendor preset: disabled)
   Active: active (running) since Fri 2022-07-22 08:50:28 CEST; 1h
   6min ago
 Main PID: 1410 (nova-novncproxy)
    Tasks: 1 (limit: 204820)
   Memory: 99.7M
      CPU: 2.940s
   CGroup: /system.slice/openstack-nova-novncproxy.service
           └─1410 /usr/bin/python3 /usr/bin/nova-novncproxy --web /usr/
             share/novnc/
```

As you can see in this example, all services are running on the same host. In the production environment, all are running on the control nodes except nova-compute and nova-compute, which are running on the compute nodes.

According to OpenStack documentation, although the compute and metadata APIs can be run using independent scripts that provide Eventlet-based HTTP servers, it is generally considered more performant and flexible to run them using a generic HTTP server that supports WSGI (such as Apache or Nginx). In particular PackStack example, web-server Apache is used as WSGI service. You can find Apache configs for WSGI services by looking at the /etc/httpd/conf.d/ directory.

```
# ls /etc/httpd/conf.d/*wsgi*
/etc/httpd/conf.d/10-aodh_wsgi.conf    /etc/httpd/conf.d/10-keystone_wsgi.
conf  /etc/httpd/conf.d/10-nova_metadata_wsgi.conf
/etc/httpd/conf.d/10-gnocchi_wsgi.conf  /etc/httpd/conf.d/10-nova_api_wsgi.
conf  /etc/httpd/conf.d/10-placement_wsgi.conf
```

Let's check for the presence of the Nova service in the Keystone services catalog.

```
$ source keystonerc_admin
$ openstack service show nova
+-------------+---------------------------------+
| Field       | Value                           |
+-------------+---------------------------------+
| description | OpenStack Compute Service       |
| enabled     | True                            |
| id          | 44cb0eddaae5494f83d07bb48278eed6 |
| name        | nova                            |
| type        | compute                         |
+-------------+---------------------------------+
```

For troubleshooting, you may also need to know where the nova endpoint is.

```
$ openstack endpoint list | grep nova
| 0b36f879db4647568c29579f1347d386 | RegionOne | nova       | com-
pute        | True    | public   | http://192.168.122.10:8774/
v2.1                   |
| 551894b71129448eb9efc934f7d1a374 | RegionOne | nova       | com-
pute        | True    | internal | http://192.168.122.10:8774/
v2.1                   |
| c1a044e51e794cf09e672a7ec29619fd | RegionOne | nova       |
compute        | True    | admin    | http://192.168.122.10:8774/
v2.1                   |
```

The Nova service listens for incoming connections at the 192.168.122.10 IP address and port 8774.

You may also want to check Nova's log files. With the help of the lsof command, you can enumerate the log files and services that are using it.

```
# lsof /var/log/nova/*
COMMAND     PID USER    FD    TYPE DEVICE SIZE/OFF      NODE NAME
nova-comp 1408 nova     3w    REG   253,0   763552 34858285 /var/log/nova/
nova-compute.log
```

```
nova-novn 1410 nova    3w   REG   253,0      16350 35522927 /var/log/nova/
nova-novncproxy.log
nova-cond 4085 nova    3w   REG   253,0   1603975 35839626 /var/log/nova/
nova-conductor.log
nova-sche 4086 nova    3w   REG   253,0   1612316 35839628 /var/log/nova/
nova-scheduler.log
httpd     4209 nova    9w   REG   253,0    490304 35839631 /var/log/nova/
nova-api.log
...
httpd     4217 nova    9w   REG   253,0     16360 34619037 /var/log/nova/
nova-metadata-api.log
...
```

Summary

OpenStack Compute is the heart of OpenStack. You cannot avoid this topic, so this chapter should be studied thoroughly. Compute topic is quite significant since it is the main goal of OpenStack to run compute resources.

The next chapter covers OpenStack's object storage.

Review Questions

1. Which service acts as a proxy service between the database and
    nova-compute services?

    A. nova-conductor

    B. nova-nonvncproxy

    C. nova-api

    D. nova-scheduler

2. Which adds a new flavor named m5.tiny that has a 5 GB disk, 2 vCPU, and 500 MB RAM?

    A. nova flavor-create --is-public true m5.tiny auto 500 2 5

    B. openstack flavor create --public --ram 500 --disk 5 --cpus 2 m5.tiny

    C. openstack flavor create --public --ram 500 --disk 5 --vcpus 2 m5.tiny

    D. openstack flavor-create --public --ram 500 --disk 5 --vcpus 2 m5.tiny

3. Which GNU/Linux permissions should be applied to the private SSH key?

    A. 640

    B. 660

    C. 600

    D. 620

4. Which lets a regular user get Nova quotes for the project?

    A. nova quota-list

    B. openstack quota show

    C. nova show-quota

    D. openstack quota show --all

Answers

    1. A

    2. C

    3. C

    4. B

## CHAPTER 8

OpenStack Object Storage

This chapter covers 5% of the Certified OpenStack Administrator exam requirements. You may expect a small number of tasks related to object storage. Moreover, not all OpenStack installations have this type of storage. However, I recommend studying this chapter carefully to maximize the chances of passing the COA exam.

Overview of Swift Object Storage

OpenStack Swift is a highly available, distributed, consistent object Software Defined Storage (SDS) system. In contrast to file storage, object storage works with an object that contains data and metadata itself. Generally, object storage provides access through an API. Objects are available via URLs and HTTP/HTTPS protocols. Object storage can distribute requests across many storage hosts. All objects are accessible in one single namespace, and object storage systems are usually highly scalable.

To pass the Certified OpenStack Administrator exam, you only need to know the basic operations with objects. With the first version of COA, the weight of this topic was 10%. Now it shrinks to just 5%.

Logically, Swift consists of three levels: accounts, containers, and objects.

Account in Swift corresponds to the Project/Tenant in other OpenStack services. Swift users are primarily people who have a username and password. Swift users correspond to accounts in other OpenStack services. Objects are stored in containers that belong to the accounts. You can imagine an account as a file system, with the container as a directory and the object as a file. Figure 8-1 illustrates this.

© Andrey Markelov 2022
A. Markelov, *Certified OpenStack Administrator Study Guide*,
https://doi.org/10.1007/978-1-4842-8804-7_8

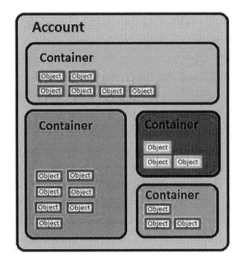

Figure 8-1. *Logical objects in Swift*

You can identify each object by its path.

/account_name/container_name/object_name

By default, the data stored in Swift is replicated three times. The main services of Swift are object, account, and container services.

With the `swift` command, you can start working with containers from the command line. This command shows the summary for the containers and objects.

```
$ source keystonerc_demo
$ swift stat
              Account: AUTH_9e0c535c2240405b989afa450681df18
           Containers: 0
              Objects: 0
                Bytes: 0
         Content-Type: text/plain; charset=utf-8
          X-Timestamp: 1658395297.47923
      X-Put-Timestamp: 1658395297.47923
                 Vary: Accept
           X-Trans-Id: tx661aafd252a347fcbb199-0062d91aa1
X-Openstack-Request-Id: tx661aafd252a347fcbb199-0062d91aa1
```

As you see, there are no objects or containers yet. Let's try to upload a file to an object store. As a part of the upload command, you need to define a container. A container is automatically created if you point to a nonexisting container.

```
$ swift upload apress_cont1 /etc/hosts
etc/hosts
$ swift stat | grep Containers
                    Containers: 1
Containers in policy "policy-0": 1
```

With the swift list command, you can list the containers and the objects within the containers.

```
$ swift list
apress_cont1
$ swift list apress_cont1
etc/hosts
```

You can use the swift stat command to check the status of the object.

```
$ swift stat apress_cont1 etc/hosts
                Account: AUTH_9e0c535c2240405b989afa450681df18
              Container: apress_cont1
                 Object: etc/hosts
           Content Type: application/octet-stream
         Content Length: 188
          Last Modified: Thu, 21 Jul 2022 09:23:24 GMT
                   ETag: ff986859745e2ad1f4be0a1136d0e82c
             Meta Mtime: 1658329953.245322
            X-Timestamp: 1658395403.32964
          Accept-Ranges: bytes
             X-Trans-Id: tx07378f4a118240c69cf7b-0062d91b3e
   X-Openstack-Request-Id: tx07378f4a118240c69cf7b-0062d91b3e
```

For downloading the content of a container, use the swift download command as shown.

```
$ swift download apress_cont1
etc/hosts [auth 0.248s, headers 0.372s, total 0.372s, 0.002 MB/s]
$ cat etc/hosts
127.0.0.1   localhost localhost.localdomain localhost4 localhost4.
localdomain4
::1         localhost localhost.localdomain localhost6 localhost6.
localdomain6
192.168.122.10 rdo.test.local
```

You may also specify a particular object in the container.

```
$ swift download apress_cont1 etc/hosts
etc/hosts [auth 0.260s, headers 0.387s, total 0.388s, 0.001 MB/s]
```

Figure 8-2 shows the Horizon web interface (Project ➤ Object Store ➤ Containers).

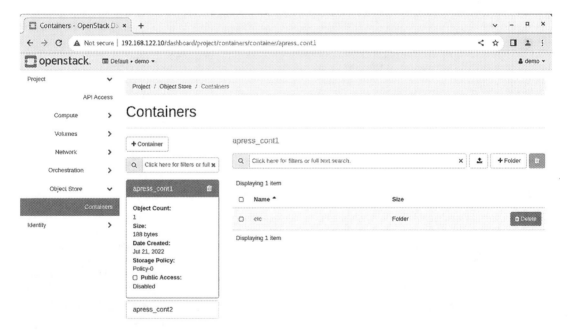

Figure 8-2. *Swift user interface in the Horizon web client*

Managing Permissions on a Container in Object Storage

Users can set up access control lists (ACLs) at the container level and define the read and write access. To successfully write to a container, a user must have both read and write access.

Here is an example of setting up a "read" ACL for users from a demo project, specifically for user8 from project1.

```
$ swift post apress_cont1 -r "demo:demo, project1:user8"
$ swift stat apress_cont1
                 Account: AUTH_9e0c535c2240405b989afa450681df18
               Container: apress_cont1
                 Objects: 1
                   Bytes: 188
                Read ACL: demo:demo,project1:user8
               Write ACL:
                 Sync To:
                Sync Key:
            Content-Type: text/plain; charset=utf-8
             X-Timestamp: 1658395402.67076
           Last-Modified: Thu, 21 Jul 2022 09:32:45 GMT
           Accept-Ranges: bytes
        X-Storage-Policy: Policy-0
                    Vary: Accept
              X-Trans-Id: tx00ddf13d043e424aa5680-0062d91d48
  X-Openstack-Request-Id: tx00ddf13d043e424aa5680-0062d91d48
```

Working with "write" ACL is similar.

```
$ swift post apress_cont1 -w "demo:demo"
$ swift stat apress_cont1
                 Account: AUTH_9e0c535c2240405b989afa450681df18
               Container: apress_cont1
                 Objects: 1
                   Bytes: 188
                Read ACL: demo:demo,project1:user8
               Write ACL: demo:demo
```

161

```
           Sync To:
          Sync Key:
      Content-Type: text/plain; charset=utf-8
       X-Timestamp: 1658395402.67076
     Last-Modified: Thu, 21 Jul 2022 09:34:19 GMT
     Accept-Ranges: bytes
   X-Storage-Policy: Policy-0
              Vary: Accept
        X-Trans-Id: tx9f19a5f891fa4e5faddfd-0062d91da5
X-Openstack-Request-Id: tx9f19a5f891fa4e5faddfd-0062d91da5
```

Using the cURL Tool for Working with Swift

A very common method of working with object storage is by using the cURL
command-line tool. cURL requests usually include an HTTP verb (such as GET, PUT),
authentication information, storage URL, data, and metadata. To get authentication
information and storage URL, use the swift auth command.

```
$ swift auth
export OS_STORAGE_URL=http://192.168.122.10:8080/v1/AUTH_9e0c535c2240405b98
9afa450681df18
export OS_AUTH_TOKEN=gAAAAABi2R3waCe9Wkj_oUMmyxCgDGwpGOo9mytrjxfd_2J_APg_3z
4RHDKTPxQgemrDXrkp5F4Hqj1UBEQ6C9zOErOpgLOKGv_sHusxSyiBqbpITZgohA3ko1rSAc-oU
FfTaZ6aPcsoyidsOaO4eTOObUFlWveCsLadEmFLlyXOX7bkh1a1onc
```

You can create a new container with the PUT verb.

```
$ curl -X PUT -H 'X-Auth-Token:gAAAAABi2R3waCe9Wkj_
oUMmyxCgDGwpGOo9mytrjxfd_2J_APg_3z4RHDKTPxQgemrDXrkp5F4Hqj1UBEQ6C9zOErOpgL
OKGv_sHusxSyiBqbpITZgohA3ko1rSAc-oUFfTaZ6aPcsoyidsOaO4eTOObUFlWveCsLadEmF
LlyXOX7bkh1a1onc' http://192.168.122.10:8080/v1/AUTH_9e0c535c2240405b989a
fa450681df18/apress_cont2
```

For simplicity, it is better to use shell variables constructed by the swift auth
command. Let's rewrite previous commands as follows.

```
$ $(swift auth)
$ curl -X PUT -H X-Auth-Token:$OS_AUTH_TOKEN $OS_STORAGE_URL/apress_cont2
```

And here is an example that is similar to using the `swift list` command.

```
$ curl -X GET -H X-Auth-Token:$OS_AUTH_TOKEN $OS_STORAGE_URL
apress_cont1
apress_cont2
```

Next, you can put the file /etc/networks into the apress_cont2 container.

```
$ curl -X PUT -H X-Auth-Token:$OS_AUTH_TOKEN $OS_STORAGE_URL/apress_cont2/
-T /etc/networks
```

For checking the content of the apress_cont2 container, use the following command.

```
$ curl -X GET -H X-Auth-Token:$OS_AUTH_TOKEN $OS_STORAGE_URL/apress_cont2/
networks
```

And at the end, you can get the contents of the object.

```
$ curl -X GET -H X-Auth-Token:$OS_AUTH_TOKEN $OS_STORAGE_URL/apress_cont2/
networks
default 0.0.0.0
loopback 127.0.0.0
link-local 169.254.0.0
```

Managing Expiring Objects

Swift object storage can schedule the deletion of an object. To do that, you must add the X-Delete-At or X-Delete-After header during an object PUT or POST command. The date and time of deletion should be in Unix Epoch timestamp format. You can use the date command to learn the current date and time in Unix Epoch timestamp format or for conversion.

```
$ date +%s
1658398821
$ date -d @1658398821
Thu Jul 21 12:20:21 PM CEST 2022
```

You could use www.epochconverter.com for conversion. The following is an example of how to automatically delete the etc/sysctl.conf object in the apress_cont1 container on Thursday, July 21, 2022, at 12:40:00 PM CEST (1658400000).

```
$ curl -X POST -H X-Auth-Token:$OS_AUTH_TOKEN -H 'X-Delete-At:1658400000'
$OS_STORAGE_URL/apress_cont2/networks <html><h1>Accepted</h1><p>The request
is accepted for processing.</p></html>
```

Note   You should change the suggested time and date to your current plus some extra minutes. You may want to use something like X-Delete-At:$(expr $(date +%s) + 60).

Swift Cluster Monitoring

For Swift cluster monitoring of the account, container, and object servers, special Swift Recon server middleware, and the swift-recon tool are used. If you installed the OpenStack lab environment with the PackStack tool, you need to do the additional configuration of the middleware server. You should change the existing pipeline option in the [pipeline:main] section and add the new [filter:recon] section in three configuration files.

Here is an example of changes made in /etc/swift/object-server.conf.

```
[pipeline:main]
pipeline = recon object-server
[filter:recon]
use = egg:swift#recon
recon_cache_path = /var/cache/swift
```

Here is an example of changes made in /etc/swift/container-server.conf.

```
[pipeline:main]
pipeline = recon container-server
[filter:recon]
use = egg:swift#recon
recon_cache_path = /var/cache/swift
```

This is an example of changes made in /etc/swift/account-server.conf.

```
[pipeline:main]
pipeline = recon account-server
[filter:recon]
use = egg:swift#recon
recon_cache_path = /var/cache/swift
```

After that, you need to check whether the cache directory exists and has the right permissions.

```
# ls -ld /var/cache/swift/
drwxr-xr-x. 2 swift swift 70 Jul 21 12:56 /var/cache/swift/
```

For tracking asynchronous pending on your object servers, you need to add a job in cron to run the swift-recon-cron script.

```
# crontab -e
*/5 * * * * swift /usr/bin/swift-recon-cron /etc/swift/object-server.conf
```

Then you must reload the Swift services. Now you can try to obtain the cluster load average stats.

```
# swift-recon -l
===============================================================================
--> Starting reconnaissance on 1 hosts (object)
===============================================================================
[2022-07-21 11:28:03] Checking load averages
[1m_load_avg] low: 2, high: 2, avg: 2.4, total: 2, Failed: 0.0%, no_result:
0, reported: 1
[5m_load_avg] low: 1, high: 1, avg: 1.2, total: 1, Failed: 0.0%, no_result:
0, reported: 1
[15m_load_avg] low: 0, high: 0, avg: 0.8, total: 0, Failed: 0.0%, no_
result: 0, reported: 1
===============================================================================
```

To obtain disk usage stats, use the -d option.

```
# swift-recon -d
===============================================================================
--> Starting reconnaissance on 1 hosts (object)
===============================================================================
[2022-07-21 11:29:01] Checking disk usage now
Distribution Graph:
  6%    1 *****************************************************************
Disk usage: space used: 124612608 of 1939709952
Disk usage: space free: 1815097344 of 1939709952
Disk usage: lowest: 6.42%, highest: 6.42%, avg: 6.4242908003598265%
===============================================================================
```

For a complete options list, see the `swift-recon(1)` main page.

Summary

This chapter was probably the most straightforward. If you follow up on the examples in this chapter, you will easily pass the corresponding tasks on the exam. Do not forget you can use the Horizon dashboard. It makes tasks even easier.

The next chapter covers block storage.

Review Questions

1. Which uploads all the files from the ~user directory to the tempcontainer container?

    A. `swift upload tempcontainer ~user/all`

    B. `swift upload tempcontainer ~user/*`

    C. `swift upload ~user/* tempcontainer`

    D. `swift upload ~user/* tempcontainer all`

2. Which checks the status of the `test` object in the `cont` container?

    A. `swift stat test cont`

    B. `swift cont test stat`

     C. `swift stat cont test`

     D. `swift test cont stat`

3.   Which gets disk usage stats in Swift?

     A. `recon -l`

     B. `swift-recon -d`

     C. `swift-recon -l`

     D. `recon -d`

4.   Which gets a list of all objects in the test container?

     A. `swift list test`

     B. `swift test list`

     C. `swift list`

     D. `swift list container test`

5.   Which gets the object with the `curl` command?

     A. `curl -X GET -H 'X-Auth-Token: token' http://server:port/`
       `AUTH_User/container/object`

     B. `curl -X GET -H 'X-Auth-Token: token' http://server:port/v1/`
       `AUTH_User/ -c container -o object`

     C. `curl -X GET -H 'X-Auth-Token: token' http://server:port/v1/`
       `AUTH_User/container/object`

     D. `curl -X GET -H 'X-Auth-Token: token' http://server:port/`
       `AUTH_User/container object`

Answers

1. B

2. C

3. B

4. A

5. C

## CHAPTER 9

Block Storage

This chapter covers 10% of the Certified OpenStack Administrator exam requirements. Block storage is an essential topic for data reliability in the private cloud. As you will learn in this chapter, you cannot build a highly available static solution without using block storage.

Cinder's Architecture and Components

Instances use an ephemeral volume by default. This kind of volume does not save the changes made on it and reverts to its original state when the current user relinquishes control. One of the methods for storing data permanently in the OpenStack cloud is using a block storage service named Cinder. This service is similar to the Amazon EBS service in its functions.

Figure 9-1 shows the main components of Cinder.

© Andrey Markelov 2022
A. Markelov, *Certified OpenStack Administrator Study Guide*,
https://doi.org/10.1007/978-1-4842-8804-7_9

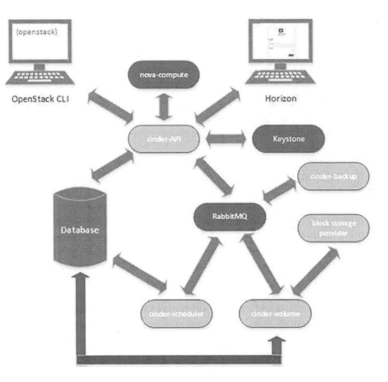

Figure 9-1. *Cinder architecture*

The OpenStack block storage service consists of four services implemented as GNU/
Linux daemons.

- **cinder-api** is an API service that provides an HTTP endpoint for API
  requests. At the time of this writing, two API versions are supported and
  required for the cloud. Cinder provides six endpoints. The cinder-api
  verifies the identity requirements for an incoming request and then
  routes them to the cinder-volume for action through the message broker.

- **cinder-scheduler** reads requests from the message queue and selects
  the optimal storage provider node to create or manage the volume.

- **cinder-volume** works with the storage back end through the drivers.
  cinder-volume gets requests from the scheduler and responds to read
  and write requests sent to the block storage service to maintain the
  state. You can use several back ends at the same time. For each back
  end, you need one or more dedicated cinder-volume services.

- **cinder-backup** works with the backup back end through the driver
  architecture.

Cinder uses block storage providers for storage. A list of supported drivers is at `https://docs.openstack.org/cinder/latest/reference/support-matrix.html`. There are a lot of storage providers for Cinder, such as LVM/iSCSI, Ceph, NFS, Swift, and vendor-specific storage from EMC, HPE, IBM, and others.

Let's look at these services in the OpenStack node.

```
# systemctl | grep cinder | grep running
  openstack-cinder-api.service
          loaded active running    OpenStack Cinder API Server
  openstack-cinder-backup.service
          loaded active running    OpenStack Cinder Backup Server
  openstack-cinder-scheduler.service
          loaded active running    OpenStack Cinder Scheduler Server
  openstack-cinder-volume.service
          loaded active running    OpenStack Cinder Volume Server
```

You can use the `openstack volume service list` command to query the status of Cinder services.

```
$ source keystonerc_admin
$ openstack volume service list
+-----------------+-------------------+------+---------+-------+
--------------------------+
| Binary          | Host              | Zone | Status  | State |
Updated At                |
+-----------------+-------------------+------+---------+-------+
--------------------------+
| cinder-scheduler | rdo.test.local    | nova | enabled | up    |
2022-07-25T11:49:23.000000 |
| cinder-volume   | rdo.test.local@lvm | nova | enabled | up    |
2022-07-25T11:49:25.000000 |
| cinder-backup   | rdo.test.local    | nova | enabled | up    |
2022-07-25T11:49:29.000000 |
+-----------------+-------------------+------+---------+-------+
--------------------------+
```

After examining the environment, you can see that all services run on one host. In the production environment, it is more common to have cinder-volume service running on separate storage nodes. In test environments, Cinder uses the Linux Logical Volume Manager (LVM) back end and the iSCSI target provided by Targetcli (http://linux-iscsi.org/wiki/Targetcli).

```
# systemctl | grep target.service
  target.serviceloaded active exited     Restore LIO kernel target
configuration
```

Now let's look through the Cinder main configuration file, /etc/cinder/cinder.conf. Table 9-1 shows the main configuration options available from the config file.

Table 9-1. *Main Configuration Options from /etc/cinder/cinder.conf*

Example of Config Options	Description
[DEFAULT] my_ip = 192.168.122.10	Default Cinder host name or IP
backup_driver=cinder.backup.drivers. swift.SwiftBackupDriver	Driver to use for backups
[keystone_authtoken] www_authenticate_uri=ht tp://192.168.122.10:5000/ auth_type=password auth_url=http://192.168.122.10:5000 username=cinder password=password user_domain_name=Default project_name=services project_domain_name=Default	Authentication parameters: endpoints and other parameters like default project name, domain name, project name for services, and account information for Cinder user

(continued)

Table 9-1. (*continued*)

Example of Config Options	Description
[DEFAULT] backup_swift_ url=http://192.168.122.10:8080/v1/AUTH_ backup_swift_container=volumebackups backup_swift_object_size = 52428800 backup_swift_retry_attempts = 3 backup_swift_retry_backoff = 2	The URL of the Swift endpoint and other Swift parameters, such as the name of the Swift container to use, maximum object size, the number of retries to make for Swift operations, and the back-off time in seconds between Swift retries
[DEFAULT] enabled_backends = lvm	A list of back-end names to use
[database] connection = mysql+pymysql:// cinder:password@10.0.2.15/cinder	The connection string used to connect to the database
transport_url=rabbit://guest:gue st@192.168.122.10:5672/	The RabbitMQ broker address, port, user name, and password
[lvm] target_helper=lioadm	iSCSI target user-land tool to use (older tgtadm is the default; lioadm used for modern LIO iSCSI support)
[lvm] volume_group=cinder-volumes target_ip_address=192.168.122.10 volume_driver=cinder.volume.drivers.lvm. LVMVolumeDriver volumes_dir=/var/lib/cinder/volumes volume_backend_name=lvm	LVM back-end options: name of LVM volume group, iSCSI target IP address, volume driver, volume configuration file storage directory, and the back-end name for a given driver implementation

Managing Volume and Mount It to a Nova Instance

Let's start our example with volume creation. Two CLI commands can be used: openstack or cinder. Also, you can use the Horizon web client. Here is an example using the cinder command.

```
$ source keystonerc_demo
$ cinder create --display-name apresstest1 1
+-----------------------------+--------------------------------------+
| Property                    | Value                                |
+-----------------------------+--------------------------------------+
| attachments                 | []                                   |
| availability_zone           | nova                                 |
| bootable                    | false                                |
| cluster_name                | None                                 |
| consistencygroup_id         | None                                 |
| consumes_quota              | True                                 |
| created_at                  | 2022-07-25T12:56:57.000000           |
| description                 | None                                 |
| encrypted                   | False                                |
| group_id                    | None                                 |
| id                          | 0f812c6f-5531-42e5-b0ff-e9f2e6492e19 |
| metadata                    | {}                                   |
| migration_status            | None                                 |
| multiattach                 | False                                |
| name                        | apresstest1                          |
| os-vol-host-attr:host       | None                                 |
| os-vol-mig-status-attr:migstat | None                              |
| os-vol-mig-status-attr:name_id | None                              |
| os-vol-tenant-attr:tenant_id | 27cdeded89d24fb49c11030b8cc87f15    |
| provider_id                 | None                                 |
| replication_status          | None                                 |
| service_uuid                | None                                 |
| shared_targets              | True                                 |
| size                        | 1                                    |
| snapshot_id                 | None                                 |
```

```
| source_volid              | None                                   |
| status                    | creating                               |
| updated_at                | None                                   |
| user_id                   | a037e26c68ba406eaf6c3a1ec87227de       |
| volume_type               | iscsi                                  |
| volume_type_id            | c046dd89-6319-4486-bdf1-455cbb2099f9   |
+---------------------------+----------------------------------------+
```

The next example shows the use of the universal openstack command.

```
$ openstack volume create --size 1 apresstest2
+--------------------+------------------------------------------+
| Field              | Value                                    |
+--------------------+------------------------------------------+
| attachments        | []                                       |
| availability_zone  | nova                                     |
| bootable           | false                                    |
| consistencygroup_id | None                                    |
| created_at         | 2022-07-25T12:57:56.570242               |
| description        | None                                     |
| encrypted          | False                                    |
| id                 | 2f223049-85da-4d72-a18d-d3212a173b94     |
| migration_status   | None                                     |
| multiattach        | False                                    |
| name               | apresstest2                              |
| properties         |                                          |
| replication_status | None                                     |
| size               | 1                                        |
| snapshot_id        | None                                     |
| source_volid       | None                                     |
| status             | creating                                 |
| type               | iscsi                                    |
| updated_at         | None                                     |
| user_id            | a037e26c68ba406eaf6c3a1ec87227de         |
+--------------------+------------------------------------------+
```

Now you can check to ensure both volumes were created and are available.

```
$ openstack volume list
+------------------------------------+------------+-----------+------+
-------------+
| ID                                 | Name       | Status    | Size |
 Attached to |
+------------------------------------+------------+-----------+------+
-------------+
| 2f223049-85da-4d72-a18d-d3212a173b94 | apresstest2 | available |    1 |
             |
| 0f812c6f-5531-42e5-b0ff-e9f2e6492e19 | apresstest1 | available |    1 |
             |
+------------------------------------+------------+-----------+------+
-------------+
```

As mentioned, Cinder uses Linux LVM in test environments. You can easily check this fact by using the lvs command. As shown next, there are two LVM volumes in the cinder-volumes group with the names that contain the OpenStack's volumes' IDs.

```
# lvs
...
  volume-0f812c6f-5531-42e5-b0ff-e9f2e6492e19 cinder-volumes Vwi-a-
tz--   1.00g cinder-volumes-pool         0.00
  volume-2f223049-85da-4d72-a18d-d3212a173b94 cinder-volumes Vwi-a-
tz--   1.00g cinder-volumes-pool         0.00
...
```

Note   The lvs command reports information about logical volumes. LVM is a common way to create the abstraction level of block devices for modern GNU/Linux distributions. LVM can create, delete, resize, mirror, or snapshot logical volumes. Logical volumes are created from volume groups, and volume groups are usually created from physical devices. If you are unfamiliar with LVM, you can start from a manual page for LVM (man lvm in the Linux prompt).

You can also manage existing and create new volumes from within the Horizon web interface. Go to Project ➤ Volume ➤ Volumes if you are working as a user or Admin ➤ Volume ➤ Volumes if you want to see all the volumes as an administrator. In each case, different subsets of options are available. Examples of the different web interface screenshots are shown in Figures 9-2 and 9-3.

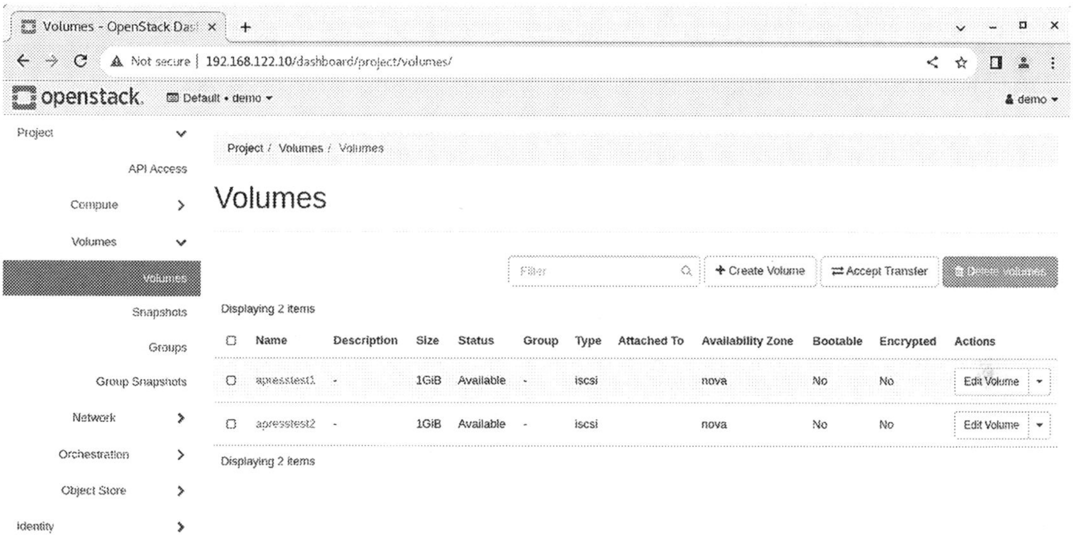

Figure 9-2. *Volumes in regular users Horizon web interface view*

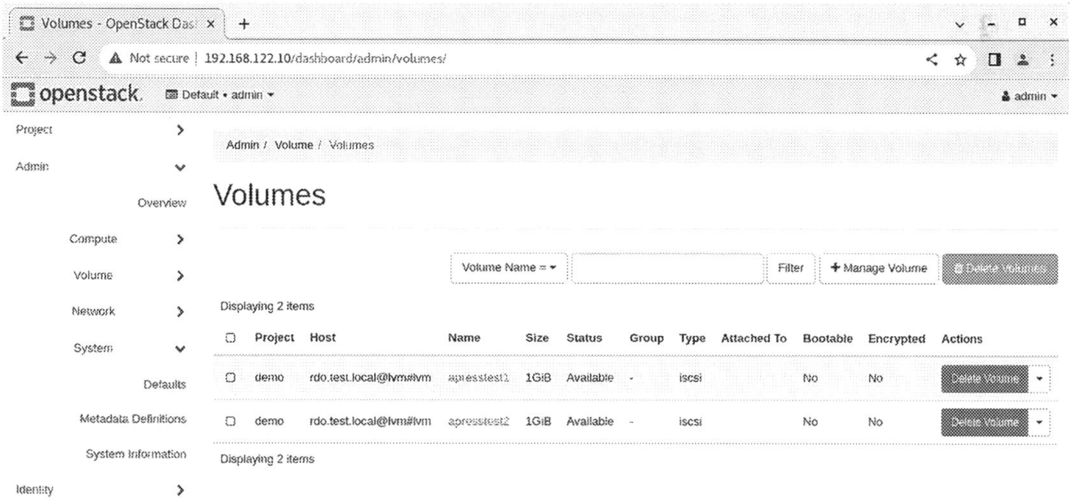

Figure 9-3. *Volumes for admin users in the Horizon web interface view*

Deleting a volume is as easy as creating one. For example, the openstack CLI command can delete a volume, as shown in the following code.

```
$ openstack volume delete apresstest2
```

Figure 9-4 shows the volume creation dialog used in the Horizon user interface. In the drop-down menu, you can see additional options for creating the image. You can create a volume from another volume or from the image by creating a volume from scratch. For these actions, the --image and --source options of the openstack CLI command are used.

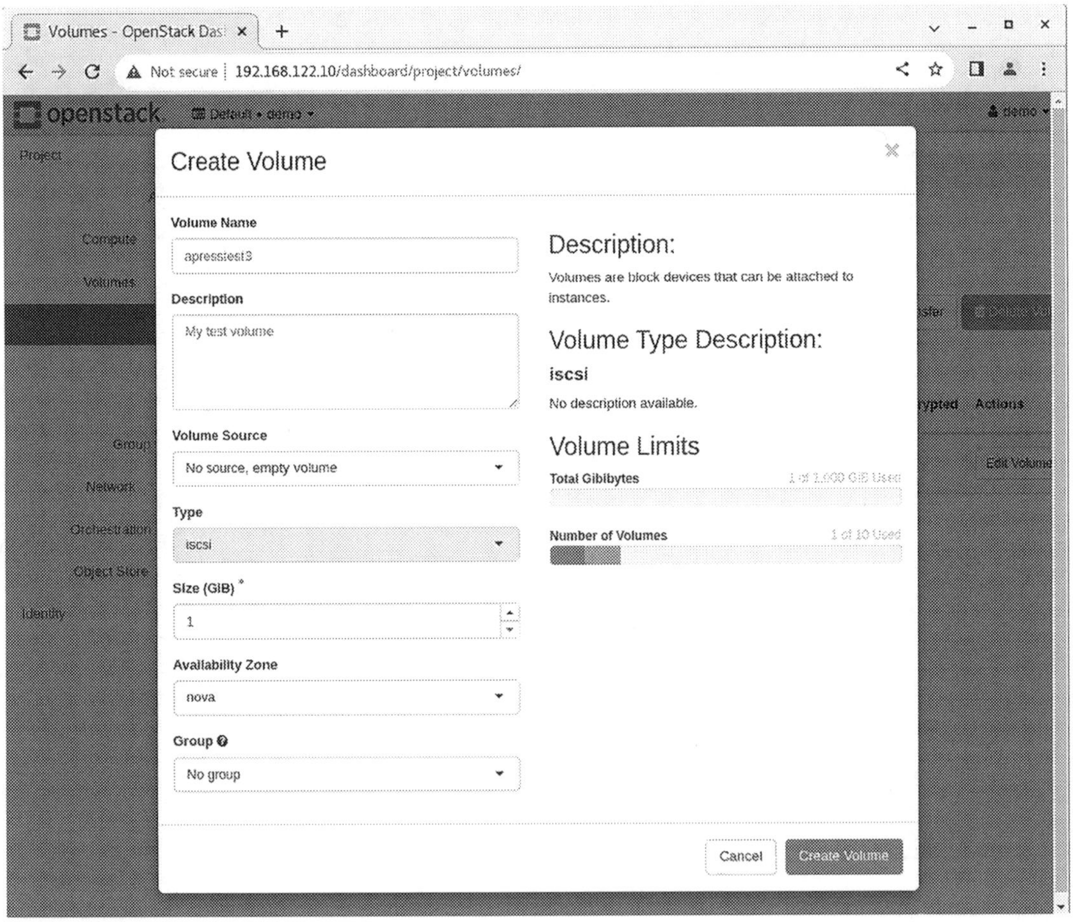

Figure 9-4. *Creation of a volume from the Horizon web interface view*

Here is an example of creating a volume from Glance's image.

```
$ openstack volume create --size 1 --image cirros-0.5.2-x86_64 apresstest3
+---------------------+--------------------------------------+
| Field               | Value                                |
+---------------------+--------------------------------------+
| attachments         | []                                   |
| availability_zone   | nova                                 |
| bootable            | false                                |
| consistencygroup_id | None                                 |
| created_at          | 2022-07-25T13:19:09.353608           |
| description         | None                                 |
| encrypted           | False                                |
| id                  | d5e3b873-44ed-4235-a492-8acef2807d67 |
| multiattach         | False                                |
| name                | apresstest3                          |
| properties          |                                      |
| replication_status  | None                                 |
| size                | 1                                    |
| snapshot_id         | None                                 |
| source_volid        | None                                 |
| status              | creating                             |
| type                | iscsi                                |
| updated_at          | None                                 |
| user_id             | a20b5a5995b740ff90034297335b330a     |
+---------------------+--------------------------------------+
```

You can use the openstack volume show command with the image name or ID to look at the volume properties.

Volumes are useless by themselves. Let's try to start a new VM instance and access a volume from within this VM.

```
$ openstack server create --image cirros-0.5.2-x86_64 --flavor m1.tiny
--network demo-net --security-group apress-sgroup --key-name apresskey1
apressinst
...
```

```
$ openstack server list
+--------------------------------------+------------+--------+
--------------------+--------------------+---------+
| ID                                   | Name       | Status |
 Networks            | Image              | Flavor  |
+--------------------------------------+------------+--------+
--------------------+--------------------+---------+
| 2f1c85bd-c680-4e7b-afa4-2367b15c9fb8 | apressinst | ACTIVE |
 demo-net=172.16.0.42 | cirros-0.5.2-x86_64 | m1.tiny |
+--------------------------------------+------------+--------+
--------------------+--------------------+---------+
```

Now you can attach the apresstest1 volume to the apresstestinstance1 instance.

```
$ openstack server add volume apressinst apresstest3
+---------------------+--------------------------------------+
| Field               | Value                                |
+---------------------+--------------------------------------+
| ID                  | d5e3b873-44ed-4235-a492-8acef2807d67 |
| Server ID           | 2f1c85bd-c680-4e7b-afa4-2367b15c9fb8 |
| Volume ID           | d5e3b873-44ed-4235-a492-8acef2807d67 |
| Device              | /dev/vdb                             |
| Tag                 | None                                 |
| Delete On Termination | False                              |
+---------------------+--------------------------------------+
$ openstack volume list
+--------------------------------------+------------+---------+------+
------------------------------------+
| ID                                   | Name       | Status  | Size |
 Attached to                        |
+--------------------------------------+------------+---------+------+
------------------------------------+
| d5e3b873-44ed-4235-a492-8acef2807d67 | apresstest3 | in-use |    1 |
 Attached to apressinst on /dev/vdb  |
+--------------------------------------+------------+---------+------+
------------------------------------+
```

You can use one of the `openstack server remove volume` commands to detach a volume, as shown in the following.

```
$ openstack server remove volume apressinst apresstest3
```

Creating Volume Group for Block Storage

One of the Certified OpenStack Administrator exam objectives is to create the LVM volume group for block storage. It is very easy, but you need to be aware of the hard disk partitions and the LVM hierarchy.

Let's assume that you do not have free space in your current storage. First, you need to add a new block device (virtual hard drive, in this case) to the controller VM. Usually, you must reboot the VM after that.

Then you need to find a new device name. A device name refers to the entire disk. Device names can be /dev/sda, /dev/sdb, and so on when using the virtualization-aware disk driver. For example, if you use the native KVM-based virtualization in GNU/Linux, this code shows the following device name.

```
# fdisk -l | grep [vs]d
Disk /dev/vda: 100 GiB, 107374182400 bytes, 209715200 sectors
/dev/vda1   *       2048    2099199    2097152    1G 83 Linux
/dev/vda2         2099200 209715199 207616000   99G 8e Linux LVM
Disk /dev/vdb: 20 GiB, 21474836480 bytes, 41943040 sectors
```

You can see that the new 20 GB /dev/vdb disk has no partitions. Let's create one partition for the whole disk.

```
# fdisk /dev/vdb
Welcome to fdisk (util-linux 2.37.4).
Changes will remain in memory only, until you decide to write them.
Be careful before using the write command.

Device does not contain a recognized partition table.
Created a new DOS disklabel with disk identifier 0x26a41428.
Command (m for help): n [ENTER]
Partition type:
```

```
  p    primary (0 primary, 0 extended, 4 free)
  e    extended
Select (default p): p  [ENTER]
Partition number (1-4, default 1): [ENTER]
First sector (2048-41943039, default 2048): [ENTER]
Last sector, +/-sectors or +/-size{K,M,G,T,P} (2048-41943039, default
41943039): [ENTER]
Partition 1 of type Linux and of size 96.7 GiB is set
```

Before saving changes to the partition table, you must change the partition type number from 83 (Linux) to 8e (Linux LVM).

```
Command (m for help): t  [ENTER]
Selected partition 1
Hex code (type L to list all codes): 8e  [ENTER]
Changed type of partition 'Linux' to 'Linux LVM'
Command (m for help): w
The partition table has been altered!
Calling ioctl() to re-read partition table.
Syncing disks.
# partprobe
```

Now you can create the new volume group for the LVM back end.

```
# vgcreate cinder-volumes-2 /dev/vdb1
  Physical volume "/dev/vdb1" successfully created
  Volume group "cinder-volumes-2" successfully created
```

The new volume group, cinder-volumes-2, is used later in this chapter.

Managing Quotas

It is possible to add quotas for Cinder volumes. Default quotas for new projects are in the Cinder configuration file. Some of them are shown in Table 9-2.

Table 9-2. *Quota Configuration Options from* /etc/cinder/cinder.conf

Example of Config Options	Description
quota_volumes = 10	The number of volumes allowed per project
quota_snapshots = 10	The number of volume snapshots allowed per project
quota_gigabytes = 1000	The total amount of storage, in gigabytes, allowed for volumes and snapshots per project
quota_backups = 10	The number of volume backups allowed per project
quota_backup_gigabytes = 1000	The total amount of storage, in gigabytes, allowed for backups per project

You can show or modify Cinder quotes using the cinder CLI command or the Horizon web interface. In Horizon, all quotas for projects that exist can be found by going to Identity ➤ Projects. Then you need to choose Modify Quotas from the drop-down menu to the right of the project name. You need to know the project ID if you work from the command line.

```
$ openstack project list
+----------------------------------+----------+
| ID                               | Name     |
+----------------------------------+----------+
| 27cdeded89d24fb49c11030b8cc87f15 | admin    |
| 3a9a59175cce4a74a72c882947e8bc86 | apress   |
| 53d4fd6c5b1d44e89e604957c4df4fc2 | services |
| 9e0c535c2240405b989afa450681df18 | demo     |
+----------------------------------+----------+
```

Then you can show the quotas for the demo project.

```
$ cinder quota-show 9e0c535c2240405b989afa450681df18
+-----------------------+-------+
| Property              | Value |
+-----------------------+-------+
| backup_gigabytes      | 1000  |
| backups               | 10    |
| gigabytes             | 1000  |
| gigabytes__DEFAULT__  | -1    |
| gigabytes_iscsi       | -1    |
| groups                | 10    |
| per_volume_gigabytes  | -1    |
| snapshots             | 10    |
| snapshots__DEFAULT__  | -1    |
| snapshots_iscsi       | -1    |
| volumes               | 10    |
| volumes__DEFAULT__    | -1    |
| volumes_iscsi         | -1    |
+-----------------------+-------+
```

The results show the current usage of the demo project's quota.

```
$ cinder quota-usage 9e0c535c2240405b989afa450681df18
+-----------------------+--------+----------+-------+-----------+
| Type                  | In_use | Reserved | Limit | Allocated |
+-----------------------+--------+----------+-------+-----------+
| backup_gigabytes      | 0      | 0        | 1000  |           |
| backups               | 0      | 0        | 10    |           |
| gigabytes             | 2      | 0        | 1000  |           |
| gigabytes__DEFAULT__  | 0      | 0        | -1    |           |
| gigabytes_iscsi       | 2      | 0        | -1    |           |
| groups                | 0      | 0        | 10    |           |
| per_volume_gigabytes  | 0      | 0        | -1    |           |
| snapshots             | 0      | 0        | 10    |           |
| snapshots__DEFAULT__  | 0      | 0        | -1    |           |
| snapshots_iscsi       | 0      | 0        | -1    |           |
```

```
| volumes               | 2      | 0        | 10    |          |
| volumes___DEFAULT__   | 0      | 0        | -1    |          |
| volumes_iscsi         | 2      | 0        | -1    |          |
+----------------------+--------+----------+------+----------+
```

You need a quota name and the suggested number to update Cinder service quotas for a selected project.

```
$ cinder quota-update --snapshots 17 9e0c535c2240405b989afa450681df18
+----------------------+-------+
| Property             | Value |
+----------------------+-------+
| backup_gigabytes     | 1000  |
| backups              | 10    |
| gigabytes            | 1000  |
| gigabytes___DEFAULT__ | -1    |
| gigabytes_iscsi      | -1    |
| groups               | 10    |
| per_volume_gigabytes | -1    |
| snapshots            | 17    |
| snapshots___DEFAULT__ | -1    |
| snapshots_iscsi      | -1    |
| volumes              | 10    |
| volumes___DEFAULT__  | -1    |
| volumes_iscsi        | -1    |
+----------------------+-------+
```

To remove all quotas for the project, use the quota-delete command.

```
$ cinder quota-delete 9e0c535c2240405b989afa450681df18
```

Backing up and Restoring Volumes and Snapshots

You can create a whole volume backup or incremental backup (starting from the Liberty release). Then you can restore a volume from a backup if the backup's associated metadata exists in the Cinder database.

You can use the `openstack volume backup create` command.

```
$ openstack volume backup create apresstest1
+-------+--------------------------------------+
| Field | Value                                |
+-------+--------------------------------------+
| id    | 9dffa586-53b4-40d4-967a-87b910dd3dbb |
| name  | None                                 |
+-------+--------------------------------------+
```

It is possible to check the status of existing backups using the following command.

```
$ openstack volume backup list
+--------------------------------------+------+-------------+----------+------+
| ID                                   | Name | Description | Status   | Size |
+--------------------------------------+------+-------------+----------+------+
| 9dffa586-53b4-40d4-967a-87b910dd3dbb | None | None        | creating |    1 |
+--------------------------------------+------+-------------+----------+------+
$ openstack volume backup list
+--------------------------------------+------+-------------+-----------+------+
| ID                                   | Name | Description | Status    | Size |
+--------------------------------------+------+-------------+-----------+------+
| 9dffa586-53b4-40d4-967a-87b910dd3dbb | None | None        | available |    1 |
+--------------------------------------+------+-------------+-----------+------+
```

All backups go to the Swift object storage by default. You can check the volumesbackup container and objects inside this container.

```
$ swift list
apress_cont1
apress_cont2
volumebackups
$ swift list volumesbackup
volume_41b8ab16-a8e0-412f-8d37-f235f3036264/20220726121502/az_nova_backup_9
dffa586-53b4-40d4-967a-87b910dd3dbb-00001
volume_41b8ab16-a8e0-412f-8d37-f235f3036264/20220726121502/az_nova_backup_9
dffa586-53b4-40d4-967a-87b910dd3dbb-00002
...
```

Restoration of an existing backup is similar to the backup procedure.

```
$ openstack volume backup restore 9dffa586-53b4-40d4-967a-87b910dd3dbb
apresstest1
+-------------+-------------------------------------+
| Field       | Value                               |
+-------------+-------------------------------------+
| backup_id   | 9dffa586-53b4-40d4-967a-87b910dd3dbb |
| volume_id   | 41b8ab16-a8e0-412f-8d37-f235f3036264 |
| volume_name | apresstest1                         |
+-------------+-------------------------------------+
```

Managing Volume Snapshots

Using volume snapshots is another way to create a backup of an existing volume. Volume snapshots provide a way to obtain a nondisruptive copy of the volume. Snapshot is stored in Cinder's back-end storage system, as opposed to Swift object storage in cases of backups. In the default installation, LVM takes care of creating snapshots. Do not confuse Cinder snapshots with Nova snapshots. You can use a snapshot when a VM uses the volume, but from a consistency point of view, it is best if the volume is not connected to an instance when the snapshot is taken. It is possible to create new volumes from snapshots.

Let's look at some examples of how to work with Cinder snapshots. First, you need to know the volume ID or name.

```
$ openstack volume list
+--------------------------------------+-------------+-----------+------+
-------------+
| ID                                   | Name        | Status    | Size |
 Attached to |
+--------------------------------------+-------------+-----------+------+
-------------+
| 41b8ab16-a8e0-412f-8d37-f235f3036264 | apresstest1 | available |    1 |
             |
+--------------------------------------+-------------+-----------+------+
-------------+
```

Next, you can enter a command to create a snapshot.

```
$ openstack volume snapshot create --volume apresstest1 apresstest1_snap1
+-------------+--------------------------------------+
| Field       | Value                                |
+-------------+--------------------------------------+
| created_at  | 2022-07-26T13:04:23.663393           |
| description | None                                 |
| id          | 1c2daa2e-8b23-4992-acb9-286c0a8c589a |
| name        | apresstest1_snap1                    |
| properties  |                                      |
| size        | 1                                    |
| status      | creating                             |
| updated_at  | None                                 |
| volume_id   | 41b8ab16-a8e0-412f-8d37-f235f3036264 |
+-------------+--------------------------------------+
```

Then you should make sure that a snapshot was created.

```
$ openstack volume snapshot list
+--------------------------------------+-------------------+-------------+
-----------+------+
| ID                                   | Name              | Description |
 Status    | Size |
+--------------------------------------+-------------------+-------------+
-----------+------+
| 1c2daa2e-8b23-4992-acb9-286c0a8c589a | apresstest1_snap1 | None        |
 available |    1 |
+--------------------------------------+-------------------+-------------+
-----------+------+
```

And now, you can show the details of the snapshot.

```
$ openstack volume snapshot show apresstest1_snap1
+-------------------------------------------+-------------------------------------+
| Field                                     | Value                               |
+-------------------------------------------+-------------------------------------+
| created_at                                | 2022-07-26T13:04:23.000000          |
| description                               | None                                |
| id                                        | 1c2daa2e-8b23-4992-acb9-286c0a8c589a |
| name                                      | apresstest1_snap1                   |
| os-extended-snapshot-attributes:progress  | 100%                                |
| os-extended-snapshot-attributes:project_id | 9e0c535c2240405b989afa450681df18   |
| properties                                |                                     |
| size                                      | 1                                   |
| status                                    | available                           |
| updated_at                                | 2022-07-26T13:04:24.000000          |
| volume_id                                 | 41b8ab16-a8e0-412f-8d37-f235f3036264 |
+-------------------------------------------+-------------------------------------+
```

At the end, you can create a new volume from the snapshot. As a part of the creation process, you can specify a new volume size in gigabytes.

```
$ openstack volume create --snapshot apresstest1_snap1 --size 1
apresstest2_from_snap
+---------------------+-------------------------------------+
| Field               | Value                               |
+---------------------+-------------------------------------+
| attachments         | []                                  |
| availability_zone   | nova                                |
| bootable            | false                               |
| consistencygroup_id | None                                |
| created_at          | 2022-07-26T13:24:52.301501          |
| description         | None                                |
| encrypted           | False                               |
| id                  | f7960041-ca6e-4b11-ade3-2df2b81d02a2 |
| multiattach         | False                               |
| name                | apresstest2_from_snap               |
```

```
| properties           |                                      |
| replication_status   | None                                 |
| size                 | 1                                    |
| snapshot_id          | 1c2daa2e-8b23-4992-acb9-286c0a8c589a |
| source_volid         | None                                 |
| status               | creating                             |
| type                 | iscsi                                |
| updated_at           | None                                 |
| user_id              | a20b5a5995b740ff90034297335b330a     |
+----------------------+--------------------------------------+
```

You can also delete the snapshot if needed.

```
$ openstack volume snapshot delete apresstest1_snap1
```

Figure 9-5 shows the Volume Snapshots tab in the Horizon web user interface.

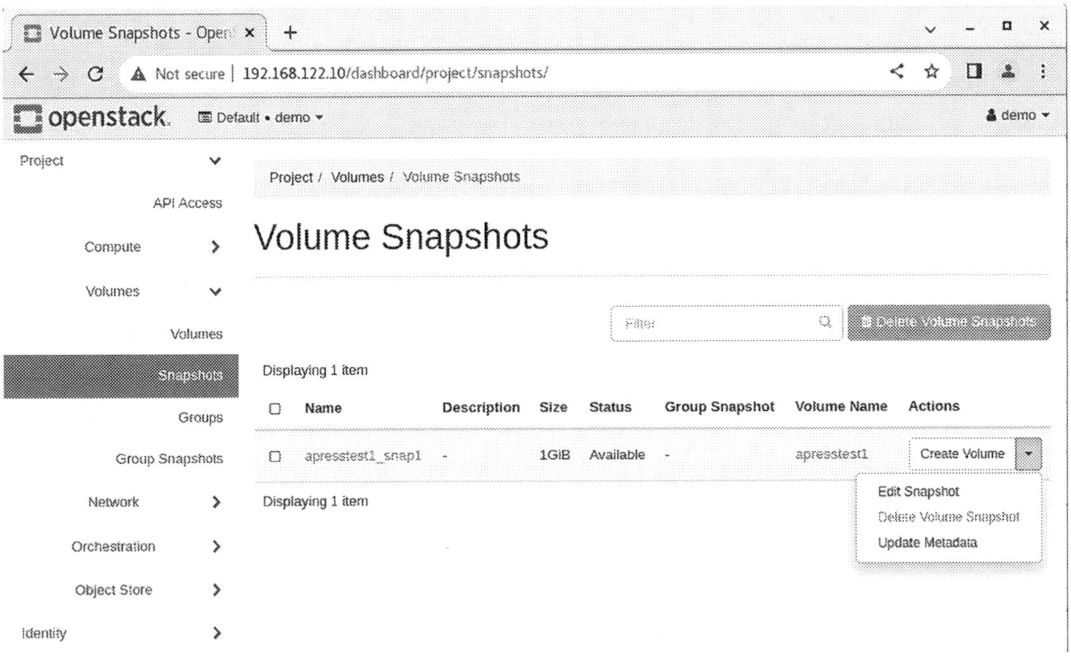

Figure 9-5. *Working with snapshots in Horizon web interface view*

Setting up Storage Pools

Cinder allows you to use multiple storage pools and storage drivers at the same time. You can find the list, which contains more than 50 storage drivers, on Cinder's Support Matrix web page (https://docs.openstack.org/cinder/latest/reference/support-matrix.html).

You must enumerate all the back ends when using two or more back ends with different or the same type of drivers in the [DEFAULT] section of the cinder.conf configuration file.

```
[DEFAULT]
enabled_backends = lvmA, lvmB, nfsA
```

You need to add sections with back-end-specific information for each back end. Here is an example for two LVM back ends and one NFS back end.

```
[lvmA]
volume_group=cinder-volumes-1
volume_driver=cinder.volume.drivers.lvm.LVMISCSIDriver
volume_backend_name=LVM
[lvmB]
volume_group=cinder-volumes-2
volume_driver=cinder.volume.drivers.lvm.LVMISCSIDriver
volume_backend_name=LVM
[nfsA]
nfs_shares_config=/etc/cinder/shares.txt
volume_driver=cinder.volume.drivers.nfs.NfsDriver
volume_backend_name=NFS
```

If you want to give the user the right to choose on which back end their volumes are created, then the admin must define a volume type.

```
$ source ~/keystonerc_admin
$ cinder type-create lvm1
$ cinder type-create lvm2
$ cinder type-create nfs1
$ cinder type-key lvm1 set volume_backend_name=lvmA
$ cinder type-key lvm2 set volume_backend_name=lvmB
$ cinder type-key nfs1 set volume_backend_name=nfsA
```

Summary

You will never find a production-grade OpenStack installation without a block storage service. Knowledge of this service will serve you well in real life after passing the exam.

The next chapter explores some troubleshooting techniques.

Review Questions

1. How many cinder-volume services exist in a typical installation?

    A. One

    B. At least three

    C. One per storage back end

    D. One per database instance

2. Which creates a volume named test with a 1 GB size?

    A. openstack volume create test 1

    B. cinder create --name test

    C. openstack volumes create --size 1 test

    D. cinder create --display-name test 1

3. What is the Linux LVM partition number?

    A. 82

    B. 8e

    C. 83

    D. 1F

4. How does Cinder backup differ from snapshots? (Choose two.)

    A. Backup is stored in Glance.

    B. Backup is stored in Swift.

    C. Backup can't be incremental.

    D. Backup can be incremental.

Answers

1. C

2. D

3. B

4. B and D

CHAPTER 10

Troubleshooting

This chapter does not cover one particular topic of the Certified OpenStack Administrator exam requirements. Instead, it shows general troubleshooting practices for OpenStack. Please note that backing up OpenStack instances is discussed in Chapter 9, and analyzing storage status is discussed in Chapters 5, 7, and 9.

The Main Principles of Troubleshooting

Troubleshooting OpenStack is not often straightforward because it consists of many separate projects that work with one another in different combinations. That is why the troubleshooting discussion is near the end of this book. You need to know the previous material before you learn the troubleshooting techniques.

It is good to stick to the scientific method during the troubleshooting exercise. The following are the primary steps to structure it as an algorithm.

1. Define the problem clearly as you can. You may want to make sure the issue is reproducible.

2. Collect all relevant information. It can be log files, debug output, etc.

3. Form a hypothesis based on observed symptoms.

4. Test the hypothesis. You can start from the easiest to test or from a theory with a higher probability or mix.

5. Try to fix issues based on tests.

6. The process must be restarted from the top of the proposed fixes that do not resolve the case.

© Andrey Markelov 2022
A. Markelov, *Certified OpenStack Administrator Study Guide*,
https://doi.org/10.1007/978-1-4842-8804-7_10

You should be aware of the concerns about generic debugging. Always make a backup copy of your configuration file before you begin changing it. It is very important to make only one change at a time. Finally, do not forget to revert your configuration files to the original if any test is unsuccessful.

OpenStack troubleshooting techniques depend to a certain extent on general GNU/Linux troubleshooting skills. That discussion is outside the scope of this book. However, Table 10-1 summarizes the main GNU/Linux troubleshooting utilities.

Table 10-1. *Basic GNU/Linux Troubleshooting Commands*

GNU/Linux Command	Useful Options and Examples
ps: Report list of the current processes	To see every process on the system, use the aux option. It can be useful with the grep command for searching exact processes, or you can use pgrep.

```
# ps aux | grep cinder
cinder      1400  0.6  0.3 354936 126036 ?        Ss    08:52    1:19 /usr/
bin/python3 /usr/bin/cinder-api --config-file /usr/share/cinder/cinder-
dist.conf --config-file /etc/cinder/cinder.conf --logfile /var/log/cinder/
api.log
```

top: Shows a dynamic view of the system processes. Unlike the ps output, this command continuously refreshes the view.	You can use interactive keystrokes in the top environment. ? - help, q - quit, l - toggles for load header line, t - toggles for threads header line, m - toggles for memory header line, u - filter process for user name, M - sorts process listing by memory usage in descending order, P - sorts process listing by processor utilization in descending order, k - kill a process.
df: Reports file system disk space usage.	Usually, df is used with the -h option, which means human-readable format (e.g., 1K 234M 2G)

(continued)

Table 10-1. (*continued*)

GNU/Linux Command	Useful Options and Examples

```
# df -h
Filesystem           Size  Used Avail Use% Mounted on
devtmpfs             16G     0   16G    0% /dev
tmpfs                16G   4.0K  16G    1% /dev/shm
tmpfs                6.3G   50M  6.3G   1% /run
/dev/mapper/cs-root  60G   9.0G  51G   15% /
/dev/vda1           1014M  266M 749M   27% /boot
/dev/mapper/cs-home  30G   331M  29G    2% /home
```

du: Estimate file space usage	The same -h option as in df is often used.

```
# du -h /var/lib/glance/images/
889M       /var/lib/glance/images/
```

ip: Show/manipulate routing, devices, policy routing, and tunnels	The most common subcommands are show - for displaying IP information, route - for showing routing information.

```
# ip addr show ens3
2: ens3: <BROADCAST,MULTICAST,UP,LOWER_UP> mtu 1500 qdisc fq_codel state
UP group default qlen 1000
  link/ether 52:54:00:4e:51:9f brd ff:ff:ff:ff:ff:ff
  altname enp0s3
  inet 192.168.122.10/24 brd 192.168.122.255 scope global dynamic
noprefixroute ens3
   valid_lft 2923sec preferred_lft 2923sec
  inet6 fe80::5054:ff:fe4e:519f/64 scope link noprefixroute
   valid_lft forever preferred_lft forever
```

(*continued*)

Table 10-1. (*continued*)

GNU/Linux Command	Useful Options and Examples
`ss` and `netstat`: Utilities to investigate sockets	The `ss` command is similar to the `netstat` command and is used to display socket statistics. They have similar options. Options are `-t` - show TCP sockets, `-u` - show UDP sockets, `-a` - show listening and established sockets, `-p` - show process using the sockets.

```
# ss -ta
State       Recv-Q  Send-Q Local   Address:Port                Peer
Address:Port
LISTEN      0       128              *:8776                     *:*
LISTEN      0       128              *:25672                    *:*
LISTEN      0       128              *:8777                     *:*
LISTEN      0       128     10.0.2.15:27017                     *:*
LISTEN      0       64      10.0.2.15:rsync                     *:*
LISTEN      0       50               *:mysql                    *:*
```

`find`: Search for files in a directory hierarchy	There are many options for the `find` utility: `-name` - find by name, `-iname` - like `-name`, but the match is case insensitive, `-group` and `-user` - find file that belongs to group or user, `-type` with f or d to find only files or directories.

```
# find /etc -name swift*
/etc/swift
/etc/swift/swift.conf
/etc/logrotate.d/openstack-swift
```

Note   Traditionally, network interfaces are enumerated as `eth0,1,2...` In most modern Linux distributions, the default naming behavior can differ. The names of interfaces can be based on device topology, type, and firmware. For example, the ethernet interface on PCI slot 0 and port 3 can be named `enp0s3`.

Checking the OpenStack Version

It is always good to know which version of the OpenStack environment you are working with. Before the Liberty version, all projects except Swift had a version based on the year and month. Starting with Liberty, all components have a traditional version structure, X.Y.Z., where X is always the same in one release.

Here is an example of Yoga.

```
# keystone-manage --version
21.0.0
# nova-manage --version
25.0.0
```

The following is an example of the old-fashioned version convention used in OpenStack Kilo.

```
# keystone-manage --version
2015.1.0
# nova-manage --version
2015.1.0
```

Also, you can find the version on the System Information tab in the Admin menu at the right corner of the page bottom. In Table 10-2, several of the latest OpenStack releases are listed.

Table 10-2. *OpenStack Releases*

Series	Releases	Initial Release Date
Victoria	Nova 22.0; Keystone 18.0; Neutron 17.0; Swift 2.26	October 14, 2020
Wallaby	Nova 23.0; Keystone 19.0; Neutron 18.0; Swift 2.27	April 14, 2021
Xena	Nova 24.0; Keystone 20.0; Neutron 19.0; Swift 2.28	October 6, 2021
Yoga	Nova 25.0; Keystone 21.0; Neutron 20.0; Swift 2.29	March 30, 2022
Zed	Nova 26.0; Keystone22.0; Neutron 21.0; Swift 2.29	October 5, 2022

Finding and Analyzing Log Files

Usually in GNU/Linux systems, log files are persistently stored in the /var/log directory. These files can be viewed using regular text utilities such as less and tail. The following is an example of this directory's content from the OpenStack controller node.

```
# ls /var/log --group-directories-first -F
anaconda/    horizon/     puppet/             boot.log-20220714  dnf.rpm.
log          secure
aodh/        httpd/       qemu-ga/            boot.log-20220717  firewalld
secure-20220717.gz
audit/       keystone/    rabbitmq/           boot.log-20220718  hawkey.
log          spooler
ceilometer/  libvirt/     redis/              boot.log-20220720  hawkey.
log-20220717    spooler-20220717.gz
chrony/      mariadb/     samba/              boot.log-20220721  kdump.
log          tallylog
cinder/      neutron/     speech-dispatcher/  boot.
log-20220722 lastlog                 wtmp
cups/        nova/        sssd/               btmp               maillog
gdm/         openvswitch/ swift/
cron                  maillog-20220717.gz
glance/      ovn/         swtpm/              cron-20220717.gz   messages
gnocchi/     placement/   tuned/              dnf.librepo.
log    messages-20220717.gz
heat/        private/     boot.log            dnf.log            README@
```

As you see, parts of the content are directories, and other parts are files. If one of the services has more than one log file, usually, such logs are placed in their own subdirectory. For example, the /var/log/cinder/ directory contains five files for several Cinder subsystems. You see that the files' names have -YYYYMMDD at the end. They are compressed by the Gzip tool. Usually, your lab must be one week old to find such compressed files. The logrotate utility renames, rotates, and compresses old logs. Instructions for logrotate are stored in the /etc/logrotate.d/ directory and /etc/logrotate.conf contains the configuration file.

The logging subsystem of GNU/Linux is based on the syslog protocol. In modern distributions the rsyslog and journald services in charge of logging.

The systemd-journald service is based on the operating system event logging architecture. It collects event messages from different sources like the Linux kernel, standard output, and standard error from daemons, boot messages, and syslog events. Then it converts them into a common format and writes them into a structured, indexed system journal. The rsyslog service reads syslog messages received by systemd-journald from the journal. It then records them to its log files under the /var/log directory or forwards them to other services according to its configuration.

There are some well-known system-wide log files.

- messages: Most of the syslog messages are stored in this file.

- secure: All authentication-related and security messages are stored here.

- cron: The log file related to periodically executed jobs.

In general, all syslog messages are categorized by type and priority. Priority can be from 0 (the system is unusable) to 7 (debug-level message). The type can be mail, cron, authpriv, etc. The RULES section of the configuration file /etc/rsyslog.conf contains directives that define where log messages are saved. The rules include type, dot symbol, priority, and destination. The following is part of a default configuration file with rules.

```
#### RULES ####
# Log all kernel messages to the console.
# Logging much else clutters up the screen.
#kern.*                 /dev/console
# Log anything (except mail) of level info or higher.
# Don't log private authentication messages!
*.info;mail.none;authpriv.none;cron.none                /var/log/messages
# The authpriv file has restricted access.
authpriv.*         /var/log/secure
# Log all the mail messages in one place.
mail.*             -/var/log/maillog
# Log cron stuff
cron.*             /var/log/cron
# Everybody gets emergency messages
*.emerg            :omusrmsg:*
# Save news errors of level crit and higher in a special file.
uucp,news.crit                                          /var/log/spooler
```

All log entries in log files are managed by the rsyslog and stored in a standard format.

```
2022-07-22 20:32:19.493 1388 INFO nova.compute.manager
[req-15841da6-61ab-47cd-bfef-cf5b7179474e - - - - -] [instance: f6fda94b-
a6d2-43cc-8e93-18a538759a22] VM Resumed (Lifecycle Event)
```

The first part of the message is the timestamp, then the priority, the name of the host, then the name of the program that sends the message, and the last part is a message.

A -f /var/log/logfilename command tail is useful for real-time log monitoring. This command prints the last ten lines of a log and continues to output new lines as they are added to this log file.

Backing up the Database Used by an OpenStack Instance

In most common cases, all OpenStack databases are on one MariaDB server. It is very easy to create a database backup then.

```
# mysqldump --opt --all-databases > /tmp/all-openstack.sql
```

Tip   The mysqldump command asks for a password. You can avoid this by adding the -p option with the password; for example, -p apress.

You can run the following if you only want to back up a single database.

```
# mysqldump --opt neutron > /tmp/neutron.sql
```

To list all database names, you can use mysql CLI.

```
# mysql
Welcome to the MariaDB monitor.  Commands end with ; or \g.
Your MariaDB connection id is 148482
Server version: 10.5.16-MariaDB MariaDB Server

Copyright (c) 2000, 2018, Oracle, MariaDB Corporation Ab and others.
```

```
Type 'help;' or '\h' for help. Type '\c' to clear the current input
statement.

MariaDB [(none)]> show databases;
+--------------------+
| Database           |
+--------------------+
| aodh               |
| cinder             |
| glance             |
| gnocchi            |
| heat               |
| information_schema |
| keystone           |
| mysql              |
| neutron            |
| nova               |
| nova_api           |
| nova_cell0         |
| performance_schema |
| placement          |
| test               |
+--------------------+
15 rows in set (0.001 sec)
```

Analyzing Host/Guest OS and Instance Status

The easiest way to check the status of OpenStack components like hosts and instances is by using the Horizon web client. The most general view of the cloud is found on the Overview tab on the Admin menu. If you are searching for information about the hypervisors, you need to use the view under Admin ➤ Compute ➤ Hypervisors. Both views are shown in Figures 10-1 and 10-2.

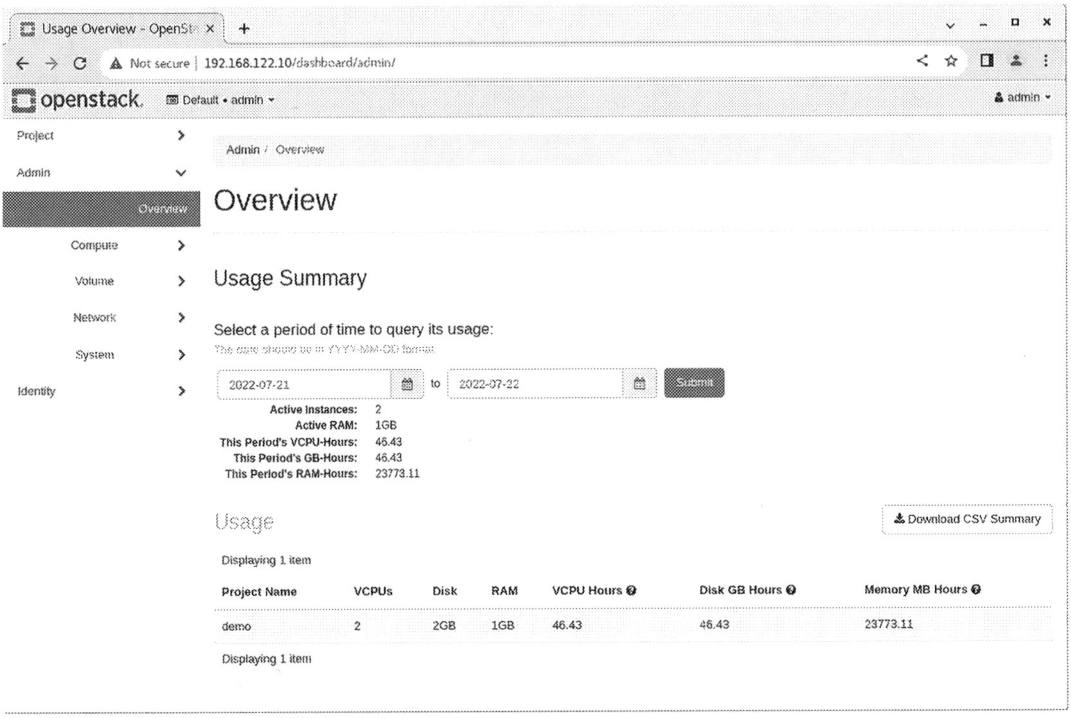

Figure 10-1. *OpenStack usage summary*

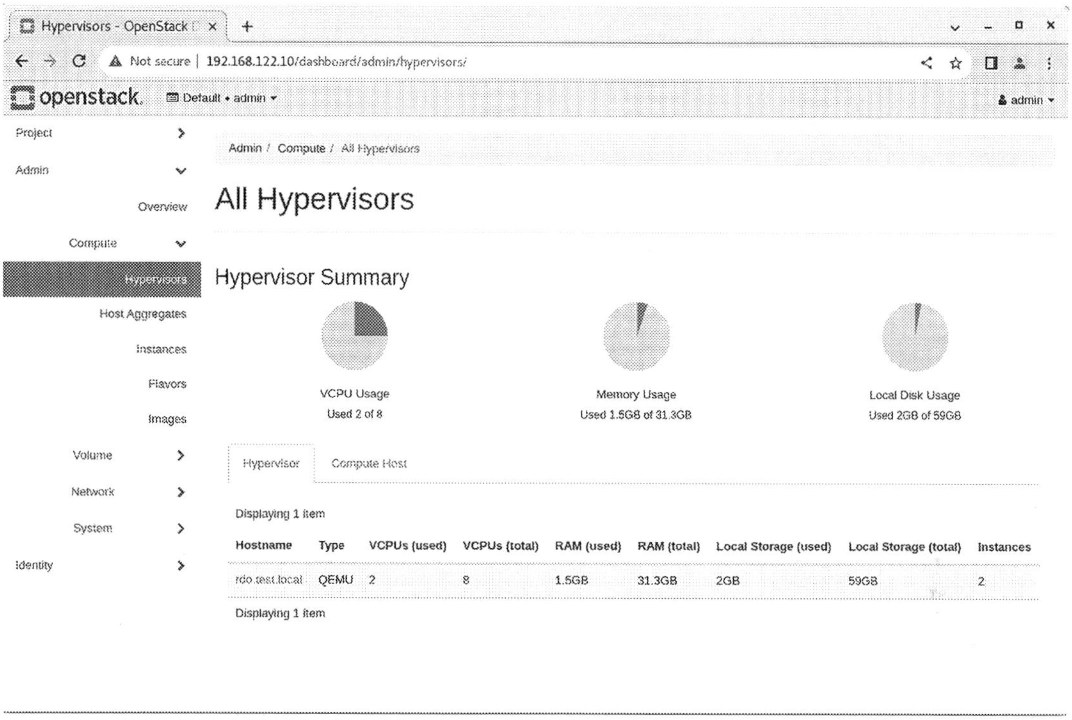

Figure 10-2. *Hypervisor usage summary*

Usually, users can find their instances in the Project menu. The administrator can view almost all instances on the Instances tab of the Admin ➤ Compute➤ Instances menu. Figure 10-3 shows an example of the Instances page.

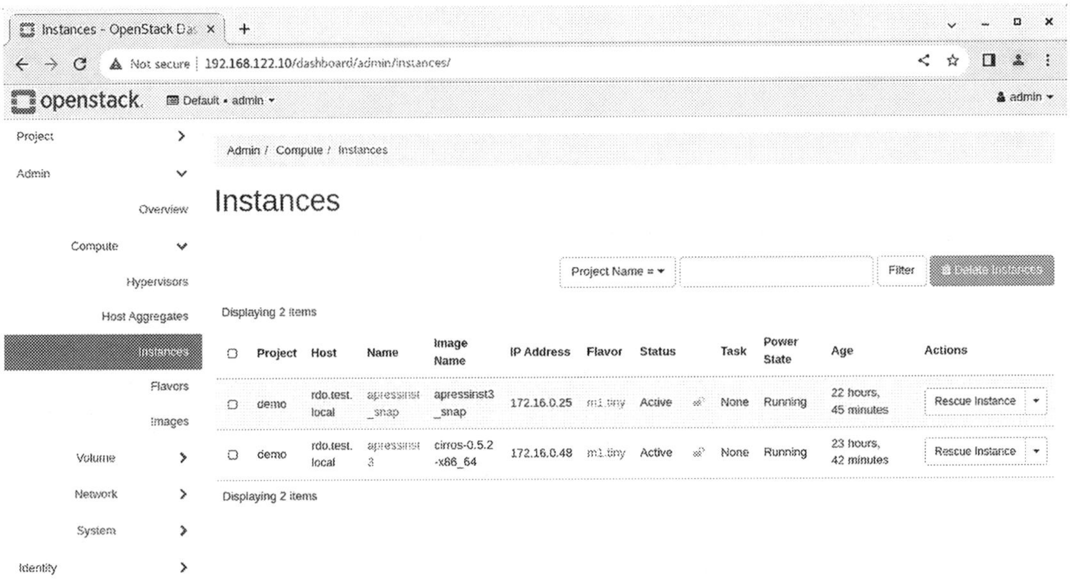

Figure 10-3. *All instances summary*

Of course, you can get the same information using a command line. Start by gathering information about the hosts. You can get the list of all hypervisors using the following command.

```
$ openstack host list
+-----------------+------------+----------+
| Host Name       | Service    | Zone     |
+-----------------+------------+----------+
| rdo.test.local  | conductor  | internal |
| rdo.test.local  | scheduler  | internal |
| rdo.test.local  | compute    | nova     |
+-----------------+------------+----------+
```

   or

```
$ nova hypervisor-list
+--------------------------------------+---------------------+-------+---------+
| ID                                   | Hypervisor hostname | State | Status  |
+--------------------------------------+---------------------+-------+---------+
| f29a98d2-389d-49b5-8582-dce34b0e89c1 | rdo.test.local      | up    | enabled |
+--------------------------------------+---------------------+-------+---------+
```

If you want more information about a specific host, the openstack host show command may help.

```
$ openstack host show rdo.test.local
+----------------+--------------------------------+-----+-----------+---------+
| Host           | Project                        | CPU | Memory MB | Disk GB |
+----------------+--------------------------------+-----+-----------+---------+
| rdo.test.local | (total)                        |   8 |     32063 |      59 |
| rdo.test.local | (used_now)                     |   2 |      1536 |       2 |
| rdo.test.local | (used_max)                     |   2 |      1024 |       2 |
| rdo.test.local | 9e0c535c2240405b989afa450681df18 |  2 |      1024 |       2 |
+----------------+--------------------------------+-----+-----------+---------+
```

With the nova command, you can get the list of all instances that are hosting each host. The following is an example.

```
$ nova hypervisor-servers rdo.test.local
+--------------------------------------+-------------------+
| ID                                   | Name              |
  Hypervisor ID                        | Hypervisor Hostname |
+--------------------------------------+-------------------+
| b360f5a5-b528-4f77-bdc7-3676ffcf0dff | instance-00000005 |
  | f29a98d2-389d-49b5-8582-dce34b0e89c1 | rdo.test.local    |
| 51ee0c05-242f-41a5-ba20-b10dc4621fdb | instance-00000006 |
  | f29a98d2-389d-49b5-8582-dce34b0e89c1 | rdo.test.local    |
+--------------------------------------+-------------------+
```

To print the list of virtual machines, you could use the openstack command.

```
$ openstack server list
+--------------------------------------+----------------+--------+
------------------+------------------+---------+
| ID                                   | Name           | Status |
Networks          | Image            | Flavor  |
+--------------------------------------+----------------+--------+
------------------+------------------+---------+
| 51ee0c05-242f-41a5-ba20-b10dc4621fdb | apressinst_snap | ACTIVE |
 demo-net=172.16.0.25 | apressinst3_snap | m1.tiny |
| b360f5a5-b528-4f77-bdc7-3676ffcf0dff | apressinst3     | ACTIVE |
 demo-net=172.16.0.48 | cirros-0.5.2-x86_64 | m1.tiny |
+--------------------------------------+----------------+--------+
------------------+------------------+---------+
```

If you want to get all information regarding a specific instance, use the following command.

```
$ openstack server show apressinst3
+---------------------------+------------------------------------------+
| Field                     | Value                                    |
+---------------------------+------------------------------------------+
| OS-DCF:diskConfig         | MANUAL                                   |
| OS-EXT-AZ:availability_zone | nova                                   |
| OS-EXT-STS:power_state    | Running                                  |
| OS-EXT-STS:task_state     | None                                     |
| OS-EXT-STS:vm_state       | active                                   |
| OS-SRV-USG:launched_at    | 2022-07-21T12:25:22.000000               |
| OS-SRV-USG:terminated_at  | None                                     |
| accessIPv4                |                                          |
| accessIPv6                |                                          |
| addresses                 | demo-net=172.16.0.48                     |
| config_drive              |                                          |
| created                   | 2022-07-21T12:25:19Z                     |
| flavor                    | m1.tiny (1)                              |
| hostId                    | 1ea0155a80f503a2aad8752d0e77968a         |
                              5f96a9975c97a6985389a988                 |
```

```
| id                | b360f5a5-b528-4f77-bdc7-3676ffcf0dff       |
| image             | cirros-0.5.2-x86_64 (7ffe1b43-7e86-        |
|                   | 4ad0-86b6-9fffa38b3c20)                    |
| key_name          | apresskey1                                 |
| name              | apressinst3                                |
| progress          | 0                                          |
| project_id        | 9e0c535c2240405b989afa450681df18           |
| properties        |                                            |
| security_groups   | name='apress-sgroup'                       |
| status            | ACTIVE                                     |
| updated           | 2022-07-22T07:48:32Z                       |
| user_id           | a20b5a5995b740ff90034297335b330a           |
| volumes_attached  |                                            |
+---------------------------+----------------------------------------+
```

Analyzing Messaging Servers

As mentioned earlier, a messaging server is used by almost all OpenStack services. Nowadays, the most common messaging server for OpenStack is RabbitMQ. Alternatives for RabbitMQ are Qpid and ZeroMQ. For transmitting information between OpenStack services, these servers use AMQP (Advanced Message Queuing Protocol). Let's briefly go over the functions of RabbitMQ.

To check RabbitMQ's status, you can use the following command.

```
# rabbitmqctl status
Status of node rabbit@rdo ...
Runtime

OS PID: 1430
OS: Linux
Uptime (seconds): 20151
Is under maintenance?: false
RabbitMQ version: 3.9.10
Node name: rabbit@rdo
Erlang configuration: Erlang/OTP 24 [erts-12.1.5] [source] [64-bit]
[smp:8:8] [ds:8:8:10] [async-threads:1] [jit]
```

Erlang processes: 1656 used, 1048576 limit
Scheduler run queue: 1
Cluster heartbeat timeout (net_ticktime): 60
...
Data directory
Node data directory: /var/lib/rabbitmq/mnesia/rabbit@rdo
Raft data directory: /var/lib/rabbitmq/mnesia/rabbit@rdo/quorum/rabbit@rdo

Config files
 * /etc/rabbitmq/rabbitmq.config

Log file(s)
 * /var/log/rabbitmq/rabbit@rdo.log
 * /var/log/rabbitmq/rabbit@rdo_upgrade.log
 * <stdout>

Memory
Total memory used: 0.3656 gb
Calculation strategy: rss
Memory high watermark setting: 0.4 of available memory, computed to:
13.4485 gb
...
Free Disk Space
Low free disk space watermark: 0.05 gb
Free disk space: 54.596 gb

Totals
Connection count: 104
Queue count: 116
Virtual host count: 1

Listeners
Interface: [::], port: 25672, protocol: clustering, purpose: inter-node and
CLI tool communication
Interface: [::], port: 5672, protocol: amqp, purpose: AMQP 0-9-1 and
AMQP 1.0

To list all users, use the following command.

```
# rabbitmqctl list_users
Listing users ...
User    tags
Guest   [administrator]
```

As you see in this demo environment, only one user guest has administrator rights. All OpenStack services use that particular user for sending and receiving messages. To check whether you can find RabbitMQ settings in the services config files.

```
# grep 'transport_url=rabbit' /etc/glance/glance-api.conf
transport_url=rabbit://guest:guest@192.168.122.10:5672/
# grep 'transport_url=rabbit' /etc/nova/nova.conf
transport_url=rabbit://guest:guest@192.168.122.10:5672/
# grep 'transport_url=rabbit' /etc/cinder/cinder.conf
transport_url=rabbit://guest:guest@192.168.122.10:5672/
# grep 'transport_url=rabbit' /etc/neutron/neutron.conf
transport_url=rabbit://guest:guest@192.168.122.10:5672/
```

This is a common part of most configuration files. For managing and monitoring the RabbitMQ server, you can activate the graphical web console.

```
# /usr/lib/rabbitmq/bin/rabbitmq-plugins enable rabbitmq_management
Enabling plugins on node rabbit@rdo:
rabbitmq_management
The following plugins have been configured:
  rabbitmq_management
  rabbitmq_management_agent
  rabbitmq_web_dispatch
Applying plugin configuration to rabbit@rdo...
The following plugins have been enabled:
  rabbitmq_management
  rabbitmq_management_agent
  rabbitmq_web_dispatch

set 3 plugins.
  Offline change; changes will take effect at broker restart.
# systemctl restart rabbitmq-server.service
```

211

Then open the web browser and point it to `http://name-of-server:15672` on the RabbitMQ server host. A screenshot of the console is shown in Figure 10-4. The login name is `guest,` and the password is also `guest` by default.

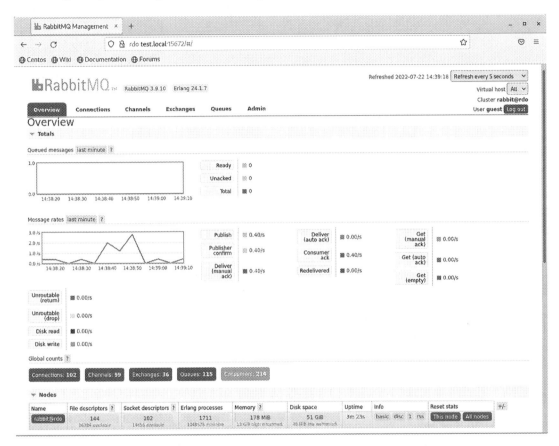

Figure 10-4. *RabbitMQ web plug-in*

Analyzing Network Status

First, you can check the list of processes that build up the Neutron service.

```
# pgrep -l neutron
971 neutron-meterin
984 neutron-server
988 neutron-metadat
1731 neutron-l3-agen
```

```
1732 neutron-openvsw
1734 neutron-dhcp-ag
1825 neutron-rootwra
2164 neutron-ns-meta
```

or

```
# pgrep -l neutron
1371 neutron-ovn-met
...
2813 neutron-server:
...
```

The exact list of processes can be different and depends on the host configuration and the type of SDN used. As you know, Neutron works through a lot of agents or plug-ins. In Horizon, the status of these plug-ins is listed on the Network Agents tab of the System Information view, as shown in Figure 10-5.

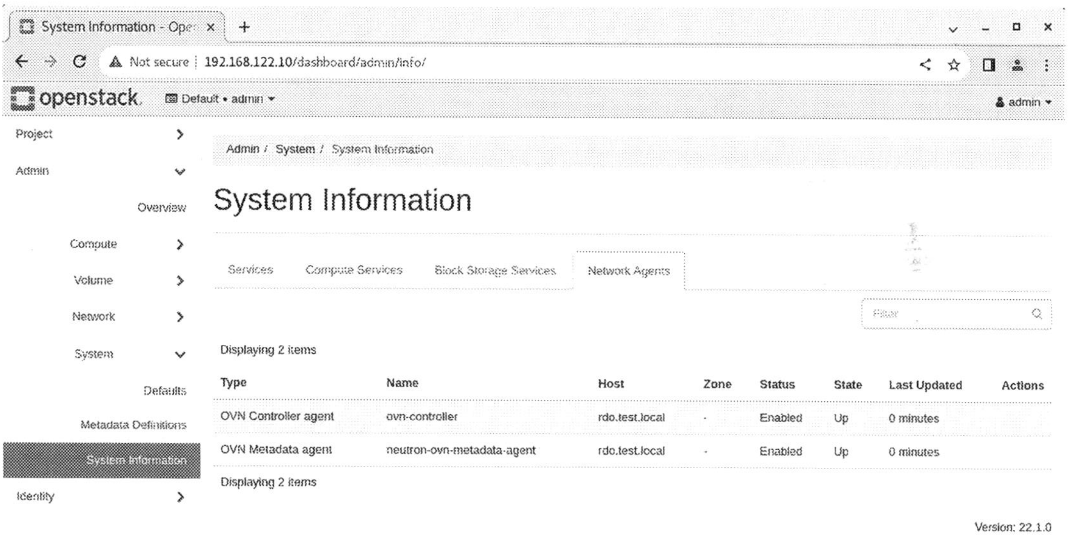

Figure 10-5. *OpenStack Neutron agents list*

The same information can be retrieved at the command line using the neutron command.

```
$
openstack network agent list
+-----------------------------------+---------------------+----------------+
-------------------+-------+-------+--------------------------+
| ID                                | Agent Type          | Host           |
Availability Zone | Alive | State | Binary                   |
+-----------------------------------+---------------------+----------------+
-------------------+-------+-------+--------------------------+
| 238f88a3-f9c6-5d22-89bb-6b9b8f369d25 | OVN Metadata agent   | rdo.test.local |
                  | :-)   | UP    | neutron-ovn-metadata-agent |
| dff0df04-e035-42cc-98a6-d2aee745b9bf | OVN Controller agent | rdo.test.local |
                  | :-)   | UP    | ovn-controller            |
+-----------------------------------+---------------------+----------------+
-------------------+-------+-------+--------------------------+
```

Neutron has a log file for each agent and OVN in separate directories.

```
# ls /var/log/neutron/ /var/log/ovn
/var/log/neutron/:
neutron-ovn-metadata-agent.log   server.log
/var/log/ovn:
ovn-controller.log               ovsdb-server-nb.log
ovn-northd.log                   ovsdb-server-sb.log
```

Let's look at the virtual networks part of the OpenStack configuration. And again, you can explore them in Horizon, as shown in Figure 10-6, or you can use a command line.

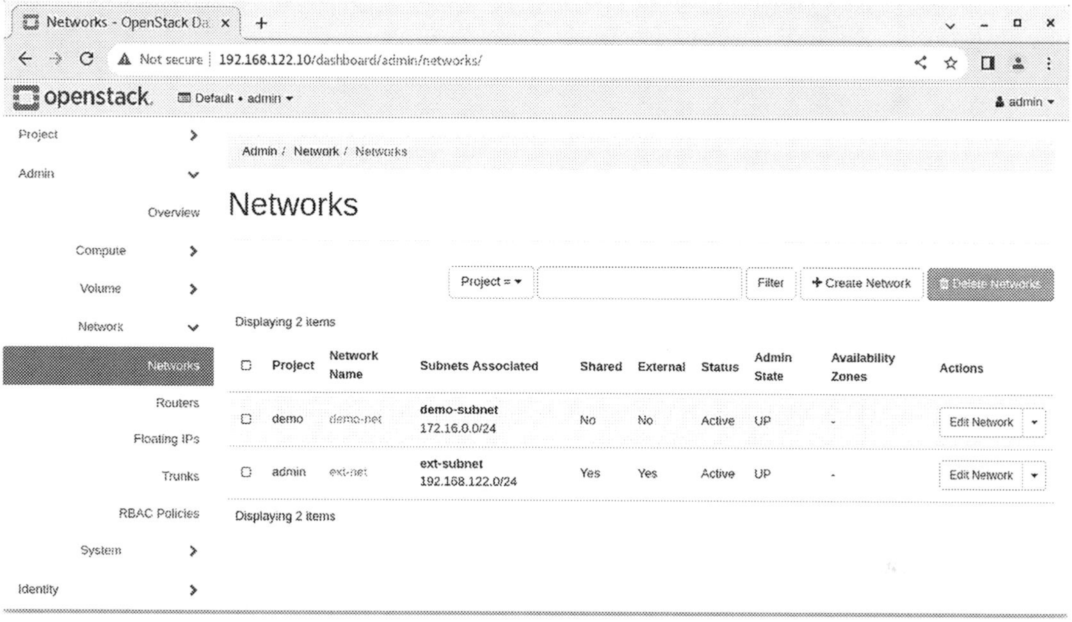

Figure 10-6. *OpenStack networks page*

```
$ openstack network list
+--------------------------------------+----------+--------------------------------------+
| ID                                   | Name     | Subnets                              |
+--------------------------------------+----------+--------------------------------------+
| 5ee4e933-de9b-4bcb-9422-83cc0d276d33 | demo-net | 18736455-80f6-4513-9d81-6cedbfe271fe |
| 5f18929b-70f6-4729-ac05-7bea494b9c5a | ext-net  | d065c027-bb60-4464-9619-7d9754535c5c |
+--------------------------------------+----------+--------------------------------------+
```

You can click the network name to get more information on a specific network. The relevant screenshot to show this is Figure 10-7. If you prefer CLI, use the following command.

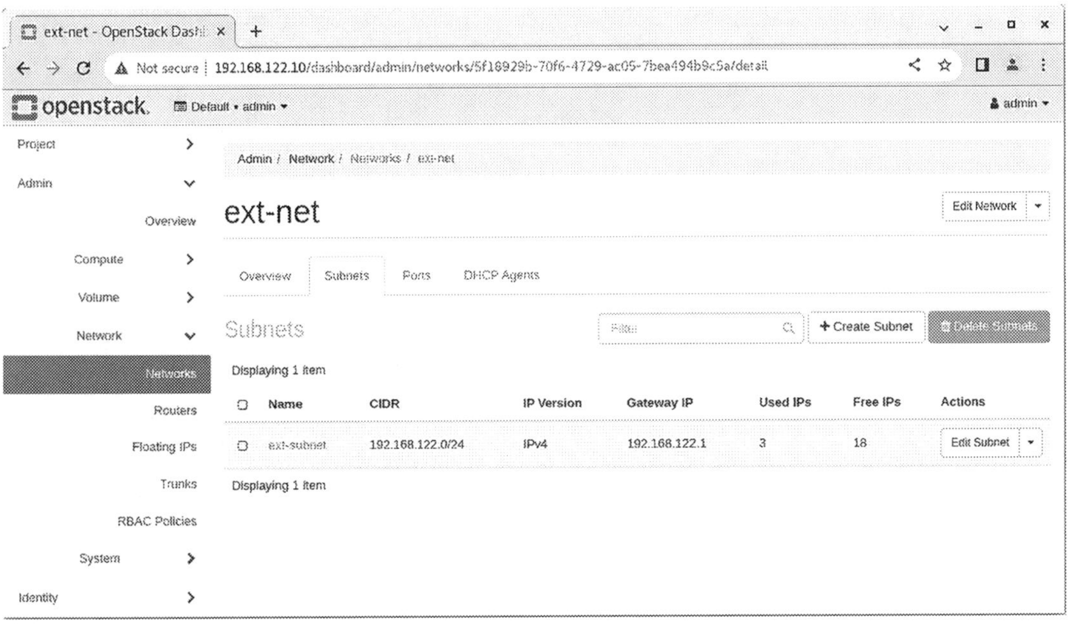

Figure 10-7. *Network overview details*

```
$ openstack network show demo-net
+---------------------------+-------------------------------------+
| Field                     | Value                               |
+---------------------------+-------------------------------------+
| admin_state_up            | UP                                  |
| availability_zone_hints   |                                     |
| availability_zones        |                                     |
| created_at                | 2022-07-17T18:12:02Z                |
| description               |                                     |
| dns_domain                | None                                |
| id                        | 5ee4e933-de9b-4bcb-9422-83cc0d276d33 |
| ipv4_address_scope        | None                                |
| ipv6_address_scope        | None                                |
| is_default                | None                                |
| is_vlan_transparent       | None                                |
| mtu                       | 1442                                |
| name                      | demo-net                            |
```

```
| port_security_enabled  | True                                 |
| project_id             | 9e0c535c2240405b989afa450681df18     |
| provider:network_type  | geneve                               |
| provider:physical_network | None                              |
| provider:segmentation_id | 30                                 |
| qos_policy_id          | None                                 |
| revision_number        | 2                                    |
| router:external        | Internal                             |
| segments               | None                                 |
| shared                 | False                                |
| status                 | ACTIVE                               |
| subnets                | 18736455-80f6-4513-9d81-6cedbfe271fe |
| tags                   |                                      |
| updated_at             | 2022-07-17T18:14:52Z                 |
+------------------------+--------------------------------------+
```

In the previous command you could use the network name, in this case demo-net, or the network ID. Figure 10-8 provides the list of virtual routers.

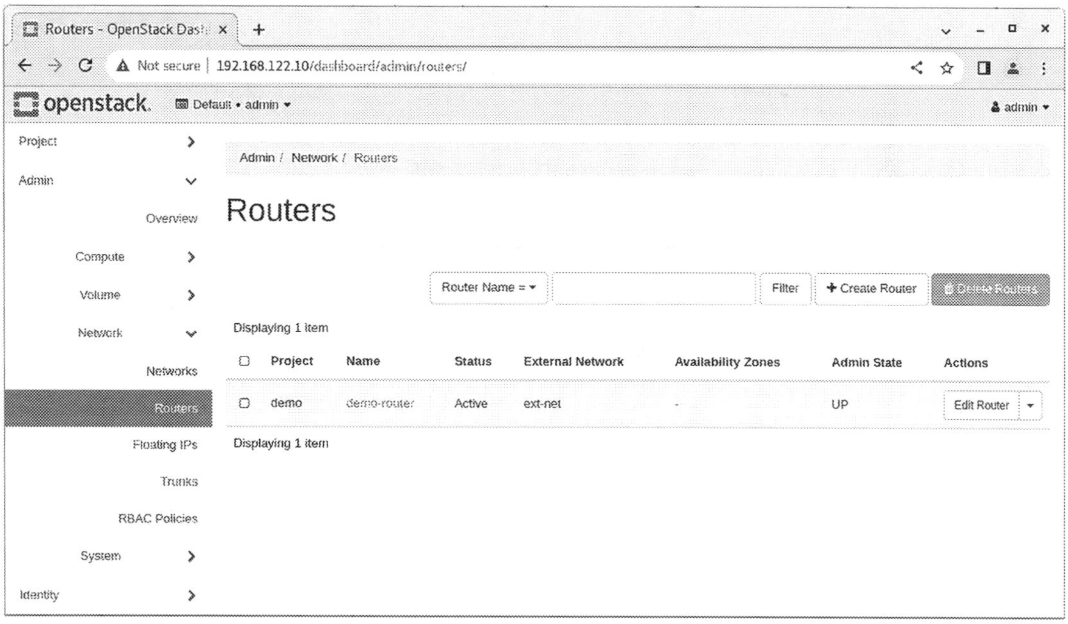

Figure 10-8. *OpenStack routers*

The corresponding CLI command to find the list of routers is.

```
$ openstack router list
+--------------------------------------+-------------+--------+-------+----------------------------------+
| ID                                   | Name        | Status | State | Project                          |
+--------------------------------------+-------------+--------+-------+----------------------------------+
| 3daad728-4075-49a4-ad05-3b279de738fa | demo-router | ACTIVE | UP    | 9e0c535c2240405b989afa450681df18 |
+--------------------------------------+-------------+--------+-------+----------------------------------+
$ openstack router show demo-router
+-----------------------+---------------------------------------------------------------------+
| Field                 | Value                                                               |
+-----------------------+---------------------------------------------------------------------+
| admin_state_up        | UP                                                                  |
| availability_zone_hints |                                                                   |
| availability_zones    |                                                                     |
| created_at            | 2022-07-17T18:16:19Z                                                |
| description           |                                                                     |
| external_gateway_info | {"network_id": "5f18929b-70f6-4729-ac05-7bea494b9c5a",              |
|                       | "external_fixed_ips": [{"subnet_id":                                |
|                       | "d065c027-bb60-4464-9619-7d9754535c5c", "ip_address":              |
|                       | "192.168.122.208"}], "enable_snat": true}                          |
| flavor_id             | None                                                                |
| id                    | 3daad728-4075-49a4-ad05-3b279de738fa                                |
| interfaces_info       | [{"port_id": "5bcc90fc-9a54-4c91-9e6a-988ac0a4a4a8",                |
|                       | "ip_address": "172.16.0.1", "subnet_id":                           |
|                       | "18736455-80f6-4513-9d81-6cedbfe271fe"}]                           |
| name                  | demo-router                                                         |
| project_id            | 9e0c535c2240405b989afa450681df18                                    |
| revision_number       | 3                                                                   |
| routes                |                                                                     |
| status                | ACTIVE                                                              |
| tags                  |                                                                     |
| updated_at            | 2022-07-17T18:21:55Z                                                |
+-----------------------+---------------------------------------------------------------------+
```

For enumerating the list of ports, use the opensrtack port list command. The openstack port show command shows the details of the port-by-port ID.

```
$ openstack port list
+------------------------------------+------+-------------------+---------------------------------------------------------------------------------------+--------+
| ID                                 | Name | MAC Address       | Fixed IP Addresses                                                                    | Status |
+------------------------------------+------+-------------------+---------------------------------------------------------------------------------------+--------+
| 01ea5959-6d71-4761-bb9d-4a7fdada1125 |      | fa:16:3e:37:cc:c8 | ip_address='172.16.0.48', subnet_id='18736455-80f6-4513-9d81-6cedbfe271fe'            | DOWN   |
| 29b05750-0c52-4fb2-88c0-f6fc7a87ecb4 |      | fa:16:3e:b6:88:ea | ip_address='172.16.0.2', subnet_id='18736455-80f6-4513-9d81-6cedbfe271fe'             | DOWN   |
| 2f0ef8d7-0219-46f8-b874-19b308dc29dd |      | fa:16:3e:24:49:cc |                                                                                      | DOWN   |
| 46050c0c-a2cb-4e56-9ad1-639f58e9e32a |      | fa:16:3e:19:3d:f9 | ip_address='172.16.0.25', subnet_id='18736455-80f6-4513-9d81-6cedbfe271fe'            | DOWN   |
| 5bcc90fc-9a54-4c91-9e6a-988ac0a4a4a8 |      | fa:16:3e:2d:7b:4d | ip_address='172.16.0.1', subnet_id='18736455-80f6-4513-9d81-6cedbfe271fe'             | ACTIVE |
| 5c2d527f-2230-4ddf-a4cd-27e71683f9aa |      | fa:16:3e:fb:f7:7e | ip_address='192.168.122.215', subnet_id='d065c027-bb60-4464-9619-7d9754535c5c'        | N/A    |
| d3838abc-14ec-4025-b808-3fe6e5ace51b |      | fa:16:3e:53:11:2c | ip_address='192.168.122.208', subnet_id='d065c027-bb60-4464-9619-7d9754535c5c'        | ACTIVE |
| ed4d0736-827e-4700-9594-41bb775e820f |      | fa:16:3e:18:49:7c | ip_address='192.168.122.213', subnet_id='d065c027-bb60-4464-9619-7d9754535c5c'        | N/A    |
+------------------------------------+------+-------------------+---------------------------------------------------------------------------------------+--------+

$ openstack port show 5bcc90fc-9a54-4c91-9e6a-988ac0a4a4a8
+-------------------------+-----------------------------------------------------------+
| Field                   | Value                                                     |
+-------------------------+-----------------------------------------------------------+
| admin_state_up          | UP                                                        |
| allowed_address_pairs   |                                                           |
| binding_host_id         |                                                           |
| binding_profile         |                                                           |
| binding_vif_details     |                                                           |
| binding_vif_type        | unbound                                                   |
| binding_vnic_type       | normal                                                    |
| created_at              | 2022-07-17T18:17:36Z                                      |
| data_plane_status       | None                                                      |
| description             |                                                           |
| device_id               | 3daad728-4075-49a4-ad05-3b279de738fa                      |
| device_owner            | network:router_interface                                  |
| device_profile          | None                                                      |
| dns_assignment          | None                                                      |
| dns_domain              | None                                                      |
| dns_name                | None                                                      |
| extra_dhcp_opts         |                                                           |
| fixed_ips               | ip_address='172.16.0.1', subnet_id='18736455-80f6-4513-   |
|                         | 9d81-6cedbfe271fe'                                        |
| id                      | 5bcc90fc-9a54-4c91-9e6a-988ac0a4a4a8                      |
| ip_allocation           | None                                                      |
```

```
+-----------------------+-------------------------------------------------------+
| mac_address           | fa:16:3e:2d:7b:4d                                     |
| name                  |                                                       |
| network_id            | 5ee4e933-de9b-4bcb-9422-83cc0d276d33                  |
| numa_affinity_policy  | None                                                  |
| port_security_enabled | False                                                 |
| project_id            | 9e0c535c2240405b989afa450681df18                      |
| propagate_uplink_status | None                                                |
| qos_network_policy_id | None                                                  |
| qos_policy_id         | None                                                  |
| resource_request      | None                                                  |
| revision_number       | 3                                                     |
| security_group_ids    |                                                       |
| status                | ACTIVE                                                |
| tags                  |                                                       |
| trunk_details         | None                                                  |
| updated_at            | 2022-07-17T18:17:37Z                                  |
+-----------------------+-------------------------------------------------------+
```

Note   For real-world network problems and troubleshooting, the utility plotnetcfg can be useful. It creates a network configuration diagram that can be visualized with the help of the dot utility. For more information, check the project website (`https://github.com/jbenc/plotnetcfg`).

The Network Topology tab is probably the best place to look for a project-level network overview. Figure 10-9 shows an example of the information provided on that page.

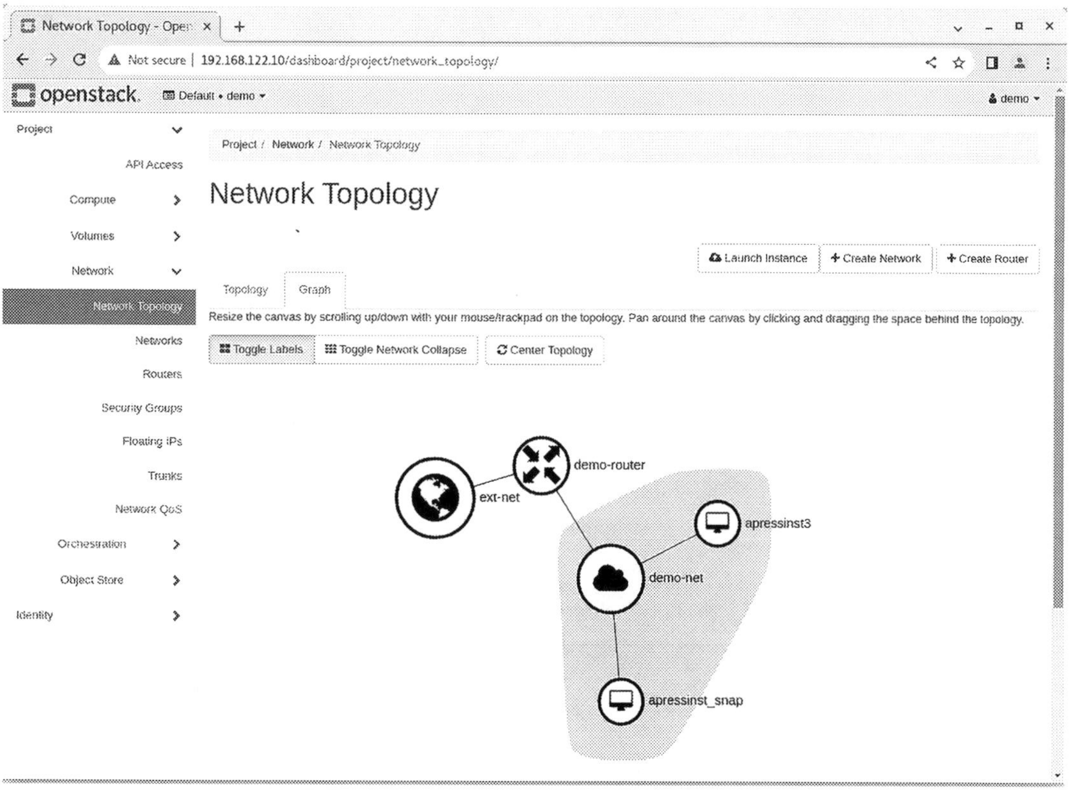

Figure 10-9. *Project Network Topology tab*

Digesting the OpenStack Environment

All OpenStack services are deployed as GNU/Linux daemons. Part of these services is represented as a single daemon, and part of them consists of two or more services. The best place to look for the status of a service is on the System Information tab on the Admin menu, as shown in Figure 10-10.

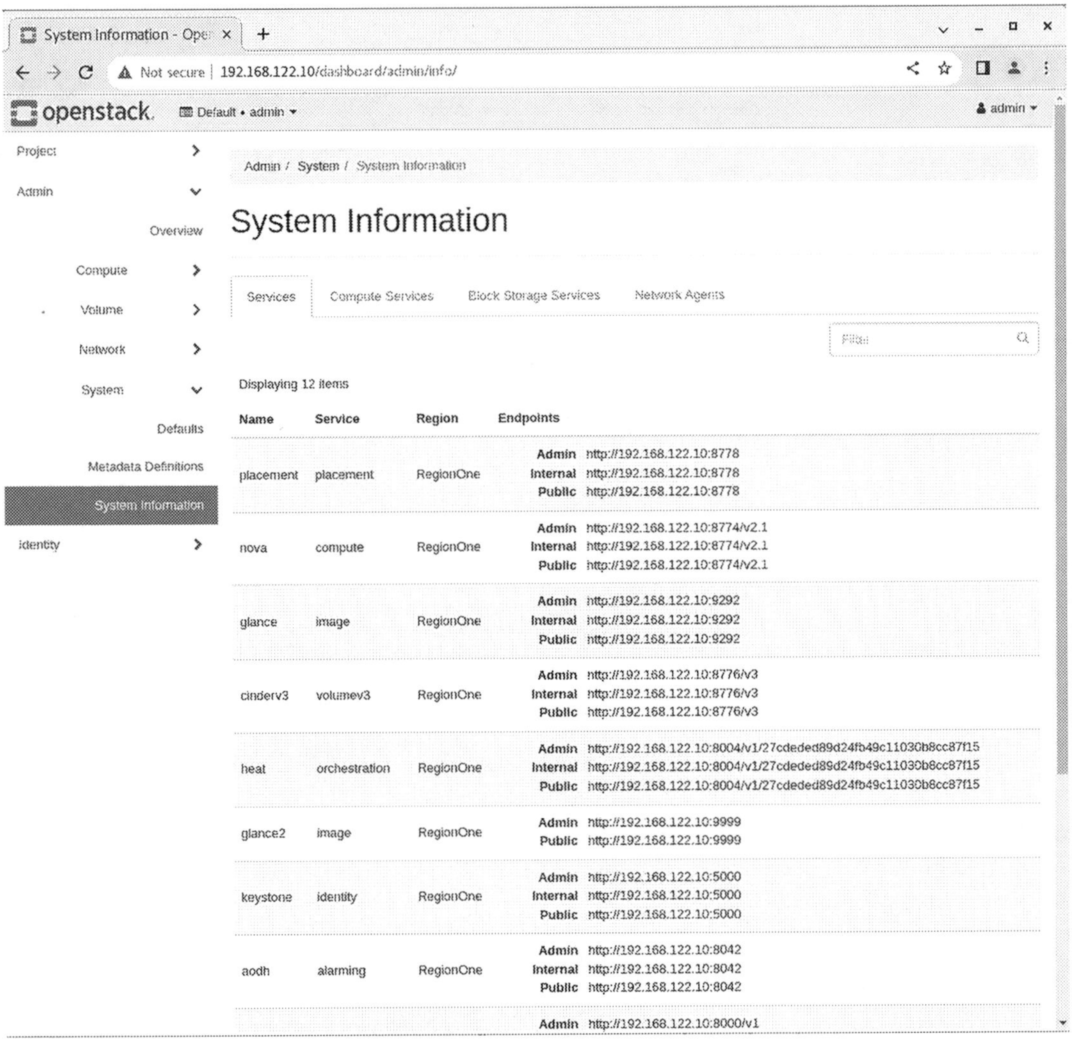

Figure 10-10. *OpenStack services information*

All the services' information and statuses are shown. To do the same thing with a command line for this demo environment based on CentOS Stream, you can use the systemctl command.

```
# systemctl | grep openstack
  openstack-aodh-evaluator.service              loaded active
running   OpenStack Alarm evaluator service
  openstack-aodh-listener.service               loaded active
running   OpenStack Alarm listener service
```

```
openstack-aodh-notifier.service                   loaded active
running    OpenStack Alarm notifier service
  openstack-ceilometer-notification.
service                                            loaded active
running    OpenStack ceilometer notification agent
  openstack-ceilometer-polling.service            loaded active
running    OpenStack ceilometer polling agent
  openstack-cinder-api.service                    loaded active
running    OpenStack Cinder API Server
...
```

In the Horizon web client, you can also check the status of the computer services and block storage services on separate subtabs on the System Information tab. Respective examples are shown in Figures 10-11 and 10-12.

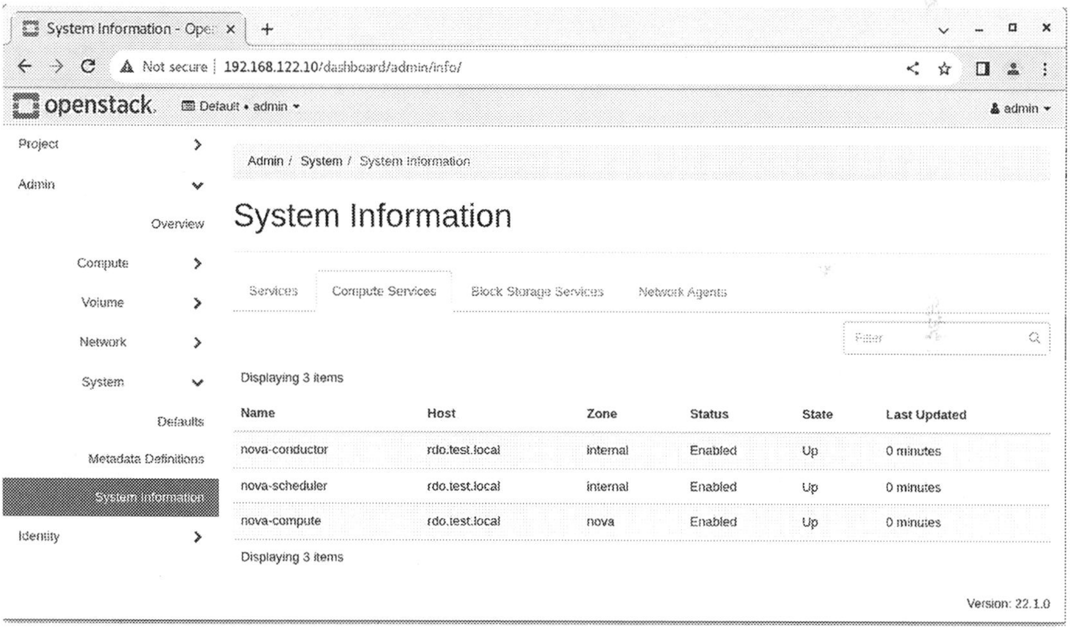

Figure 10-11. *OpenStack compute services*

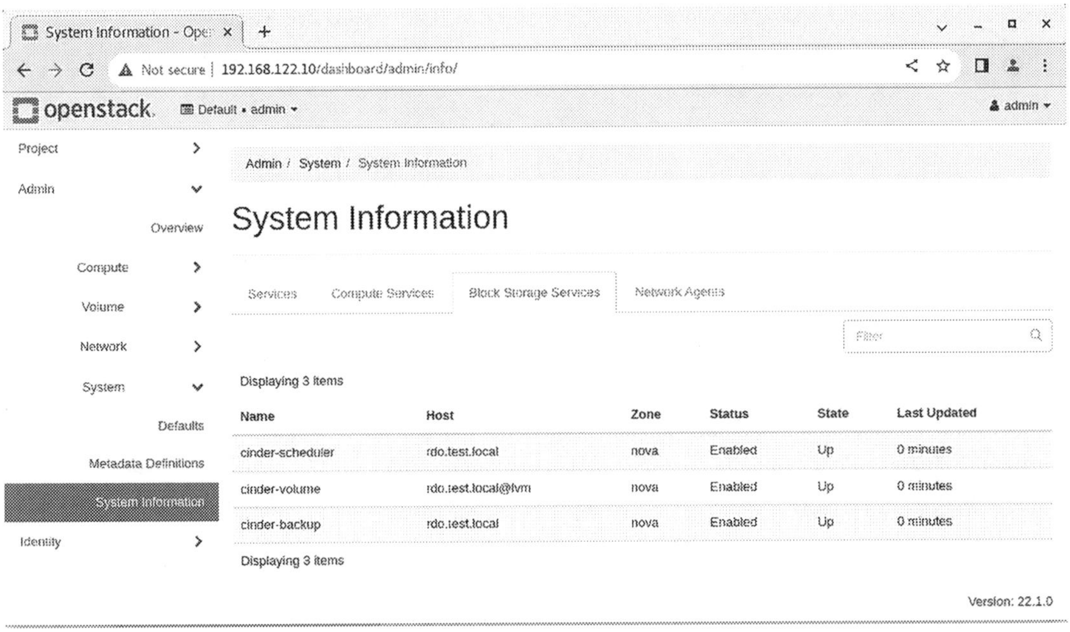

Figure 10-12. *OpenStack block storage services*

Summary

A troubleshooting topic is bigger than one particular chapter or even book. Solid knowledge of GNU/Linux is needed. In the past, troubleshooting was a separate topic of the exam. In general, you still need troubleshooting skills as part of the exam.

Review Questions

1. Which do you use to search for the identity service configuration files in a configuration directory hierarchy?

   A. find /etc -name *keystone.*

   B. find /etc --name heat.*

   C. find /var --name *keystone.*

   D. find / --name heat.*

2. Where would you find the messages from the Cinder service? (Choose all that are applicable.)

   A. /var/log/messages

   B. /var/log/cinder/api.log

   C. /var/log/cinder/scheduler.log

   D. /var/log/cinder/backup.log

3. Which backs up all the OpenStack databases?

   A. mysqlbackup --opt --all-db > /tmp/all-openstack.sql

   B. mysqlbackup --opt --all-databases > /tmp/all-openstack.sql

   C. mysqldump --opt --all-db > /tmp/all-openstack.sql

   D. mysqldump --opt --all-databases > /tmp/all-openstack.sql

4. Which enumerates all the compute hosts? (Choose all that are applicable.)

   A. openstack hypervisor list

   B. openstack host list

   C. nova host-enumerate

   D. nova hypervisor-list

5. Which provides a list of all virtual machines?

   A. openstack vm list

   B. openstack server list

   C. openstack host list

   D. openstack instance list

6. Which checks the status of the RabbitMQ messaging server?

   A. rabbitmqctl stat

   B. rabbitmq status

   C. rabbitmqctl status

   D. rabbitmq state

7. Which checks the status of the Neutron agents?

    A. openstack network agent list

    B. neutron plugin-list

    C. openstack agent list

    D. openstack network list

8. Which gives the details of a given router?

    A. neutron router list router

    B. neutron router show router

    C. openstack router list router

    D. openstack router show router

Answers

1. A

2. A, B, C, D

3. D

4. B, D

5. B

6. C

7. A

8. D

CHAPTER 11

Conclusion

If you've read this far and understand what was presented, you are close to being ready to take the Certified OpenStack Administrator exam. The next step should be studying the official OpenStack documentation at `http://docs.openstack.org` (see Figure 11-1), which includes the following.

- Installation guides for three GNU/Linux distributions: SUSE Linux, CentOS/RHEL, and Ubuntu Linux

- Deployment guides categorized by deployment tools: Charms (Canonical's stack), TripleO (Tool driven by Red Hat), and Ansible

- Administrator guide

- Operations guide

- Security guide

- Virtual machine image guide

- Architecture guide

- Configuration reference

- API complete references

© Andrey Markelov 2022
A. Markelov, *Certified OpenStack Administrator Study Guide*,
https://doi.org/10.1007/978-1-4842-8804-7_11

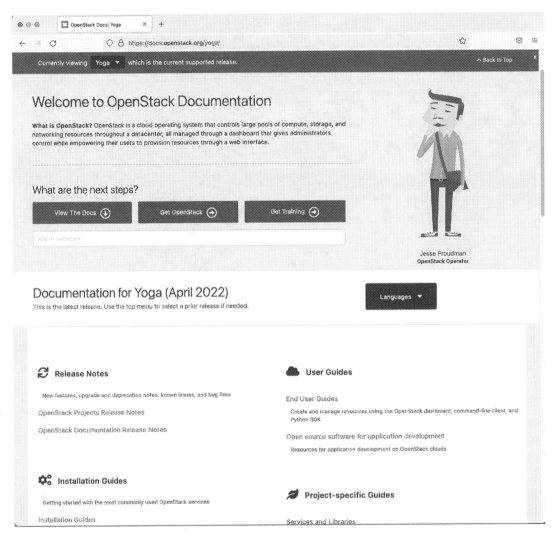

Figure 11-1. OpenStack documentation site

In the GNU/Linux world, there's the Linux From Scratch (LFS) project. It is the guide on how to build your own GNU/Linux installation from nothing to a working instance. Generally, it is not suitable for production and used for learning purposes only. Installation guides at the OpenStack website are like "OpenStack from scratch." These materials are very useful for learning. You will build your own cloud step by step, configuration file by configuration file. I highly recommend you follow these guides at least once without any automation tools.

The next valuable source of information is mailing lists. Check out `https://wiki.openstack.org/wiki/Mailing_Lists`. This archive engine for mailing lists has internal searchability, so before asking a question, check previous conversations. Most of the interesting lists are called *operators*, which are for cloud operator discussions and announcements and project announcements.

I also recommend *Superuser*, an online magazine by the OpenStack marketing team, available at `http://superuser.openstack.org`. The OpenInfra Foundation created the publication to facilitate knowledge sharing and collaborative problem solving among individuals who are running OpenStack clouds and the cloud-based infrastructure across all industries.

More documentation is produced by specific OpenStack vendors, which is vendor specific and describes a particular distribution.

The complete Red Hat documentation, including the knowledge base and reference architectures, is available only to customers, but the basic product documentation can be downloaded from `https://access.redhat.com/products`. Select the Red Hat OpenStack Platform documentation on the landing page. You can access it online or download it in EPUB or PDF format.

I have included lists of OpenStack supporting services and the network ports used by OpenStack, respectively, in Tables 11-1 and 11-2.

Table 11-1. *OpenStack and Supporting Services*

Service	Description
rabbitmq-server	RabbitMQ: AMQP message broker.
mariadb	MariaDB: One of the most popular database servers. Used by most OpenStack services.
glance-api	Glance API: Gives access to image service REST API.
cinder-api	Cinder API: Gives access to block storage service REST API.
cinder-scheduler	Cinder scheduler: Selects the optimal storage provider node on which to create the volume.
cinder-volume	Cinder volumes: Responds to read and write requests sent to the block storage service to maintain a state. Interacts with a variety of storage providers through a driver architecture.
cinder-backup	Cinder backup: Provides backup volumes of any type to a backup storage provider.
nova-api	Nova API: Accepts and responds to end-user compute API calls.
nova-scheduler	Nova scheduler: Takes a virtual machine instance request from the queue and determines on which compute server host it runs.
nova-conductor	Nova conductor: Mediates interactions between the nova-compute service and the database.
nova-consoleauth	Nova console authorization: Authorizes tokens for users that console proxies provide.
nova-novncproxy	Nova noVNC proxy: Provides a proxy for accessing running instances through a VNC connection.
nova-compute	Nova compute: A worker daemon that creates and terminates virtual machine instances through hypervisor APIs.
mongodb	NoSQL database used for the Ceilometer service.
ceilometer-central	Ceilometer central: Runs on a central management server to poll for resource utilization statistics for resources not tied to instances or compute nodes.

(continued)

Table 11-1. (*continued*)

Service	Description
httpd	Apache web server: Used for Horizon and Keystone.
heat-engine	Heat engine: Orchestrates the launching of templates and provides events back to the API consumer.
heat-api	Heat API: An OpenStack-native REST API that processes API requests by sending them to the Heat engine over the Remote Procedure Call (RPC).
heat-api-cfn	Heat API for cloud formation: An AWS Query API compatible with AWS CloudFormation. It processes API requests by sending them to the Heat engine over RPC.
neutron-server	Neutron server: Accepts and routes API requests to the appropriate OpenStack networking plug-in for action.
neutron-l3-agent	Neutron l3 Agent: Agent for routing and NAT service.
neutron-dhcp-agent	Neutron DHCP agent: With the help of dnsmasq processes, it provides DHCP service for instances.
neutron-metadata-agent	Neutron metadata agent: Works with Nova to provide metadata information into running instances.
openvswitch	Open vSwitch: An open source implementation of a distributed virtual multilayer switch.
neutron-openvswitch-agent	Neutron Open vSwitch agent: Works with neutron-server and sends through message broker commands to OVS.
openstack-swift-proxy	OpenStack Swift proxy: Accepts the OpenStack Object Storage API and raw HTTP requests to upload files, modifies metadata, and creates containers.
openstack-swift-account	OpenStack Swift account: Manages accounts defined with Object Storage.
openstack-swift-container	OpenStack Swift container: Manages the mapping of containers or folders within Object Storage.
openstack-swift-object	OpenStack Swift object: Manages actual objects, such as files, on the storage nodes.

Table 11-2. *Network Ports Used by OpenStack*

Service	Port Number
Keystone admins API endpoint	35357
Keystone public API endpoint	5000
Glance API endpoint	9292
Cinder block storage and iSCSI target	8776, 3260
Nova compute service	8774
Nova API	8773, 8775
Access to instances by VNC protocol	5900–5999
VNC proxy for browser access	6080
HTML5 proxy for browser access	6082
Swift object storage and rsync	8080, 6000, 6001, 6002, 873
Heat orchestration service	8004
Neutron network service	9696
RabbitMQ AMQP message broker	5672
MariaDB database	3306

I want to thank all of you readers. I hope you have found this book interesting and useful and enjoyed the reading as much as I enjoyed writing it.

APPENDIX A

OpenStack Orchestration

OpenStack's orchestration service was excluded from the Certified OpenStack Administrator exam requirements. However, I decided to keep this topic in the book as an annex and parity with the first exam version amount of knowledge.

Heat's Architecture and Components

The last (but certainly not the least) service covered in this book is Heat. OpenStack's orchestration service is the "one ring to rule them all." Heat's main purpose is to manage the entire infrastructure and applications life cycle within OpenStack clouds. Heat uses templates describing instances, networks, volumes, and so forth for orchestration. Heat can also rule scale-in/scale-out scenarios with Ceilometer's help.

Two formats of templates can be used.

- **HOT (Heat Orchestration Template)** is an OpenStack-native YAML-based template format.

- **CFT (AWS CloudFormation Template)** is compatible with AWS CloudFormation (`http://aws.amazon.com/cloudformation/`) JSON-based template format. You can use a lot of templates designed for AWS. A good starting point for research is `https://aws.amazon.com/cloudformation/resources/templates/`.

OpenStack's orchestration architecture is shown in Figure A-1. Heat consists of several services implemented as GNU/Linux daemons and CLI commands.

- **heat-api** accepts an OpenStack-native REST API call for template processing. After receiving API calls, heat-api processes them by sending them to the heat-engine via the AMQP protocol.

© Andrey Markelov 2022
A. Markelov, *Certified OpenStack Administrator Study Guide*,
https://doi.org/10.1007/978-1-4842-8804-7

- **heat-api-cfn** is a CloudFormation API service. It is similar to heat-api by function.

- **heat-engine** is Heat's main service. The engine does all the work of orchestrating, launching templates, and providing feedback to the client.

- **heat** is a CLI tool that communicates with the heat-api.

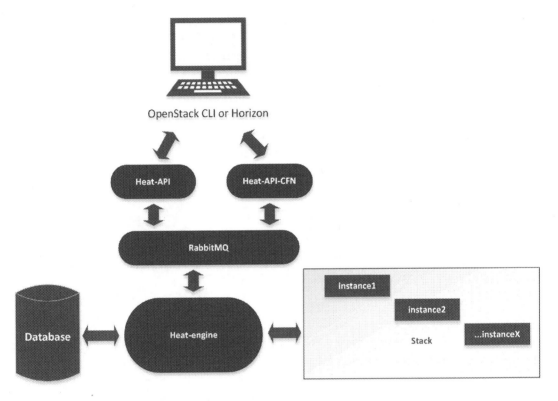

Figure A-1. *OpenStack Orchestration architecture*

Introducing the Heat OpenStack Template

The input information for Heat is a template that describes the stack. Stack is the branch of OpenStack resources that creates an application. Applications can consist of several instances and networks. HOT (Heat OpenStack Template) was originally introduced in the Icehouse release, and it acts as a primary standard for Heat.

Have a look at Figure A-2, where the structure of the HOT is shown. The template is divided into four parts. The first part is a template header. It consists of the HOT version and an optional description for the OpenStack operator. Table A-1 lists the most recent versions of HOT.

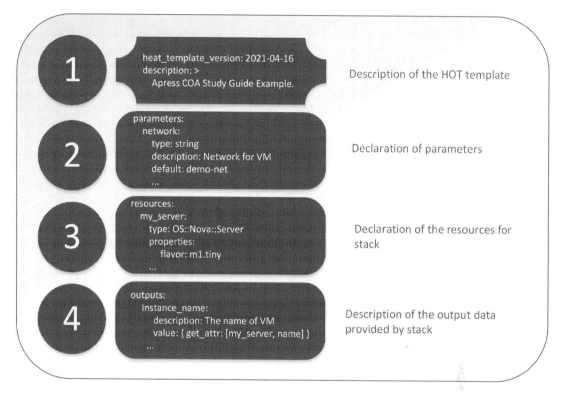

Figure A-2. *Example of the Heat OpenStack Template (HOT) format*

Table A-1. *OpenStack Heat OpenStack Templates Versions*

Series	HOT Version
Liberty	heat_template_version: 2015-10-15
Mitaka	heat_template_version: 2016-04-08
Newton	heat_template_version: 2016-04-08
Ocata	heat_template_version: 2017-02-24
Pike	heat_template_version: 2018-09-01
Queens	heat_template_version: 2018-03-02
Rocky	heat_template_version: 2016-04-08
Wallaby	heat_template_version: 2021-04-16

The second optional section is the parameters. This section allows you to customize the deployment and specify the input parameters that must be provided when instantiating the template.

The third section is always mandatory. It starts from general resources and defines actual resources that make up a stack. There are more than 100 resource types that can be defined here. You can find a full description of HOT at the OpenStack documentation project site (`http://docs.openstack.org/developer/heat/template_guide/index.html`). There should be at least one resource definition in this section.

The last section defines the output parameters that should be available to the user after a stack has been created. These output parameters are available from CLI and in the Horizon web client.

Launching a Stack Using a HOT

You can check the template examples at `https://github.com/openstack/heat--templates/`. There you can find examples of templates that demonstrate core Heat functionality. Here is a listing of a slightly modified "Hello world" example from this repository.

```
heat_template_version: 2015-10-15
description: >
  Apress Certified OpenStack Administrator Study Guide.
  One VM Example
parameters:
  network:
    type: string
    description: Network for VM
    default: private
  image:
    type: string
    description: Cirros Image for VM
    default: cirros
resources:
```

```
my_server:
  type: OS::Nova::Server
  properties:
    flavor: m1.tiny
    key_name: mykey
    networks:
    - network: { get_param: network }
    image: { get_param: image }
    user_data: |
      #!/bin/sh
      echo "Instance started :)"
    user_data_format: RAW
outputs:
  instance_name:
    description: The name of VM
    value: { get_attr: [my_server, name] }
  private_ip:
    description: The private IP of VM
    value: { get_attr: [ my_server, first_address ] }
```

The example consists of all four main parts of the template. There are two parameters defined: network and image. They have default values, but you can redefine them at the time of stack launching. The only described resource type OS::Nova::Server in this stack is my_server. By the way, you can find descriptions of all the resource types in the Horizon web interface. The results of this example are shown in Figure A-3. The most interesting part of the definition is the example of how to run a specific script when starting the instance. And at the end of the template, the virtual machine's name and IP output are defined.

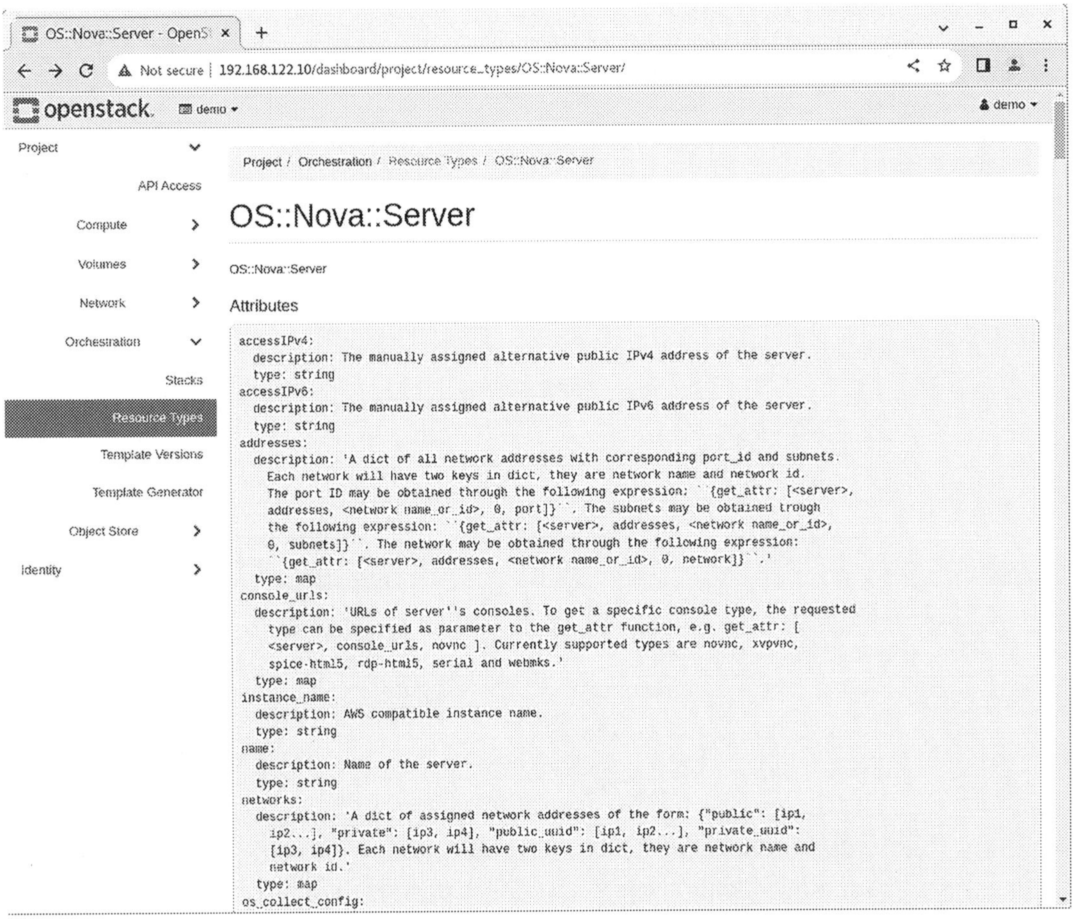

Figure A-3. *Example of the resource types' description in Horizon*

You can start the stack either in Horizon or in the command line. If you choose Horizon, go to Project ➤ Orchestration ➤ Stacks and click the Launch Stack button. You can use the -P option to define parameters if you use the command line.

```
$ openstack stack create -t Hello-World.yml --parameter network=private
--parameter image=cirros mystack
+---------------------+------------------------------------------+
| Field               | Value                                    |
+---------------------+------------------------------------------+
| id                  | 37160ce4-d98e-4950-82af-873eabd1573e     |
| stack_name          | mystack                                  |
| description         | Apress Certified OpenStack Administrator |
|                     | Study Guide. One VM Example              |
|                     |                                          |
| creation_time       | 2022-07-28T14:42:09Z                     |
| updated_time        | None                                     |
| stack_status        | CREATE_IN_PROGRESS                       |
| stack_status_reason | Stack CREATE started                     |
+---------------------+------------------------------------------+
```

Then you can issue the openstack stack list command to make sure the stack creation is completed.

```
$ openstack stack list
+--------------------------------------+------------+-----------------+
----------------------+--------------+
| ID                                   | Stack Name | Stack Status    |
 Creation Time        | Updated Time |
+--------------------------------------+------------+-----------------+
----------------------+--------------+
| 37160ce4-d98e-4950-82af-873eabd1573e | mystack    | CREATE_COMPLETE |
 2022-07-28T14:42:09Z | None         |
+--------------------------------------+------------+-----------------+
----------------------+--------------+
```

You also see the new instance in Nova.

```
$ openstack server list
+-----------+-----------+--------+----------+--------+---------+
| ID                                   | Name                         |
Status | Networks            | Image  | Flavor  |
+-----------+-----------+--------+----------+--------+---------+
| d6b2e228-46a7-4d85-85b9-40623f90ee58 | mystack-my_server-rn4jl7eg3uko |
ACTIVE | private=10.0.0.155 | cirros | m1.tiny |
+-----------+-----------+--------+----------+--------+---------+
```

The name of the instance consists of the stack name, instance name, and automatically generated alpha-number appendix. You can show detailed information about running the stack.

```
$ openstack stack show mystack
+----------------------+---------------------------------------------------+
| Field                | Value                                             |
+----------------------+---------------------------------------------------+
| id                   | 37160ce4-d98e-4950-82af-873eabd1573e              |
| stack_name           | mystack                                           |
| description          | Apress Certified OpenStack Administrator Study     |
|                      | Guide. One VM Example                             |
|                      |                                                   |
| creation_time        | 2022-07-28T14:42:09Z                              |
| updated_time         | None                                              |
| stack_status         | CREATE_COMPLETE                                   |
| stack_status_reason  | Stack CREATE completed successfully              |
| parameters           | OS::project_id: 7c8be1bdcc544e5fa8191b6095e5e595|
|                      | OS::stack_id: 37160ce4-d98e-4950-82af-873eabd1573e |
|                      | OS::stack_name: mystack                           |
|                      | image: cirros                                     |
|                      | network: private                                  |
|                      |                                                   |
| outputs              | - description: The name of VM                     |
|                      |   output_key: instance_name                       |
```

```
|                       |   output_value: mystack-my_server-rn4jl7eg3uko  |
|                       | - description: The private IP of VM             |
|                       |   output_key: private_ip                        |
|                       |   output_value: 10.0.0.155                       |
|                       |                                                  |
| links                 | - href: http://192.168.122.10:8004/v1/7c        |
|                       |   8be1bdcc544e5fa8191b6095e5e595/stacks/        |
|                       |   mystack/37160ce4-d98e-4950-82af-873eabd1573e  |
|                       |   rel: self                                     |
|                       |                                                  |
| deletion_time         | None                                            |
| notification_topics   | []                                              |
| capabilities          | []                                              |
| disable_rollback      | True                                            |
| timeout_mins          | None                                            |
| stack_owner           | demo                                            |
| parent                | None                                            |
| stack_user_project_id | 2affe18a371844afab2b4cdb685a93fb                |
| tags                  | []                                              |
|                       |                                                  |
+-----------------------+-------------------------------------------------+
```

This information is also available in the Horizon web interface (see Figure A-4).

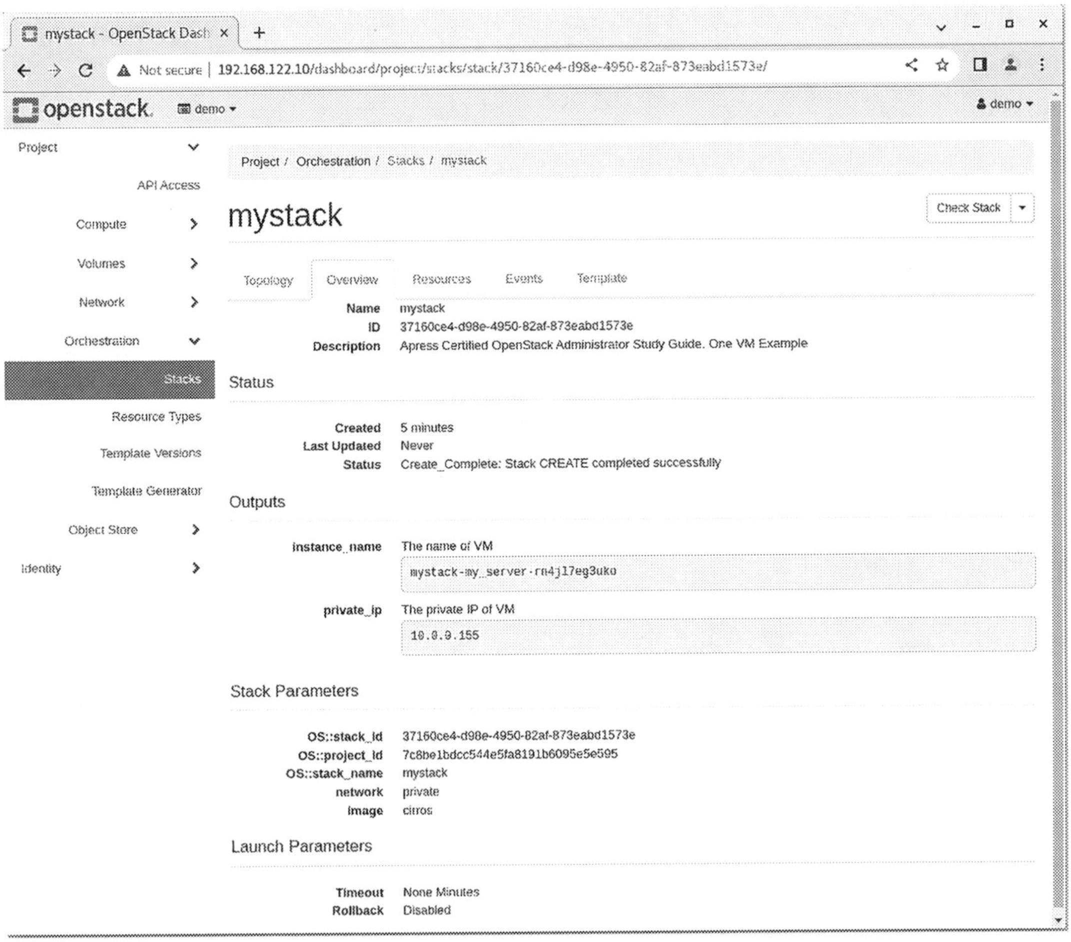

Figure A-4. *Example of the stack details in the Horizon web interface*

Using CLI and the Dashboard for Heat Service Operations

Let's examine the most common operations with stacks. If you troubleshoot the stack and want to see what happens with the resources, the heat event-list command is very useful.

```
$ openstack stack event list mystack
2022-07-28 14:42:09Z [mystack]: CREATE_IN_PROGRESS  Stack CREATE started
2022-07-28 14:42:09Z [mystack.my_server]: CREATE_IN_PROGRESS  state changed
2022-07-28 14:42:15Z [mystack.my_server]: CREATE_COMPLETE  state changed
2022-07-28 14:42:15Z [mystack]: CREATE_COMPLETE  Stack CREATE completed
successfully
```

Figure A-5 shows the list of events in the Horizon web interface.

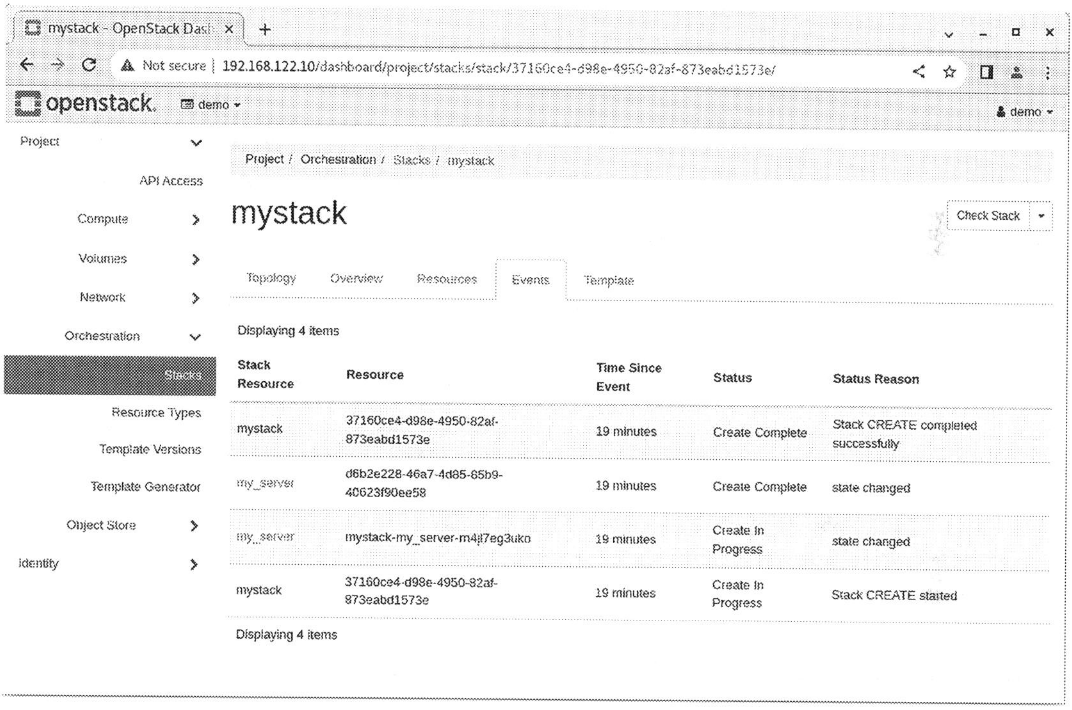

Figure A-5. *Example of the stack events list in the Horizon web interface*

As the owner of the stack, you can suspend and resume your stacks again.

```
$ openstack stack suspend mystack
```

```
+-----------+------+-----------+------+--------+
| ID                                        | Stack Name | Stack Status     |
Creation Time          | Updated Time |
+-----------+------+-----------+------+--------+
| 37160ce4-d98e-4950-82af-873eabd1573e | mystack     | SUSPEND_IN_PROGRESS |
2022-07-28T14:42:09Z | None          |
+-----------+------+-----------+------+--------+
$ openstack stack resume mystack
+-----------+------+-----------+------+--------+
| ID                                        | Stack Name | Stack Status     |
Creation Time          | Updated Time |
+-----------+------+-----------+------+--------+
| 37160ce4-d98e-4950-82af-873eabd1573e | mystack     | RESUME_IN_PROGRESS |
2022-07-28T14:42:09Z | None          |
+-----------+------+-----------+------+--------+
```

With Horizon and CLI, it is possible to see the resources of your stack.

```
$ openstack stack resource list mystack
+---------+-----------+------------+-----------+------+
| resource_name | physical_resource_id               | resource_type    |
resource_status | updated_time         |
+---------+-----------+------------+-----------+------+
| my_server     | d6b2e228-46a7-4d85-85b9-40623f90ee58 | OS::Nova::Server |
RESUME_COMPLETE | 2022-07-28T14:42:09Z |
+---------+-----------+------------+-----------+------+
```

If you prefer to work with Horizon, you can see the same information. An example of the stack resources in Horizon is shown in Figure A-6.

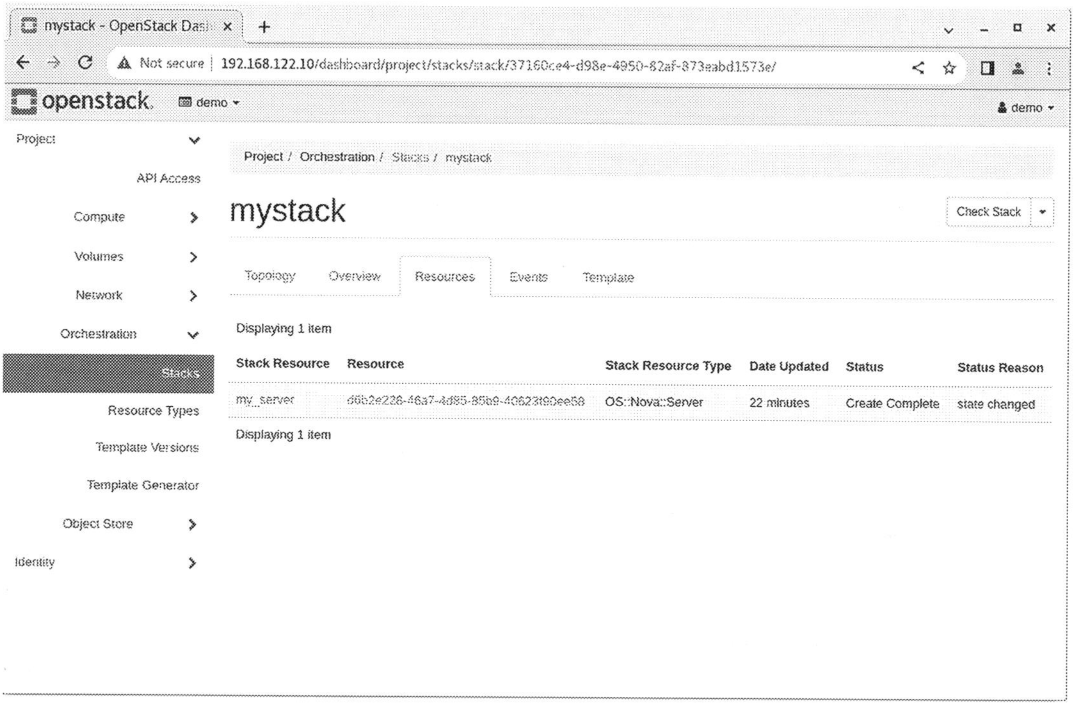

Figure A-6. *Example of the stack resources as shown in the Horizon web interface*

As mentioned, `openstack stack show mystack` shows the information for all the stacks' properties, including output. You can use another command if you want to see output only.

```
$ openstack stack output show mystack --all
+----------------+------------------------------------------------------+
| Field          | Value                                                |
+----------------+------------------------------------------------------+
| instance_name  | {                                                    |
|                |     "output_key": "instance_name",                   |
|                |     "description": "The name of VM",                 |
|                |     "output_value": "mystack-my_server-rn4jl7eg3uko" |
|                | }                                                    |
| private_ip     | {                                                    |
|                |     "output_key": "private_ip",                      |
|                |     "description": "The private IP of VM",           |
|                |     "output_value": "10.0.0.155"                     |
|                | }                                                    |
+----------------+------------------------------------------------------+
```

245

Also, you can see the template using the command.

```
$ openstack stack template show mystack
```

If you update the text of the template file, you may also want to update a stack. Run the following command to update an existing stack from a modified template file.

```
$ openstack stack update -t Hello-World.yml --parameter network=private
--parameter image=cirros mystack
+--------------------+---------------------------------------------------+
| Field              | Value                                             |
+--------------------+---------------------------------------------------+
| id                 | 37160ce4-d98e-4950-82af-873eabd1573e              |
| stack_name         | mystack                                           |
| description        | Apress Certified OpenStack Administrator Study    |
|                    | Guide. One VM Example                             |
|                    |                                                   |
| creation_time      | 2022-07-28T14:42:09Z                              |
| updated_time       | 2022-07-28T16:01:34Z                              |
| stack_status       | UPDATE_IN_PROGRESS                                |
| stack_status_reason | Stack UPDATE started                             |
+--------------------+---------------------------------------------------+
```

Some resources are updated in place, while others are replaced with new resources. Finally, you can also delete a stack.

```
$ openstack stack delete mystack
Are you sure you want to delete this stack(s) [y/N]? y
```

The Topology subtab on the Project details page is very useful for an overall view of the stack resources and links between them. An example of a two-instance stack topology is shown in Figure A-7.

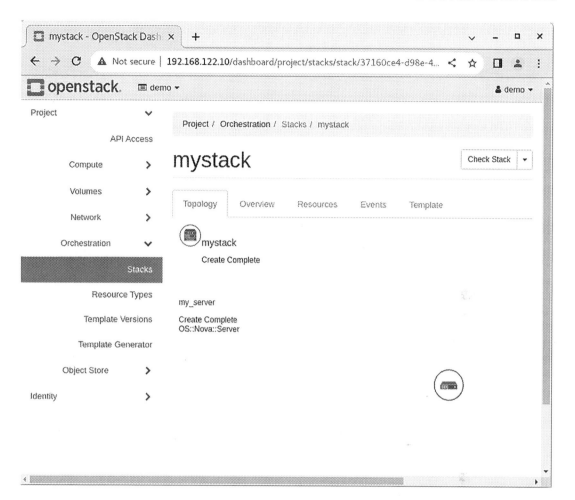

Figure A-7. *Example of the stack topology*

Index

A, B

Access control lists (ACLs), 161

C

Ceilometer, 13
Certified OpenStack
    Administrator (COA), 1
  architecture and components, 9
  command key bindings, 5
  commands, 3
  distributions, 14
  download links, 14
  exam facts, 1, 2
  exam requirements, 2
  hypervisor, 10
  kernel modules, 10
  KVM, 10
  Nova, 9
  production operations, enterprises, 14
  vs. Red Hat, 6
  services, 12, 13
  technical documentation, 3
  tmux multiplexers, 3, 4
  vendor's contribution, 14
  versions, 13
  virtualization hardware support, 10–12
  website, 2
Cinder, 13
  architecture, 169, 170
  configuration options, 172, 173
  LVM volume group, 181, 182
  OpenStack node, 171
  openstack volume service list, 171
  quotas
    configuration options, 182, 183
    demo project, 183, 184
    Horizon, 183
    name/number, 185
    results, 184
  services, 170
  snapshots
    backing up, 185, 186
    volume, 187, 189, 190
  storage pools, 191
  storage providers, 171
  test environments, 172
  volumes
    admin users, 177
    apresstest1, 180, 181
    backing up, 185, 186
    cinder command, 174
    creation, 178
    deletion, 178
    Glance's image, 179
    lvs command, 176
    openstack command, 175
    regular users, 177
    VM instance, 179
CloudFormation Template (CFT), 233
Cloud service models, 8
Command-line interface (CLI)
  clients, 30
  help option, 30

© Andrey Markelov 2022
A. Markelov, *Certified OpenStack Administrator Study Guide*,
https://doi.org/10.1007/978-1-4842-8804-7

Printed in the United States
by Baker & Taylor Publisher Services